5/16/08

To ~~[redacted]~~
~~[redacted]~~
~~[redacted]~~ - Thank-you
for your interest -
God Bless -
O servant of the O [signature]

FAILURE TO ATONE

The True Story of a Jungle
Surgeon in Vietnam

By Allen Hassan
MD, JD, DVM

As told to David Drum

Failure to Atone Press
Sacramento, California

FAILURE TO ATONE

© Allen Hassan 2006

Publisher's Cataloging-in-Publication
(Provided by Quality Books, Inc.)

Hassan, Allen.
Failure to atone : the true story of a jungle surgeon
in Vietnam / by Allen Hassan ; as told to David Drum.
p. cm.
ISBN 0-9776049-0-X

1. Hassan, Allen. 2. Vietnamese Conflict, 1961-1975
—Personal narratives, American. 3. Vietnamese
Conflict, 1961-1975—Medical care. 4. Vietnamese
Conflict, 1961-1975—Campaigns—Vietnam—Quang Tri
(Province) 5. Surgeons—United States—Biography.
6. Surgeons—Vietnam—Biography. 7. Quang Tri (Vietnam :
Province)—History. I. Drum, David, II. Title.

DS559.5.H375 2006   959.704'3'092
                            QBI05-600221

Failure to Atone Press
www.vietnamfailuretoatone.com

Book design by www.KarenRoss.com

Acknowledgements

The author would like to thank the following individuals whose support has been invaluable in the preparation of this book:

First, I want to thank my family who I've often neglected, but who have always been supportive of me. These include my sister Miriam, my half brothers and sisters Rey, El Maza, and Leila, and my aunt and uncle Nancy and Jerry, who were like brother and sister to me.

I would also like to thank my professional colleagues without whom I could not have had success in my field and any success with this book. These include Superior Court Judge James Long, a true brother; Jack Friedman, MD, a good friend since our first day in medical school at the University of Iowa; Mark Winchester, cardiologist; Joe Cooper, JD, David F. Smith, thoracic surgeon; Philip Riley, MD; Johnny Griffin, JD; Charles Bonneau, JD; the fleet-footed John Virga, JD; and my old friend Jimmy Higa, DVM.

A special heartfelt thanks to my editor, Richard W. Smith, who accompanied me to Vietnam several times and tenaciously searched for the truth.

Thanks also to my good friends in Vietnam, including one of my best friends, Dick Hughes of Shoeshine Boys of Vietnam; Don Luce, a courageous Christian; and Crystal Erhart, a sensitive soul. This book is in memoriam to the approximately 135 journalists and photojournalists from both sides who were killed in the Vietnam War, and specifically to my traveling buddy Steve Erhart, to John Steinbeck IV, and to Dana Stone and Sean Flynn, valiant American journalists who died in the line of duty.

I would also like to thank my Auburn friends, Ben and Marguerite of Golden Swan, who stuck with me through thick and thin, and to acknowledge the assistance and patience of my gracious office staff including Sharon, Xee, Larissa, and Michelle, former Corporal Richard Baughman, as well as the Botello family, Luis, Estella, Alex and Fernando, who care for my ranch and have become my family.

Last but not least, I would like to thank my unheralded thoroughbred racehorses "Majestic Kid" and "Heritor," who helped earn money to sustain me in times of crisis.

Dedication

This book is dedicated to all the

Marines, Soldiers, Sailors,

Air Force personnel and Journalists

who lost their lives during the

Vietnam War. It is equally

dedicated to the people of

Vietnam who struggled and died to

liberate their country.

Also by Allen Hassan

Evaluation, Treatment and Prevention of Head and/or Spinal Injury Problems. Edited by Gervase Flick, MD, JD

Also by David Drum

Alternative Therapies for Managing Diabetes

The Chronic Pain Management Sourcebook

What Your Doctor Might Not Tell You About Uterine Fibroids. Co-written with Scott Goodwin, MD, and Michael Broder, MD

The Type 2 Diabetes Sourcebook. Co-written with Terry Zierenberg, RN, CDE

Making the Chemotherapy Decision

Table of Contents

FAILURE TO ATONE

The True Story of a Jungle
Surgeon in Vietnam

Allen Hassan
MD, JD, DVM

*"Wars are not paid for in wartime;
the bills come later."*

– Benjamin Franklin

Forward

From my first harrowing days as a volunteer surgeon-doctor at Quang Tri Provincial Hospital, the Vietnam War and everything around it was a remarkable life-defining experience. My life was changed forever by my two tours of war-ravaged Vietnam.

As one of 774 doctors with the American Medical Association's Volunteer Physicians for Vietnam program, I saw a great many extraordinary events in just a few short months, including extraordinary displays of courage, and sickening displays of man's inhumanity to man. Many of my volunteer physician colleagues also witnessed extraordinary events during these times, and their letters and reflections on the Vietnam experience are included in this book. *Failure to Atone* is in large part the story of selfless humanitarian service by this group of American medical doctors, men and women who volunteered to help people in a far away land.

Failure to Atone is also an attempt to come to terms with everything I saw as a civilian doctor in Vietnam–the terrible atrocities, the wasted lives and money, and the continuing sorrow that haunts many of us to this day.

The Vietnam War has never been far away for those of us who have solemn and vivid memories of that painful era. There are profound and essential lessons to be learned from the experiences of the wise old sages who came of age during those turbulent times, when America was debating the wisdom of a divisive, bloody war in Southeast Asia. The historical and moral issues that were raised by our involvement in Vietnam are with us today. Those issues, and the issues of how medical doctors and the medical establishment should conduct themselves ethically and morally during times of war, need to be re-examined now more than ever before.

Failure to Atone has been more than a decade in development, but was delayed by the demands of my busy and successful medical-legal practice in Sacramento, California. For many years, I also tended to repress memories of what I saw during my two humanitarian tours of Vietnam in 1968 and 1969. Completing *Failure to Atone* has been liberating and therapeutic for me, and I offer it as one doctor's contribution to our continuing national dialogue on issues of war and peace.

— Allen Hassan, MD

1

One Afternoon in May

"Ye shall know the truth and the
truth shall set you free." - John 8:32
Inscribed over entrance of CIA
administration building

I have a recurring dream of the past, or perhaps it is a nightmare. It is late May 1968, and I am a doctor in the jungles of South Vietnam, near heavy fighting and the demilitarized zone. I hear the familiar loud sound of a military helicopter landing in the courtyard of Quang Tri Provincial Hospital where I am the only doctor.

Suddenly, three uniformed helicopter pilots hurry into the foyer of the hospital, carrying stretchers heaped with young children. Three and four children are piled upon each stretcher, and the pilots bring in stretcher after stretcher. Finally, the soldiers lay the last of the young victims on the marble floor.

"Here they are, doc," one says, glancing at me as they leave.

I am a doctor. I know this is Vietnam, and this is war. But as I hear the chopper fly away over the jungle, I cannot believe the grotesque tableau on the floor around me.

Spread out before me are the writhing, dying forms of approximately 40 very young Vietnamese children. Many are infants, the oldest perhaps five years of age. The children all wear plastic medical arm bands. They are struggling to stay alive. Many of the children try to move their arms and legs, but blood spurts from small, round wounds in their heads. Each beautiful little boy or girl has an untreated head wound. They have all been shot through the head. I quickly realize that these young children were probably lined up and shot, execution style.

I am the only doctor in Quang Tri Provincial Hospital. All around me, innocent children are dying. I yell as if in a dream for Gelfoam, an absorbent material which helps control bleeding. I desperately stuff Gelfoam into the bullet holes in the children's heads, trying desperately to save them. Some of the children, I see, are already dead. Other children are taking their last breaths before my eyes. I realize after several desperate minutes of trying to save them that none of these little children can possibly live.

I remember that moment of cold despair, a moment every doctor feels after fighting to save a patient only to see them slip away. I am losing forty patients at one time, and I cannot save even one. I am not only a doctor, I am a former Marine. I take a look at one of the arm bands on the children. The arm bands say, "Interrogated USMC."

My entire body shakes. Did the US Marines have something to do with this massacre? My head explodes with questions. I feel as if I am under attack, as if mortar shells are falling on the roof of the hospital. The sight of several dozen executed babies is forever imprinted upon my brain. As the last innocent child quietly dies, I wonder if it will ever be possible to atone for such an inhuman slaughter, one of the many continuing atrocities of war.

2

My Early Years

"The only purpose for which power can be rightly exercised over any member of a civilized community against his will is to prevent harm to others."
- John Stewart Mill, On Liberty

I did not come into the world prepared to become a battlefield surgeon, operating day and night to save lives in the primitive jungles of Vietnam. I doubt that anyone in Red Oak, Iowa, where I was born, had even heard of Vietnam. There were no other doctors in my family; I was destined to become the first doctor, the first lawyer, and even the first veterinarian in my family. On the day I was born, in the middle of the Great Depression, Red Oak, Iowa, was a town of 7,500 in the rolling hills of the bucolic Nishnabotna Valley, in the heart of rural America.

My last name, Hassan, is an unusual name in the Midwest. Although my Iowa-born mother had been of Swedish and Irish descent, my father was born outside the United States, on the West Bank of what was then called Palestine-in-Bethlehem. My father was a hard-working Muslim immigrant running a fashionable women's clothing store in Chicago when he met my grandmother, a pilot who would sometimes fly from Red Oak to Chicago to go shopping. On one of these trips, my grandmother met my father, a handsome and successful businessman. My grandmother couldn't understand why this handsome, debonair man wasn't married. My father told her he wanted a clean-living woman who didn't drink, and who would follow the tenets of his religion, but he couldn't find any women like that in America. Before too long my grandmother brought her daughter, my mother, an impetuous debutante intending to study art at the Art Institute of Chicago. When my mother met my father, they immediately fell in love and after a whirlwind courtship they were married. There must have been some problems. My mother never finished art school. She did not completely give up drinking, and my Muslim father disapproved of this, but I don't know what really happened between them. My mother was still a young woman of twenty-one when she shot herself near the cash register in my father's clothing store, perhaps suffering from post-partum depression. Although I don't remember it, I was said to have been present at the moment when she took her own life. My grandfather instinctively took charge of the situation, and my sister and I were brought back to Red Oak to grow up in rural America.

My older sister and I were more or less adopted by our grandparents, Pete and Milly Tuttle. I spent much of my youth on their 240-acre farm. I had an idyllic, hard-working youth in Red Oak. When I think of Red Oak now, it reminds me of something as decent and American as a Norman Rockwell painting. In high school, I got up at 4:30 a.m. to milk the cows, gather eggs, feed the cows and horses, and begin my other daily chores. I was an officer in the Future Farmers of America or FFA, dreaming of becoming the best dairy farmer in Iowa. Since I was energetic and industrious, I had a paper route in town, too. We ate well and worked hard in Red Oak. Although a lot was expected of me, and I was worked hard throughout my youth, I grew up feeling I was loved.

The most important man in my life was my Irish grandfather, Clarence "Pete" Tuttle. My character was formed in his giant shadow. A New Deal Democrat, a math savant, and an entrepreneur, Pete Tuttle was a lion of a man who radiated masculine confidence and power. His deep, powerful voice could silence a room with a couple of words. He had once wanted to become a minister, but he loved the ladies a little too much to succeed in that profession. A visionary who was often a step or two ahead of his times, my grandfather had once been asked to run for governor of the state of Iowa, but he declined because he did some time in jail for bootlegging during Prohibition. To me, he seemed solid as a monument.

My grandfather was active in the earliest days of aviation as a stunt pilot. When he was barnstorming with Charles Lindbergh, one of his men could walk from wing to wing between two flying biplanes, one of them piloted by him. My grandfather owned several airplanes for stunt flying, which were also a front for his bootlegging activities. Among his good works, he successfully lobbied Congress to have lights installed at all airfields, so planes could land at night. But my grandfather quit barnstorming when his wing man fell off his airplane and tumbled to a terrible death. Both my grandfather and grandmother had already made flying a part of their lifestyle, and they didn't stop flying. Either one of them would hop in a plane to go shopping in Chicago, or to see a major league baseball game in New York.

Grandfather Clarence "Pete" Tuttle was the patriarch of my family.

My grandfather had a knack for spotting and taking advantage of trends. He built radio station KICK in Red Oak, one of the first radio stations in the United States. He served on the Federal Communications Board, but got kicked off a year after I was born for promoting a boxing match that never happened. Pete Tuttle built the first motel in Red Oak, three soda pop factories, chicken and turkey hatcheries, and more. During World War II, he built a 400-home subdivision in Downey,

My mother's family made flying in planes like this a part of their lifestyle. Pictured here are my grandmother and her two children, my mother Dorothea and my aunt.

Ready to take off from Chicago are pilot Tip Wagner, top left, co-pilot and my Grandmother Minnie Tuttle, seated behind him in cockpit, and my Aunt Nancy Marks, whose war hero son Mortimer Marks influenced my decision to join the Marines.

California, which he aptly named Tuttleville. Although my grandfather taught my sister and me to always tell the truth, he had me lie about my age so I could enroll in school at the same time as my older sister. My grandfather was constantly going places and doing things, and I'm sure my sister and I got in his way, but I do remember that he defended me and my sister with his booming ministerial voice, his furious Irish temper, and his generous heart. He loved me and my sister when it seemed like no one else in the world did.

Growing up, even with my olive skin, dark hair, and dark eyes, I was pretty much accepted as just another person by the blue-eyed Scandinavians of Red Oak. We attended the Congregational Church, and went to public schools. However, when I was about nine years old, I felt the sting of discrimination when somebody saw my dark skin and assumed I was Jewish. This incident happened when I tried to buy a candy bar at a local gas station. The attendant refused to sell me the candy. Instead, he took the candy back from me, and gruffly announced, "We don't serve Jews here."

I went home crestfallen, and somewhat confused. My grandfather was reading the newspaper when I entered the house.

"Grandpa," I asked. "What's a Jew?"

"Why do you ask?" he said, lowering his newspaper.

I told him the story. My grandfather quietly folded up his newspaper. He took me out to the truck, and we drove back to the gas station. While I waited in the pickup, my grandfather went inside to talk to the owner face to face.

I don't know what happened inside. But when he returned, he told me, "You want to buy a candy bar there, you can. You won't have a problem again."

About three weeks later, a sign appeared on the gas station that said, "Out of Business." I always wondered if my grandfather had anything to do with that, since he seemed so powerful to me.

One summer, when we were vacationing at Lake Okiboji in northern Iowa, my sister and I were walking peacefully along the shore of the lake. My big sister was thirteen, a budding woman, and a future beauty contest winner with her dark hair and golden bronze skin. We walked by a bunch of boys, and one of them said, "Ain't that nigger girl purty!"

When his buddies quickly joined in, making more rude and nasty comments, I realized they were insulting my sister. There on the shore of the lake, I could see Miriam was frozen with fear. Miriam was already sensitive about our last name, which she would later change, and when I glanced at her I could see she was humiliated and heartbroken by the comments directed at her because of her brown skin.

I sprang to Miriam's defense. I yelled and stepped between my sister and the boys. The young bullies and I almost came to blows, but fortunately an older boy came over and broke it up. I was learning lessons about the cruelty of racism and intolerance which would stay with me for my entire life.

Pete Tuttle also hated intolerance. I saw it in the way he lived. As one of twenty-one children, he grew up feeling like he had to help out the underdog. His generosity was legend in Red Oak, as was his insistence on a hard day's work for his handouts. Having survived the Great Depression, my grandfather valued money, but he valued people, too. One story he told was that, after the Depression, several local farmers owed him money for baby chicks he hatched out in his hatchery. Since most of the chicken ranchers had already gone broke trying to raise chickens and couldn't pay for the chicks, Pete Tuttle forgave them all. He only asked them to pay him back if and when they could.

I had a hard, physical life on the farm in Red Oak. From an early age, I milked cows, tended pigs, raised and rode horses, and took care of baby chicks, chickens and turkeys. I rode a tractor to plant and cultivate our fields of corn and oats. I mowed and baled hay to feed the cows and horses. I drove a pickup all over the farm, taking care of the animals and crops, more or less a typical Iowa farm boy. As a young man, I already knew how to run the place. My granddad laughed when I told him when I grew up, I wanted to be "a gentleman farmer like him."

At the age of fourteen, however, my life changed when I was kicked in the head by my favorite horse, Jeanie. My skull was broken by her powerful kick. I sustained serious brain trauma. When I came to, I remember the sight of my grandfather crying.

"He'll be mentally retarded. He won't be able to see out of his right eye, and he won't be able to smell," was the doctor's grim prognosis at the hospital.

From over my right eye, a good neurosurgeon in Omaha removed a portion of my skull the size of a fifty-cent piece. He also removed a massive blood clot and part of the frontal lobe of my brain.

Me, Miriam, and my Uncle Jerry on the farm in Red Oak.

This was a delicate surgery without a good prognosis at that time, but fortunately I recovered. Medical textbooks say this kind of brain trauma often leads to mental retardation. Recovery is quite slow, and even when recovery occurs, some problems may persist. These can include increased irritability, borderline personality, difficulty processing thoughts, difficulty reasoning abstractly, and short- or long-term memory loss.

On the farm with my favorite horse, Jeannie.

But I was young and in good shape, we ate well, and I experienced a slow but miraculous recovery. After the horse kicked me, my grades fell from As and Bs down to Cs and Ds. I got an F in Algebra. I had difficulty thinking. I knew my mental processes were not quite right. But in time I recovered completely enough to earn three advanced degrees, a recovery so remarkable that another doctor told me my case should be written up in a medical journal.

After the surgery, my grandparents worried about me, and they restricted my activities. In high school I was five feet seven inches tall and growing fast, and at 146 pounds fairly well-built. Under other circumstances I would probably have been an athlete. Instead, I was kept away from contact sports like football. All through high school, although I was working hard on the farm, I was not allowed to participate in team sports. Instead, I had to settle for being manager of the sports teams, cheering my classmates on to victory.

Eventually, as I applied myself, my grades came back. I was able to graduate from high school at the age of sixteen. I joined my sister Miriam at Iowa State University in Ames. I began to major in agriculture, specifically dairy animal husbandry. I had always made and saved a little money in high school, and I tried to pay my own way by milking cows part-time on the school farm, but I was seventeen years old trying to work and make it in college, and I ran out of money. Government loans were not easily available at that time, and I was too proud to ask my family for financial help. I didn't want to tell my grandfather I had run out of money, and I was horrified to ask him for a loan. I knew my sister would try to help me stay in school, so I told her I flunked out before I left.

When I was eighteen, without much encouragement from anyone in the family, I joined the United States Marine Corps. My friends at Iowa State warned me that if I joined the Marines I'd never make it back to college, but I didn't believe them. I left school with $22 in my pocket and became a Marine.

I suppose I joined the Marines because I wanted to prove that I could survive by myself in the world. I already knew I didn't want to spend my life working on the farm. The Marines had a reputation of being the toughest of the armed forces, and I wanted to make up for those lost years in high school when I had been kept out of the macho camaraderie of team sports. I knew some people discriminated against Arabs, too, and I wanted to prove I was as good as anybody else.

As a boy, I vividly remember hearing Franklin Roosevelt's speech castigating Japan for the bombing of Pearl Harbor, calling it "a day that will live in infamy." Like everybody else, I witnessed the American military's heroic efforts to win the war. I often heard my grandparents speak of my uncle, Mortimer M. Marks, a US Marine who the family believed to be dead, since he was forced to participate in the brutal Bataan Death March. One day, after we presumed he was dead, we heard my uncle was alive, in a prisoner of war camp in Japan. With the family back home worrying about his safety, my uncle survived three years in a Japanese prison camp. He earned his way up to the rank of Lieutenant Colonel in the Marines, and returned to the United States a war hero. In my own case, on a practical level, I also knew there was the GI Bill, which could help me pay my own way to finish college after a few years in the Marines.

I loved the Marine Corps in the way that only a young man can love the Marines. I loved the unique sense of pride, discipline, and the high standards of honor that are built into military service. I felt the Marines saved me from a life of farm labor, and pointed me in a new direction of honor and service. As a US Marine recruit in 1954, I was trained to defend myself and to kill in 12 unbelievably brutal weeks of boot camp at Camp Pendelton, California. Drill instructors yelled at us and physically beat us for the smallest infractions. The other motley recruits and I survived and bonded in the primitive, barbaric, confrontational atmosphere of boot camp. We woke up early, worked all day, and slept like logs. We carried our 121-pound machine gun and ammunition belts up and down the desert hills around Camp Pendelton, and practiced as a team loading and firing 550 rounds a minute by belt. When we'd all had so much abuse and humiliation we wanted to quit, we'd reach inside and find a hidden reserve that helped us keep going. The Marine Corps helped form my character. It taught me discipline, bravery, courage, self-preservation, and honesty. The Marines also showed me I could do more than I thought I could do.

Two weeks into boot camp, a drill instructor came up to me and poked me in the chest as we were standing in formation. By this time I'd grown to six feet tall, and became a heavyweight at 182 pounds.

"Son, have you ever boxed?" the drill instructor asked.

"No, sir," I replied.

"Well, you are now this platoon's boxer."

I thought about this afterwards. I was in good shape, having worked all my life on the farm. But the guy I was going to box, for my first match, was a Golden Gloves boxer. And I had that old head wound, from being kicked in the head by a horse. I went back to see the drill instructor privately, in his office.

"Sir, I will not be able to box," I said.

"What's the matter? What do you mean, you won't be able to box, shithead?"

"Sir, I've had a bone removed from my head. If I get hit, I might be killed."

"Are you a yellow-bellied asshole, shithead? Are you yellow? Are you chicken?"

"No, sir."

"Did you join the Marine Corps?"

"Yes, sir."

"Did you lie to get into the Marine Corps?"

"No, sir."

"They let you in the Marine Corps?"

"Yes, sir."

"Then you're a Marine."

"Yes, sir."

"Get the fuck out of my office."

Fortunately, boxers in the Marine Corps were required to wear protective headgear. The headgear was constructed so that a piece of leather cushioning fell neatly in place over the soft spot above my right eye. Although I trained for a month, I felt weak in the knees when I stepped into the ring with the Golden Gloves boxer. He wasn't much better than I was. We mixed it up pretty good, and although neither of us won a trophy for our display of boxing prowess, I was awarded the victory. I got the highest score ever attained in the .45 pistol shoot, I came in second in the combat course run, and I helped our platoon become Merit Platoon 204. In many ways, the Marine Corps taught me I could do more than I thought I could do.

My Marine Corps buddies and I lugged this 121-pound machine gun up and down hills at Camp Pendelton. I am standing, third from left, with squad members Unger, Jackson, Robertson, and Frost.

I served on the USS *Toledo*, the flagship of the 7th Fleet, shipping out for four months at a time with a landing party of 45 other combat-ready Marines. At sea, the Marines' primary job in wartime was to be the front line gunners for attacking aircraft. As part of a landing party, you also have to continue training day in and day out, six and a half days a week. Standing four-hour watches every other day could be a grind in itself, especially when you are standing watch from midnight to four after a full day's work.

As a Marine, I was prepared to hit the beach in Korea if necessary. I was ready to see action when we shipped out for Cairo in 1956, during the Suez Canal crisis. Egyptian President Gamel Abdul Nasser had taken control of the canal from the British and the French, and it was possible we would go to war to retake the canal. But before we reached Cairo, President Eisenhower cancelled our order and said to hell with the French and English, deciding not to help them become a colonial power all over again. Breaking with my staunchly Democratic grandfather, I had supported Eisenhower for president. When I showed him my "I Like Ike" button, he asked me to take it off or get out of the house. To me, this was a way of declaring my independence. Still, on the way to Egypt, the captain of the USS *Toledo* confronted me.

"Hassan, are you a Marine or an Arab?" he asked me.

"Sir, I'm a Marine first, and an Arab second," I responded.

"Okay, we'll keep our eye on you," he said. "You're qualified to be a squad leader, so I expect, like a good Marine, Corporal Hassan, you'll know what's to be done when we get to the Mediterranean."

I took this as a vote of confidence at the time, but later I wondered why he'd ever brought it up in the first place.

On another tour, during the crisis over the islands of Quemoy and Matsu, we were prepared to fight, standing call for up to twenty-four hours a day, followed by six hours to sleep. We were all loaded with grenades, and expecting shells the size of Volkswagen Beetles to land on our deck. Civilians were fleeing the islands, and the Communist Chinese, and our job was to help civilians board ships for Taiwan.

Our ship docked in Hong Kong, China, Korea, and the Japanese ports of Kobe, Nagoya, Sasebo, and Yokusuku. We also docked in Bataan and Corregidor in the Philippines, and helped lay a ceremonial wreath at Surabachi on the island of Guadalcanal. I was an expert rifleman, a sniper, but I had many other duties aboard ship including a stint as a military policeman. My MOS 2900 meant that I was basically a machine gunner, .50 caliber air-cooled, and along the way I taught Korean Marines my skills in Chin Hae, South Korea. I was also honored to wait on Naval and Marine captains and even admirals at sea, to serve as their chauffeur in port, and sometimes to serve as a chauffeur for their daughters. I had many memorable exchanges with these proud patriotic men.

Basically, I saw the world at taxpayers' expense. And being an industrious sort, I gave my shipmates haircuts, or did their laundry or ironing for a dollar or two. While some of my shipmates were in port, carousing in bars, and hustling chicks, I sometimes stood watch in their place for a fee of $20 a night. I initiated prayer services on board ship, where we studied not only the Bible, but also the Torah and other religious tracts. I was hoarding up as much of my $75-a-month salary as I could, and constantly trying to better myself. One night, the commanding officer made a surprise inspection after lights were supposed to be out at nine o'clock, and found me studying a correspondence course for law school. He was so impressed by the grade on one of my papers that he allowed me to use the dispensary to study after lights out from then on.

First and foremost, I was a loyal Marine. I was promoted to corporal, and then to sergeant. My years in the Marine Corps were my glory days. I loved the motto of *Semper Fidelis,* always faithful. The idea that I was a warrior who would give my life defending my country was a concept filled with honor and glory to me.

One day, Naval Captain Thomas, the captain of the ship, called me into his cabin on the USS *Toledo* and gave me an unexpected oral examination shortly before I was promoted to sergeant. Captain Thomas put a hypothetical situation before me.

"Corporal Hassan, I'm going to ask you a few questions because I have an appointment to Annapolis arranged for you. Here is the oral examination," he said.

Coming out of the blue, as it were, I was struck by a lightening bolt of excitement and a deepened sense of honor and commitment to my fellow comrades in arms at the greatest honor that could possibly be bestowed upon me during my lifetime.

"Yes, sir," I replied, although I had no idea of what was coming.

"You are now in Korea and you're holding Hill 827. The enemy wants that hill and they are coming after you. You have fourteen men with you and you are told to hold it. They are coming up that hill and they are pushing women and children before them. Now, what are you going to do?" Captain Thomas asked.

"Sir, I would ask my snipers, my riflemen, to selectively shoot at the leaders, officers, and enlisted men who are leading the charge," I replied.

"They are still coming," he said.

"Sir, I would summon my mortar squad. We'd mortar behind the civilians. We'd continue mortaring and we'd set up a main line of resistance or MLR."

"Corporal Hassan, they are still coming."

"Well, sir, if they are breaking through my MLR, I would give the order to bring out the bazookas and fix bayonets, because war is hell."

I had heard the phrase war is hell in a movie somewhere, but my answers reflected the way I saw war — as man-to-man combat, a battle of warriors, fought using all the available tools of war. And if civilians were used as pawns, as they were in the captain's scenario, killing them was to be avoided if at all possible. My responses must have satisfied Captain Thomas, and I also must have satisfied my other ranking superior officer, Marine Captain Thompson. At the end of my tour of duty I was flattered to be appointed to the United States Naval Academy at Annapolis, the only one of 190,000 Marines so chosen in the 7th Fleet. Both my Naval and Marine captains advised me I had been given the chance of a lifetime, and I felt that way, too.

In Hong Kong, as I said goodbye to Captain Thomas, I introduced him to a lovely young girl with whom I had fallen in love, the beautiful Monica Thirwell. Monica was only seventeen, but she spoke five languages, and I thought that since she was smarter than I was, we could get married and have a nice bunch of babies. But the captain pulled me out of earshot, and told me in an indirect way that he wanted me to go to Annapolis, and not to get married.

"Sgt. Hassan, if you marry this young lady, I am going to tear your arm off and beat you over the head with the bloody stump," he hissed in my ear.

"Yes, sir, I understand," I said.

I didn't get married. I would soon go to Annapolis, a proud but also a very lonely man.

Even before I left for Annapolis, I learned my grandfather had leukemia. I flew back to Iowa to see him. I told him I was going to Annapolis to become a Marine officer. He had told me before that he thought I'd be a good doctor, and he told me that again. I knew he was sick, but I didn't realize how serious it was because he drove me back to the airport himself. He had already had eighteen blood transfusions.

Flying back to Korea, I fell asleep and missed my plane at Travis Air Force Base. I tried to run after the plane, but an airman grabbed me.

"I can't miss ship's movement - it's a court-martial offense!" I gasped. But I'd already missed the plane. I later found out the plane I missed had gone down in the Pacific Ocean, near Wake Island.

Sixty-nine Marines and other soldiers died. The wreckage of the plane was never found, only a few pillow cases.

I was a proud young Marine aboard the USS Toledo.

After a long series of adventures, including a month of serving as an air courier and a guard in Korea, I eventually made it back to the ship, and on to Annapolis. I had been at Annapolis for only a month when my sister Miriam called me to tell me my grandfather's leukemia had gotten worse. He was in the hospital, she said, dying from chronic leucocytic leukemia. Although I took the first plane I could get, I was not able to get back to Red Oak before he died. He was seventy-three. I felt guilty, because I hadn't had time to talk to him, and to tell him how much I loved him, before he died. For years, I would think about him every day.

"Your grandfather depended on you to come back to take over the farm," one of my aunts told me, driving a knife of guilt into my heart. "Your grandmother thinks you killed your grandfather by telling him you wouldn't come back to the farm."

These words filled me with remorse as I took time off from Annapolis and stayed in Iowa to help my grandmother Millie Tuttle sell off the stock. I was the only one in the family who knew the bloodlines, and what each animal was worth, and I didn't want my grandmother to get ripped off. I stayed in Iowa to sell off the registered Black Angus and Brown Swiss cattle, the registered Duroc hogs, the Beltsville turkeys, the big Morgan riding horse we bought from a traveling circus, the magnificent Belgian pulling team my grandfather and I raised to compete in the Iowa State Fair in Des Moines, Belgian mares, and the stud Apollo. I was overwhelmed with guilt as I sold off these animals, because my grandfather had trained me all my life to run the farm, and I had not done so.

By the time I returned to Annapolis, I'd missed too much class. I was told I'd have to start class the following year. They told me I could wait around for the next fall semester, the only semester students were allowed to enter the academy. I stayed at Annapolis for a while, helping make training films, but I missed the camaraderie of the ship, I wasn't in school, I mourned my grandfather, and I felt my life was standing still.

When I was in Red Oak, my sister's husband, a veterinarian, had urged me to return to Iowa and complete my education.

"You'd be better off as a veterinarian than going to Annapolis," Richard Houck said. "You're a farm boy."

In Annapolis, where I was impatiently marking time, his words suddenly made sense to me. I was only twenty-one years old, and somewhat impatient. I called Iowa State University, and with the help of my brother-in-law, I was re-admitted there, even though I'd missed the first two weeks of classes. Although I was honorably discharged from the Marines, I have always regretted leaving Annapolis. I felt I let the people who nominated me down.

I hobbled back to Iowa State University on crutches from a diving accident that occurred just before I left, carrying my seabag. In addition to $3,500 in savings and $3,000 my grandfather left me, I had $110 a month from the GI Bill. Since I got a late start, my mid-term grades were terrible; in fact, I was failing everything. I was advised by the smartest professor I had to drop out, because I was too far behind. Professor O'Mara, the red-haired genetics professor, was reputed to have an IQ of 187, the highest on campus, and I listened carefully to what he said.

"Allen, you are too far behind. You're smart but I don't think you'll be able to make it. You've gotten terrible grades in my class," he said.

I asked Professor O'Mara to let me finish the semester, because I felt that, despite my dismal grades, the "lights were starting to come on."

"Well, you better have a very good electrical system to overcome the deficits you have with your other professors and myself," said Professor O'Mara.

I threw myself into my work, studying constantly, with only short bouts of sleep. My classmates generously invited me into study groups, which helped fill in the blank spots. My grades improved considerably. By the end of the quarter I had a B average. I had made the Dean's list before enlisting in the Marines, so the faculty ws kind enough to allow me into veterinary school.

In veterinary school at Iowa State, I served on our school's Supreme Court as chairman, top right. My colleagues included future presidential candidate and Senator Thomas Harkin, top left, and other student justices Sergeant, and Stifel on the back row. Front row includes Student Supreme Court members Cramer, Humphrey, and Timm.

Once I got going, veterinary school was difficult but I could do it. I'd run my grandfather's farm, I loved animals, and I knew how to take care of them. My classmates were other smart, high-achieving farm kids, and you had to be tenacious to survive the competitive grind. We were taught that you could judge a civilization by the way it treated its animals. We memorized the all the bacteria and diseases which could be transferred from animals to humans, and vice versa. We learned all the symptoms of all of these diseases in animals. We did many, many dissections and surgeries, of animals large and small. As much as anything else, all those delicate and precise surgeries prepared me for the demands of trying to save the civilian wounded in Vietnam.

In vet school, with sure-fingered Jimmy Higa, Richard Okey, and other members of my surgery team, we did exotic procedures on dogs and cats. We did delicate surgery on intestinal tracts, pulling them out, cutting them apart, and putting them carefully back together while the animals were still alive and under anesthesia, extremely difficult and sensitive procedures that gave me experience that would be invaluable when I went to Vietnam. We removed the spleen, kidneys, ovaries, uterus, part of a liver, part of a pancreas, and more on our test dogs. Once, a vet student tried to remove a tumor protruding from the nostril of a parrot with electricity, and the bird exploded. I remember waking up one morning on the anatomy table, next to a dead horse that I'd been dissecting for an examination the next morning. I remember our professors assuring us that we would know more than any damned MD in the country when we finished school, and besides that, we'd be more sober, too, since our school had a zero tolerance for alcohol.

While studying to be a veterinarian, I was admitted to the Acacia Scholarship Fraternity, an honor fraternity on campus. After I was elected vice president and pledge trainer of Acacia, one of my tasks was to pick up the world-famous Olympic hero, Jesse Owens, a black man who is judged by many to be the greatest American athlete ever. On the way back to school, Jesse Owens asked me if I was in a fraternity, and I said, yes, I was in the Acacia fraternity.

"As a man named Hassan, an Arab, you shouldn't be in a fraternity. Fraternities don't allow Negroes into their ranks," he said. "Do you realize fraternities are a major bastion of racism in the United States?"

I thought about this famous athlete's words over the next few weeks. Then I recommended a black football player, a personal friend, with a 3.6 GPA, to join our fraternity. I was appalled to see a minority of the active members line up to "blackball" this intelligent guy, saying they'd once heard him say the word "fuck." This hypocrisy frosted me, since I'd heard many of my fraternity brothers use the same language. At that moment, it seemed like an example of the racism Jesse Owens talked about to me.

In angry protest, I moved out of the fraternity house. I have always been able to connect with people, and from outside the fraternity house I began a campaign to talk to my more open-minded brothers about the unfairness of the selection procedure. Eventually, a large group of them came to my apartment and told me that the supervisor of the fraternity had agreed to change the bylaws so there would be no more exclusionary commentary. They asked me to come back as vice president, but I said I wouldn't return unless my football player friend was just as welcome as I. I guess I had made a point.

Although I was preparing to become a veterinarian, people I respected saw me as a doctor. Acacia's kindly housemother, Mother Dinsmore, had been watching me. One day, she took me aside and told me she thought my skills would be more useful as a medical doctor than as a veterinarian. I took her words to heart, as these were the same words I'd heard from my beloved grandfather, Pete Tuttle.

"You have too much to give to humans to waste it on animals," Mother Dinsmore told me.

"But I love animals as much as I love humans," I said.

"Love all God's creatures," Mother Dinsmore said. "But maximize your potential. Do not do less than what is your best."

Mother Dinsmore helped get me into medical school. She called the university and told them I had just graduated from veterinary school with very high grades, that I was extremely likeable, and that she thought I'd prosper better as a physician than as an animal doctor. I applied to medical school at the University of Iowa, in Iowa City, Iowa. While working part-time as a vet at the US Department of Agriculture's Animal Disease Eradication Program, I went to medical school as my grandfather had wanted me to do. Medicine was fifty percent listening to professors and reading, and the rest examining patients, smelling patients, touching patients, looking at patients, listening to patients.

For a while I thought I wanted to be a neurosurgeon. As a part of my surgical rotation, I worked in several hospital emergency rooms in California, ranging from hospitals in the inner city of Oakland, to a Native American tribal clinic on the Hoopa Reservation in Humboldt County. Not counting the many surgeries and dissections I performed in vet school, I must have assisted in hundreds of human surgeries of various kinds, ranging from many types of cancer surgeries and eye tumors, to emergency chest and abdominal wounds, fractures, and amputated limbs. Along the way, I even delivered a few babies.

I believe medicine is a noble calling. I have always liked a particular quote by the writer Robert Lewis Stevenson, who suffered from tuberculosis and had many dealings with doctors. "There are men and classes of men that stand above the common herd: the soldier, the sailor and the shepherd not unfrequently; the artist rarely; rarer still, the clergyman, the physician almost as a rule. He is the flower (such as it is) of our civilisation; and when that stage of man is done with, and only remembered to be marvelled at in history, he will be thought to have shared as little as any in the defects of the period, and most notably exhibited the virtues of the race. Generosity he has, such as is possible to those who practise an art, never to those who drive a trade; discretion, tested by a hundred secrets; tact, tried in a thousand embarrassments; and what are more important, Heraclean cheerfulness and courage. So it is that he brings air and cheer into the sickroom, and often enough, though not so often as he wishes, brings healing," Stevenson wrote.

After the rigorous discipline of medical school, and an externship in neurology, I settled on the field of psychiatry. Psychiatry was an area in which I could learn about people without judging them, I told my friends. Academically, I found psychiatry to be the easiest discipline I had attempted in school. I was particularly interested in transcultural psychiatry, a branch of psychiatry which deals not only with minority inmates in prison but also with understanding the culture and customs of other peoples in the world. I had a dream I could integrate experiential learning with theory, and eventually pursue a world public health career. In 1966, I moved to Northern California for a rotating internship at Mount Zion Hospital in San Francisco and a residency in psychiatry and neurology at Mendocino State Hospital, a state mental hospital near San Francisco. My bad experiences in California eventually propelled me to Vietnam.

I worked in the Mercy San Juan Hospital emergency room in Sacramento as an "ER doctor" on weekends, and did some independent research at nearby universities, but almost all the rest of the time I lived at the mental hospital. I threw myself into the psychiatric literature, learning all I could about the various mental illnesses. I thought psychiatrists could do the greatest good by working with the poor and disadvantaged, and the most seriously mentally ill, but one of the doctors at Mount Zion told me that, unless I had an office at the top of Nob Hill in San Francisco, I wouldn't be considered a good psychiatrist. After studying psychiatry at Mendocino State Hospital for two and a half years, I was disillusioned by the hostile environment the hospital staff created for the mental patients. Basically, I felt, we were warehousing people. None of us residents received much teaching, and after leaving Mendocino, many had to study an extra year to catch up on what they hadn't been taught.

Often, one of the residents would serve as a doctor for an entire ward of schizophrenic patients. As a resident, I was the only doctor assigned to a ward for young drug abusers for six months. The hospital administration seemed primarily interested in controlling the patients, using heavyweight psychiatric drugs such as Thorazine and Mellaril along with various types of punishment and confinement that sometimes bordered on the medieval.

It was my job, I believed, to understand the mentally ill people under our care, and to treat their illnesses without judging them. My attitude made things uncomfortable for me, and brought some clashes with my supervisors, who never managed to earn my respect. One of my supervisors, had let three of his horses die of starvation, and, as a former veterinarian and farm boy, this cruelty and neglect of dependent animals truly appalled me.

My other supervisors had some problems with me, too. Once, I took a busload of kids from a locked ward in the hospital on an outing to the Pacific Coast at Mendocino. The children functioned beautifully, without being loaded up with psychotropic drugs. We played softball, roasted hot dogs, and set up lifeguards so the kids could swim in the Pacific Ocean. I paid for this trip out of my own pocket, because I thought it would help the patients, and was a direction in which psychiatry ought to go.

Not long afterwards, Dr. John Gonda, a Stanford psychiatrist who was a visiting instructor in the program, visited Mendocino and told me he'd heard about me. He said I'd opened the windows and let the sun shine into Mendocino State Hospital because of activities like this. Keep doing what you're doing, he said, you'll be a great psychiatrist.

But not everyone approved of my humanitarian approach. When the administrators at Mendocino State Hospital found out about the outing to the beach, they put a memo in my file citing me for "unprofessional conduct." Another time, after I took a young autistic boy out of Mount Zion Hospital for an ice cream cone, another critical memo went into my file.

On still another occasion, I was appalled at the treatment of a teenage girl who had been placed in the schizophrenic ward, and I took action to rescue her. The girl had been admitted to the hospital a few days before for extreme anxiety, and "acting-out" behavior. Two days after being admitted, she was found having sex with another patient under some bushes. For punishment, she was placed in the schizophrenia ward, with patients who were much older, mostly over the age of sixty, and under very heavy medication.

I was horrified when I heard about this placement. The patients in that ward threw feces at each other, used foul language, and often assaulted each other. It was no place for a young girl. I asked that the girl be moved to a more compatible ward, with people closer to her age and her diagnosis. I was told to mind my own business. I went back to my ward, found a hatchet, and stood at the door to the schizophrenia ward, proclaiming, "If you don't release that girl from this ward, I'm going to chop the door down!"

For rescuing a damsel in distress, I was reprimanded severely and more memos went into the file. Disillusioning experiences like these led me to wonder if I was doing any good in the world as a doctor and a psychiatrist, or not. I had completed thirteen straight years of education, and I had two medical degrees. I was educated almost to the point of absurdity. Yet I was bored, and I didn't feel I'd really accomplished anything worthwhile in my life. I yearned to give something back. My very soul was malnourished.

A defining moment in my life was approaching. Outside the little world of the Mendocino State Hospital, the Vietnam War was heating up. I had read bits and pieces about the war and I was personally against it, although I believed strongly in the goodness and greatness of America. I was curious to learn more about Vietnam. And when a call for help came, this former Marine was more than ready to get off the sidelines, and plunge into the belly of the beast.

3

Volunteer Doctors for Vietnam

*"The truly great man is he who would master
no one and who would be mastered by none."
- Khalil Gilbran*

*"I find war detestable but those who praise it
without participating in it even more so."
- Romain Rolland*

*I*n January 1968, I noticed a short advertisement in the prestigious *Journal of the American Medical Association.* It said, "We need volunteer doctors in the Republic of Vietnam (South Vietnam) to provide health care for the civilian population, sponsored by the American Medical Association."

That year, I was one of about two hundred US doctors who answered the American Medical Association's humanitarian call. The Volunteer Physicians for Vietnam or VPVN program had been started three years before. It was supported by funds from the US Agency for International Development, and administered by the American Medical Association. Not many young doctors fresh out of medical training volunteered. Most of the volunteer doctors were middle-aged, and a few were over the age of seventy.

At that time, the civilian population of war-torn Vietnam was desperately in need of doctors. Until the Volunteer Physicians in Vietnam program was terminated in June 1973, it needed thirty-two doctors to volunteer every two months. Many American doctors responded. Altogether, some 774 physicians served unpaid, two-month tours of duty in Vietnam, given only per diem expenses of $10 per day and $50,000 insurance policies. I am proud to be counted among the American doctors who volunteered for the Volunteer Physicians for Vietnam, and one of about seventeen percent who returned to Vietnam for a second tour. In the process of preparing this book, I wrote other doctors who volunteered, and several were kind enough to respond with insightful comments which are excerpted in these chapters, and printed in full in the last chapter of this book.

One of the first doctors to volunteer for Vietnam was Dr. William Shaw, who was seventy-two years old when he went to Vietnam in 1965. Although Dr. Shaw died in 1973, after having received many honors as a family doctor and a military surgeon, he recorded some telling statistics about the practice of medicine during the Vietnam War. South Vietnam was a country of 17 million people, with only 700 licensed physicians. Of these, 500 served with South Vietnam's armed forces, leaving only 200 doctors to treat millions of civilians in a country being blown apart by war. A few doctors from other countries such as Australia, New Zealand, the Philippines, Korea, Italy and Iran were already present and trying to help fill the gap when Dr. Shaw arrived in Vietnam. In the cities, Dr. Shaw noted, Vietnam had one doctor per 25,000 people. In the rural areas, he estimated, it was closer to one doctor per 100,000 people. This compared to the US ratio of one doctor per 700 people, and Japan's ratio of one physician per every 920 people at the time.

When I volunteered to help through the American Medical Association, I didn't realize that a relatively short stint of medical duty in Vietnam would become a defining moment in my life. As a Marine, I had developed a fondness for the Far East, having landed in Hong Kong, Macao, Japan, South Korea, and other exotic ports of call in the Pacific. I spoke some Chinese, Japanese, and Korean. Vividly bound up with my Marine Corps days, and my service on the USS *Toledo*, the East was a fascinating region of the world for me. Probably most of all, I volunteered because I desperately needed a change from my frustrating and unrewarding residency at Mendocino State Hospital.

Although I didn't know it at the time, Vietnam would eventually finish my residency in psychiatry. I had only three months to go in my residency when I volunteered for Vietnam. I may have acted impulsively, but I badly needed a break. I was drawn toward the war not only as a former Marine, but as a doctor looking for useful work to do.

My supervisors at the mental hospital were not happy about the break in my residency. The doctors who supervised me had a meeting and vetoed my going to Vietnam. But I was finally able to persuade them when I told them my training would be enhanced by the paper I was going to write on the Vietnamese psychiatric system. Then I took an unpaid leave of absence, and prepared to go to South Vietnam.

Vietnam was a divided country at that time, the center of a bitter war between the Communist government of North Vietnam and the South Vietnamese government supported by the United States. The French called that part of the world Indochina. Vietnam had been a very rural country, producing commodities like rice and rubber on a sort of plantation system run by the French until the end of the French Indochinese War in 1954. When the French withdrew, the Geneva Accords temporarily partitioned Vietnam into two parts. Ho Chi Minh, a nationalist hero, quickly established a Communist government in North Vietnam. This caused nearly a million Catholics to flee to South Vietnam. As war continued, people from the farms of South Vietnam migrated or were forced into urban areas, transforming the South Vietnamese population from rural to urban. As advisors and then American troops poured in to support South Vietnam during a long and bitter war, North Vietnamese troops along with guerillas from the National Liberation Front or Viet Cong fought to reunite Vietnam. Although nobody realized it in 1968, this bloody, brutal civil war would grind on and on like a bad dream, producing more and more casualties until a cease fire halted the fighting in January 1973.

The American Medical Association sent instructions to its volunteer doctors in a series of short letters. The letters spelled out which vaccinations to receive, which pills to take, how to deal with passport requirements, and so on. One letter suggested that we study up on both the French and Vietnamese languages. As doctors, we were warned that we would encounter tropical diseases we didn't see in the United States, such as bubonic plague, malaria, and typhoid fever, which were rampant in the villages. We also expected to treat people for bullet and shrapnel wounds and infections which were a natural result of the war.

I was excited to be going to an exotic land, and to be getting a break from my work at the state mental hospital. I was excited to be contributing something useful to the world as a medical doctor. But I tried to prepare, since I knew I wouldn't have the same pristine working conditions I had as a doctor in the United States when working in the jungle villages of Vietnam.

I packed books on tropical medicine, trauma surgery, orthopedic surgery, and how to maintain electrolyte balance in emergency rooms. The most useful of these was a thick little book entitled *Emergency War*

Surgery, NATO Handbook, Department of Defense, United States of America, which I'd picked up for $2.25 in a San Francisco bookstore near Mount Zion Hospital. I naively expected to be able to read my medical books in the evenings, after a day of medical work. I didn't realize that the unending stream of traumatic emergencies I would deal with during the daylight hours would frequently exhaust me, and leave no time or energy for even necessary reading. I didn't appreciate how little can actually be seen by candlelight in a bunker, and how any light at all can make you a target for incoming mortar fire. Like many of the doctors who volunteered for service, I was somewhat naive about actual conditions in Vietnam.

"Arrived alone and a little scared in Nha Trang," recalls Dr. William P. Levonian of his arrival to serve in one of Vietnam's provincial hospitals. "No one at the airport to meet me. Not sure I even got off the plane in the right town. No one around who spoke English, having no idea which way to town. Hitched ride with suitcase in hand to Provincial Hospital, having no idea who was VC or otherwise. The hospital thought I was to arrive the next day."

Dr. William Shaw set down his thoughts regarding his time as a volunteer physician in Nha Trang: "In one month in my hospital, diseases included hepatitis, tonsilitis, diphtheria, Ascaris, leprosy, encephalitis, bubonic plague, myopathy, dysentery, malnutrition, cholera, and worms. On the survey of my surgical ward of thirty, thirteen of the group were listed as battle casualties. Generally 50% of our patients were battle casualties, but many times the number of casualties we saw died before being admitted to the hospital. In one instance, four out of six injured civilians died before surgery could be done."

"The first day was my hardest," recalled Dr. Carnes Weeks, who at the age of forty-three left a busy rural medical practice to help out in Vietnam. Unfortunately, he arrived in Phan Rang suffering from serious stomach pain. "While suffering acute gastroenteritis made worse by the smell of the hospital population, a line of patients stretching for three blocks (many traveling all night by foot and ox cart). On this day, I was very happy and thankful for the local custom of siesta during the hot afternoon. I had a chance to lie down for a couple of hours and get refreshed with liquids and some rest. In the next month, we became quite adept at triaging, improvising, and empathizing. We treated bubonic plague, cholera, tetanus, polio and TB, to name only a few."

Dr. Bill Owen recalls his first impressions of the hospital to which he was assigned in Bac Lieu, in the southeast part of Vietnam: "There was no running water. Pigs and sheep wandered through the empty wards. I saw 120 children in the first outpatient clinic I had. A mother came in and handed me a baby who died in my arms."

Dr. Marvin H. Lottman, a surgeon, recalls his arrival in Go Cong to assist a team of Spanish doctors as "the most depressing point in my entire medical career." Arriving in the Mekong Delta hospital, he looked around and realized, "the only instruments available are old, rusty and poorly sterilized. What there is available is for abdominal surgery along with some GU and rectal instruments. There are no orthopedic tools at all. There is no traction available. Little or no suture is present and what's there is #3 linen. The only antibiotics available were those I brought with me. There is no ventilation in the wards, no IV solution, no blood bank, no hygiene – the more I look, the more problems become apparent. It will probably get worse as I learn more about it."

In Quang Ngai, Dr. Gilbert Lee was seeing 600 new patients a day in a hospital with no sewage disposal, a trickle of water, and naked light bulbs. Dr. Lee added: "I was shocked by this temple of misery, a whirlpool of blood and pus. The lines of sick and wounded trailing in and streams of refugees flowing out. By the end of my first week in Vietnam, I was convinced Vietnamese medicine was a different profession from the one I had practiced in the US."

"When I first hit the ground at my Mekong Delta hospital, I saw a lady lying on a stretcher just outside with her right arm severed below the shoulder joint," recalls Dr. John McCann, who served in Phu Vinh. "No dressing had been applied. According to the interpreter, the Viet Cong had questioned this lady at great length. They felt she had some knowledge they needed, but she stubbornly refused to answer their questions, so the VC cut off her arm. They left her here to bleed to death. Her family carried her many miles to the hospital. She was eighty-three years old and she did survive."

About this time, ready to join my volunteer colleagues, I was making plans to catch the next plane for Vietnam.

4

Arriving in Saigon

"Can anything be more ridiculous than that a man should have the right to kill me because he lives on the other side of the ocean and because his ruler has a quarrel with my ruler though I have none with him?" - Pascal, 1670

I boarded a plane in San Francisco on May 3, 1968, and arrived in Hong Kong on May 5. On May 7, I left the Peninsula Hotel and boarded a commercial airline flight to Vietnam containing about a dozen other volunteer doctors and several soldiers. We rose into the air over Hong Kong and headed across the deep blue sea toward Saigon, the capital of South Vietnam.

When we entered Vietnamese airspace, the plane began to swerve violently from side to side. Four airplanes had been shot down in the past two years, a stewardess told me. The zigging and zagging was a necessary if gut-wrenching precaution to help us avoid being shot down.

Only a few months earlier, the Tet offensive had been a huge and unexpected reversal in the Vietnam war. Many South Vietnamese cities had been attacked simultaneously by North Vietnamese and Viet Cong forces, and enemy forces were beaten back at great cost. As our plane prepared to land, another, smaller Tet-type offensive was underway in parts of the city, including attacks on the Chinese or Cholon district in the heart of Saigon.

Below us, approaching Saigon, I could see an expanse of lush Vietnamese jungle, cut by a maze of rivers snaking their way through the rich green delta to the pale blue South China Sea. The landscape below us was peaceful, a giant postcard of serenity. But the landing was not peaceful at all.

The way our plane landed confirmed we were in a war zone. Over Saigon, our pilot made a sudden nosedive, an extremely fast descent, and a sudden screeching landing that felt to me as if the plane might turn over on its nose. We were hurried out of the plane at Ton Son Nhut Airport, and into the aircraft terminal. We were obviously in a war zone. Damaged planes sat off the runway and in hangars. The airport and terminal were ringed with barbed concertina wire. Sandbagged machine gun bunkers were visible every forty feet. Every area around the airport was blocked and configured for visual surveillance to thwart Viet Cong infiltrators.

As we made for the bus, we all began to sweat in the high humidity of Vietnam. The first things I noticed were the thin metal screens on the open bus windows of the bus that took us to the hotel. I was told these were to protect against grenades being tossed into our bus. Later in the war, the Viet Cong learned to circumvent this rudimentary protection by attaching fish hooks to their grenades.

Saigon, the picturesque French provincial capital, had become the capital of South Vietnam. The historic old city was built almost entirely by the French during colonial times, and it had a kind of bright, colorful, colonial charm. The streets were crowded with pedestrians and people in cars and on bicycles and rickshaws, some in light flowing garments, many wearing distinctive cone-shaped Vietnamese straw hats to protect them from the sun. Many French-style chateaus remained from the colonial era. But the other doctors and I also saw a city pockmarked by sporadic fighting. Saigon was already an armed fortress. We saw craters in the streets and a few bombed-out buildings. People wandered and bicycled through the streets, trying to go about their business. The nearby hills and jungle were full of Viet Cong guerillas pressing the attack daily.

We passed dozens of bunkers, machine gun nests made of stacked-up sandbags and rimmed with barbed wire. The machine gun nests were manned by tough, grimacing South Vietnamese soldiers wearing dark sunglasses. The "Tet II" offensive began May 7, the day we arrived. Fighting was underway in Saigon, and it would continue for nearly a month more through most of Vietnam. It was a relief to reach the elegantly beautiful old French hotel. The Caravelle Hotel was the headquarters of the Volunteer Physicians in Vietnam. At the Caravelle, we were met by a stunningly beautiful Vietnamese hostess, a lovely angel of grace who never smiled, but treated us all like royalty for two days. And the meals were sumptuous.

"During our briefing in Saigon, we were told there were three reasons for our being there," recalled Dr. Victor S. Falk, who would be stationed in Vinh Binh. "The first was psychological impact, both on the Vietnamese and the home front. The second was to teach and train the Vietnamese in the provincial hospitals to which we were assigned. Perhaps some of our methods and practices could rub off on the observers. The third was immediate medical care. The last proved to be the most important and consumed our time."

Inside the Caravelle Hotel, meeting some of the other volunteer doctors, I learned that none of us had been assigned a specific duty location yet. We discussed the situation in Vietnam, and the possible assignments that were open. In a few days, we knew, we'd all be assigned somewhere, most of us shipped out of the city to new surroundings in South Vietnam.

That night, as I lay in the presumed safety of my bed in the Caravelle Hotel, my bed was shaken and rocked by the sound of exploding bombs nearby. On a later visit to Saigon, I would find out I could stand on the roof of the hotel and literally watch the war around us.

At breakfast I ran into Jim Cavanaugh, a volunteer doctor I'd bunked and partied with in Hong Kong. Jim was ten years older than I, but we became fast friends in Hong Kong. Jim was a former US Army paratrooper, and I was a former Marine. We were advised to stay in the hotel, but Jim and I decided to see what happened the night before. We caught a taxi to the site of the bombing which was not far away. On the way, Jim showed me a pistol he'd brought over from the US.

"You never know when you might need this in 'Nam," he said, flashing a 45-caliber pistol.

Jim was an adventurous, hard-drinking former soldier, a paratrooper during the Korean War and a doctor who loved living on the edge. While in Vietnam, he ventured into many wild and dangerous areas in the company of American Green Berets. Before long, he would have the distinction of being the only VPVN doctor expelled from Vietnam, but we would remain friends. Back in the US, we would briefly share a medical office and practice together.

Stepping out of our cab, Dr. Cavanaugh and I looked over the Cholon section of Saigon which had been bombed the night before.

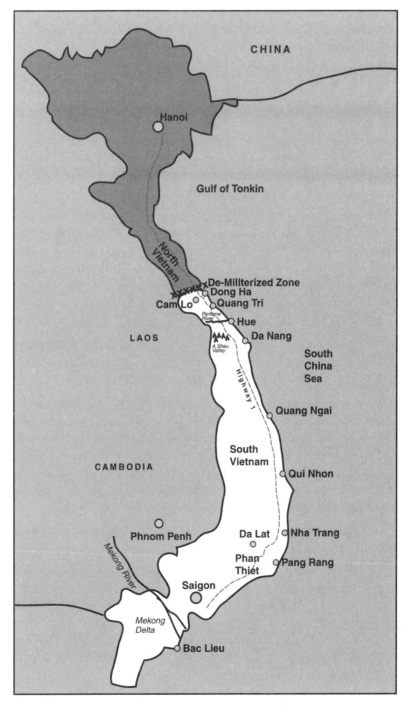

Map of Indochina, North and South Vietnam

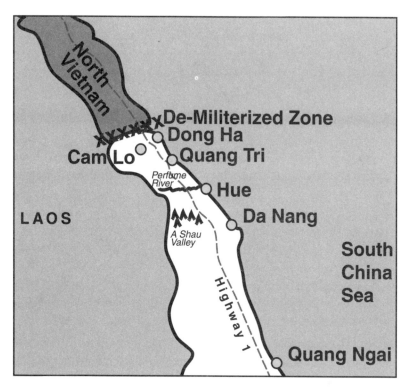

Area around the De-miterized Zone.

Low-flying jets had strafed an area where a clandestine guerrilla encampment was said to be located. Powerful bombs had been dropped on the Viet Cong hideout. The area was still warm and smoldering when we stepped out of the taxi. It was our first look at the devastation of the Vietnam war.

An entire city block had been bombed. The first thing I saw was a smoldering bed mattress, still hot and slowly burning, emitting a strange smell I would later recognize as napalm. Although we saw no bodies, as doctors we recognized the familiar smell of death in the air. The dead and wounded must have been evacuated, we thought. To me, the bombing seemed indiscriminate, dropping bombs on a densely populated area in the center of a big city. I wondered, who did this? What was its purpose? Why did it seem so reckless? Answers to questions like this did not come easily in Vietnam, if they came at all.

Jim and I returned to the Caravelle Hotel feeling more like veterans than we did before.

Over the next couple of days, the new contingent of volunteer physicians met informally to get to know each other, and to exchange notes and ideas. Many of my fellow volunteers were experienced surgeons. Several very experienced neurosurgeons, orthopedic surgeons, and other specialists had volunteered. Most were in their forties and fifties, some in their sixties. I was easily the youngest man in the group, and I felt like it. In stark contrast to these men around me, I was a young psychiatrist in training with very little surgical experience, about to be assigned as a medical doctor somewhere in Vietnam. But all of us had something in common, something that brought us to Vietnam.

"I will never be quite sure why I volunteered," recalled Dr. William P. Levonian, another volunteer physician. "The State Department's Agency for International Development planned to help civilians in Vietnam. I just thought it was the right thing to do. I was unsure if I had the right to risk sacrificing the happiness and future well-being of my entire family as I waved goodbye through the airplane window. My wife and kids standing there waving goodbye gave me good reason to question my judgment," Dr. Levonian recalled.

"As nearly as I can tell, there are many reasons for serving as a volunteer physician in Vietnam," observed Dr. William J. Rogers III, who served as a volunteer physician in Da Nang. "In talking with American volunteers, I found that the reasons for their being there could not be easily verbalized, but all said it was something they wanted to do, and maybe had to do, without being able to say why. These people are different. Their motivation is not quelled by riding in the latest model luxury car, or by getting a hard-bargained-for salary raise, or gaining the position of no longer having to take a night call, or a thousand and one things that sometimes seem to be the ultimate goal of physicians."

The other volunteer doctors and I were given a briefing by the US State Department, covering the history, economic and military situation in Vietnam. Final duty assignments were handed out by Dr. Charles H. Mosley, at that time the program's field director in Saigon. One of the areas that needed a civilian doctor, what the Vietnamese call "Bac Si," was the distant Quang Tri province, to the far north end of South Vietnam. Quang Tri needed a general practitioner. Our briefers informed us Quang Tri was a highly sensitive, insecure area near the demilitarized zone. It was about twenty-five miles south of the border between North and South Vietnam, and in the midst of the fierce fighting. The volunteer assigned to Quang Tri hospital should have military experience, we were told, preferably as a paratrooper or another combat field. Not having immediate family would also be preferred.

"I'll go to Quang Tri," I found myself saying, as I raised my hand. "I was in the Marines. I can take care of myself."

My colleagues looked at me with blank stares, which at the time I didn't notice too much. No one else volunteered for this position, so I more or less got the job by default. Since I had been a Marine, I felt I could handle any situation in Vietnam, however precarious. I wasn't married, which was another plus. Most of the other doctors would be assigned to areas of Vietnam where there was less risk of personal injury or death, but I became the first volunteer physician to go to Quang Tri. Many times during my stay in Vietnam I would remember and act on the motto of the Volunteer Physicians, "If it comes to you, do it!"

The weather was warm and humid as I boarded the plane to leave Saigon.

5

Open Heart Surgery in Hue

"When the rich wage war, it is the poor who die."
- Jean Paul Sartre

*V*ietnam's Highway One, also known as the Street Without Joy, is a long, treacherous highway. It is the major north-south road in Vietnam. It was built by the French, who gave it the sadly appropriate name *La Rue Sans Joie.* Running from Saigon north to Hue, to Quang Tri, and beyond, the Street Without Joy carried American and South Vietnamese military convoys which were attacked day and night by enemy snipers during the Vietnam War. Leaving Saigon, I flew into a small jungle airfield in Phu Bai, a secured Marine base a few miles from Hue. In Hue, I was to meet up with some other Volunteer Physicians before heading on by Jeep to Quang Tri.

I remember stepping off a small ten-passenger Air Vietnam airplane onto a steaming black runway. The jungle around the Phu Bai Airport was partially destroyed by defoliants and bombs, but the black asphalt runway was pristine. I carried a knapsack containing a toothbrush, shaving kit, toothpaste, three clean T-shirts, an extra pair of Levi's, the NATO surgery book, a tropical disease book, two apples, an orange, and a banana. A colonel gave me a quick tour of a small one-story military hospital in a Quonset hut at Phu Bai. It was a bright, orderly little military hospital. I remember the quietness, the antiseptic smell. I remember the neat rows of beds, each containing a wounded Marine or soldier. Some of the soldiers' legs were up in slings, but most wounds were not visible, hidden under dull brownish-green Army blankets.

"Hey doc, over here!" a male voice called.

Who in Phu Bai knew I was a doctor? Not far away, under a blanket, I saw a familiar clean-shaven face over a pair of broad shoulders. The man had a military haircut and sad eyes. It was a man I knew only as Jerry, a handsome, square-jawed Marine lieutenant. Only a few months before, we met at the Shadowbox Bar in San Francisco, a watering hole for interns near Mount Zion Hospital. I had commented on Jerry's full dress-blue Marine uniform, and told him I'd been a Marine. We talked and had a few drinks together while checking out the girls and talking. I had my doubts about the war, and he had his doubts, too, he said, but he was a loyal Marine lieutenant and he went where they sent him. And here he was in a hospital in Vietnam.

"Just a moment, sir," I said, breaking ranks with the colonel and approaching his bed.

"Jerry!" I said. "What the hell are you here for?"

He told me he'd been in Dong Ha a few weeks before, in early May, during the Tet offensive. Dong Ha was approximately seven or eight miles north of Quang Tri, the site of my assignment. Jerry said it was like hell up there, too many enemy, American soldiers couldn't hold the front line. Jerry had jumped into a bomb crater for protection. A mortar followed him and exploded. They were still picking shrapnel out of his back, he said. He was paralyzed from the waist down, and he said he had trouble moving his arms.

"But you look great," I said.

"I don't look great under here," he said, lifting the blanket a bit.

The colonel let me know we had to leave. I told Jerry I'd meet him in San Francisco, that we'd do some drinking and dancing and girl-chasing. I told him that the military doctors were excellent, and that he'd get better. Jerry said maybe he'd drink with me, but he didn't think he'd be dancing anymore.

The short drive from the airport to the old city of Hue was a hair-raising speed dash through the jungle by Jeep. My driver said he had to go fast to avoid Viet Cong snipers, who regularly attacked any American vehicle. As we roared down the Street Without Joy, we passed along a jungle river, the beautiful *Song Huong*, the River of Perfumes. The winding jungle river was named for the exotic and fragrant flowers springing from lush tropical vegetation that lined its banks.

Hue was a university town of more than 100,000 people. It was surrounded by traditional Vietnamese architecture including palatial villas and monuments, many of which were eventually destroyed or damaged in the war. A center of learning and culture, Hue was the old Imperial capital of Vietnam. It contained a "Forbidden City," or citadel, at the heart of the city. The culture of Vietnam was 4,000 years old. Throughout the reign of thirteen emperors, Hue had been a home to Vietnam's most important scholars, artists, philosophers, and doctors. While the French occupation of Indochina from 1889-1954 was exploitative and cruel, and kept most Vietnamese in horrible poverty, there were some outstanding humanitarian gestures by the French. For instance, protegees of Louis Pasteur built the first two Pasteur Institutes outside Paris in Vietnam, in the late 19th century.

Hue was also the site of the large Hue University Hospital, perhaps the best hospital in South Vietnam. The 1,000-bed hospital, built by the French to reduce disease by cleanliness, trained highly skilled Vietnamese doctors to perform some of the most remarkable work in all of Southeast Asia. Doctors in Hue were able to maintain some degree of sterility, and to control flies, mosquitoes, and other disease-carrying insects.

In Hue, I met several American doctors, including Dr. Howard Detwiler, a portly ear, nose and throat specialist who would become my mentor. The kindly Dr. Detwiler was sixty-five years old when he left a good practice in Michigan and volunteered to serve as a doctor in Vietnam. He was nearly retired. His medical team in Hue consisted of three other volunteer doctors: Dr. Grant Raitt, a radiologist, Dr. Ralf Young, a pediatrician, and Dr. Joe Nettles, an orthopedic surgeon.

The city of Hue had been overrun by North Vietnamese Army troops during the Tet offensive just weeks before. Before Dr. Nettles and the three other American doctors arrived, four German doctors hired by the South Vietnamese government to teach there had been found in shallow graves, having been mutilated and shot, execution-style. Dr. Nettles vividly remembers his first look at the crowded Hue hospital which was desperately in need of doctors when they arrived.

"There were literally two to three patients per bed in this thousand bed hospital," Dr. Nettles wrote, years later. "Included in this was a chronic leprosy wing. The hospital was secured by day, but incoming mortar rounds came in several times at night. We were advised to sleep in the pediatric ward with our M16s and hand grenades close by in case of a repeat overrun. Each morning at daybreak, new casualties from the B-52 bombings during the night would be lined up at the compound gate."

"The horrific wounds were sometimes hard to describe and certainly harder to treat," Dr. Nettles recalled. "I was busy from dawn to dusk each day and remember that when the weather got real hot one late afternoon I went across the road in front of the hospital and jumped into the Perfume River in my scrubs to cool off. I was swimming along quite refreshed until I hit a warm current and realized I was swimming through the effluent from the hospital sewage."

During my first few days of training in Hue, I got a taste of what awaited me in Quang Tri. There was a sort of insanity in the air.

I met Dr. Detwiler when he was hiding under a hospital bed. An angry South Vietnamese soldier was stalking through the halls of the hospital with an M16 rifle, trying to find him. The soldier shouted that he was going to kill Dr. Detwiler. The kindly old specialist had killed the man's son. Dr. Detwiler had surgically corrected the boy's cleft palate – a common problem in Vietnam – but the boy had a loose tooth. After the surgery, in post-op, the boy had aspirated the tooth. The tooth lodged in his windpipe and the boy suffocated, probably because the nurses weren't paying attention. The 240-pound doctor escaped death by hiding under a small bed in one of the unused hospital rooms, and the angry South Vietnamese soldier eventually cooled down.

Three days later, Dr. Detwiler and I had stepped out when we found a twenty-one-year-old Vietnamese soldier collapsed on the hospital steps. There was a small red spot over his heart, and blood spreading out over the fabric of his South Vietnamese army uniform. His stitched name tag read "Corp. Binh." The young soldier was nearly dead. Dr. Detwiler noticed his distended neck veins.

"We got a cardiac tamponade here," Dr. Detwiler said. "Let's get him into the emergency surgery suite immediately."

Dr. Detwiler and I carried the young soldier into the Hue University Hospital surgical suite and placed him onto the operating table. The young soldier weighed about 120 pounds and we got him there in about a minute, but he was dying. This was the same operating room where Dr. Detwiler had lost the boy.

"Bring me scalpels! Bring me fluids! Bring me blood, universal donor, whatever you have, gallons of it!" Dr. Detwiler shouted. We were joined by Dr. Nettles, and several Vietnamese nurses magically appeared, seemingly out of nowhere.

"Open his femoral vein," Dr. Detwiler snapped. "We need a femoral on the right and a femoral on the left! We need to pour fluid in him! He's losing blood! Get ready to crack his chest!"

We sloshed alcohol over his chest, and strapped the young man onto the operating table. Although he was already semi-comatose, Dr. Detwiler didn't want the soldier moving around during surgery. He called for ether, which was all we had for anesthesia except for Pentothal which might have put him too far under. We isolated two veins in the thighs and put catheters in them, to expedite transfusion of blood to the heart. Luckily, the man hadn't lost too much blood.

The most important thing was to get him in the correct position, on his back, with his head hyper-extended so that he wouldn't choke to death. We put a tube through his nose into his trachea so he would be able to breathe.

"Do you know where to open him?" Dr. Detwiler asked me.

"I think so," I said.

I slashed between ribs six and seven, a long slash from the edge of the sternum to the midaxillary line between the ribs. I remembered my medical school training: nerve, artery, vein. I remembered that the nerves, veins, and arteries lie at the inferior edge of the rib, and that if you hit them the patient will bleed to death or suffer severe nerve damage. That day, for some reason, I associated the letters N, A, and V in my mind with the North Vietnamese Army. I sliced the patient's chest; we cracked the ribcage open, and put in chest retractors. As I opened him up, a fountain of red blood hit the ceiling of the operating room. The soldier's blood dripped down on us as we worked.

The blood that spurted up to the ceiling showed us that the heart we pulled out of his chest was still alive, and that it was strong enough for its rhythm to be restored. We had hit the pericardial sac around the heart, which had filled with blood and stopped the heart from beating. This had distended the veins up into the neck, which Dr. Detwiler recognized as a cardiac tamponade.

Although Hue Hospital was the best facility in Vietnam, we didn't have a heart monitor to observe his heart functions, and no oxyometer. As doctors often did in Vietnam, we proceeded based on intuition and experience. Dr. Detwiler ordered more fluid into the femoral veins, to replace the blood he was losing, and to lower the probability of shock.

While the patient was receiving fluids, Dr. Detwiler called for more ether. We were anxious to avoid as much shock as possible, since shock can be a major cause of death in these situations. Turning the patient from side to side during surgery can induce or aggravate shock. Shock may appear immediately or insidiously. Shock is a defensive reaction which increases heartbeat and impairs the efficiency of the circulating blood, producing paleness, a lack of oxygen to the brain, and a suppression of function in the body. In severe shock, the liver and kidneys can shut down and cause death.

We probed and discovered a three-centimeter wound through his heart. Apparently, the soldier took a bayonet between his sixth and seventh ribs. It was a low-velocity wound, and not as nasty as the wounds I would see later from shrapnel, bullets, and bombs. However, the tip of the bayonet went completely through his heart – penetrating the pericardium, both heart ventricles, the interventricular muscle, and nicking his diaphragm. As a result of these wounds, we saw that his pierced, bleeding heart had stopped beating.

"I'll take the right and you take the left," Dr. Detwiler said.

"What should I use, 4-0 chromic?"

"No, use 3-0 chromic," he said, instructing me to use a thicker, stronger surgical thread. "We've got to make it last."

To keep the young man alive, we had to stitch up the holes in his heart. We worked quickly to save him. If the patient lived, we could worry later about complications such as a ventrical septal defect, or adhesions forming around the pericardium that could adhere to the heart. Dr. Detwiler worked on the left wound and I started on the right, as blood oozed from both wounds.

Miraculously, it seemed, as we were sewing up the holes on both sides of his heart, the young soldier's heart started beating again. Because the heart was moving now, we had to wait, and sew on the beat. Beat, take a stitch, try to tie the knot, beat, try to take another stitch, try to tie the knot, and so on. It was like trying to sew up a live, warm, wet wiggling frog that was trying to jump out of your hands. Meanwhile, blood continued to ooze out of his heart.

With every beat of his heart, I felt we got closer to success. The possibility of saving his life came closer and closer. We thought the patient might live if we could close the holes in both sides of his beating, bleeding heart.

We worked as quickly and carefully as possible. We were pouring in the fluids, normal saline. The patient had lost at least three liters of blood, and was probably down to a 6 of hemoglobin, less than half of normal. We didn't have replacement blood. The important thing was, the man was still alive.

Within ten minutes of when we'd begun, the ventricle and heart wounds were closed. It seemed like we'd been working for hours. We took a deep breath. We approached the next step, the pericardial sac. Dr. Detwiler said, "I'm no heart surgeon, but I think we ought to leave it open."

"Sure enough," I said.

We put small drains in the right and left, little pieces of iodoform gauze measuring one centimeter by six centimeters, which would allow the blood to come out of the pericardial sac while the heart healed. We had to do something, because if the oozing blood didn't drain off we'd be right back where we were before, and he'd need a second surgery.

We began closing up his chest. I noticed Dr. Detwiler sweating profusely. His face was pale.

Suddenly, the ether wore off. The soldier woke up. He tried to sit up, moaning and groaning. Fortunately, he was still groggy from the ether and weak from loss of blood. Our corpsmen were able to hold him down until we finished.

The soldier wanted to get up and go home as soon as the operation was complete. But our Vietnamese nurses talked to him, and gently coaxed him to stay the night. I relaxed for a moment, and took a deep breath. It had come to me, and I had done it. However, when Dr. Detwiler and I returned to the hospital the next morning, we found that our first open-heart surgery patient was gone. Patients who walked out of the hospital after surgery were not uncommon in Vietnam.

"Rounds in the morning showed many patients missing," recalled Dr. Carnes Weeks, a volunteer physician in Phan Rang, another part of Vietnam. "If they died, they were taken home to their village. Likewise, if they had gotten slightly better they took them home on their own and discharged themselves. We had to ask the night nurse, if she hadn't left already, what happened to whom, and when and why."

"Customarily several family members would remain with their patients during their hospitalization," recalls Dr. R.B. Richards, a volunteer physician who served in rural Ban Mi Thout. "They would cook their meals on a small fire on the ground. Frequently, on making my rounds, I found one or two very ill patients were not in the ward. I asked the nurse what happened. She said that the family had taken the patients away to die at home rather than in the hospital."

After a few days of orientation and training from my American colleagues in Hue, I was on my way by Jeep to Quang Tri Hospital. We hurried north, up the Street Without Joy. I was to join a military doctor who was stationed Quang Tri. My colleagues in Hue had told me they thought that I was out of my mind to go to Quang Tri, which was surrounded with heavy fighting. Looking back, maybe I was a little too gung-ho as I left Hue. After I arrived, I would find out that Quang Tri could be one of the most dangerous places on the planet.

6

Quang Tri Provincial Hospital

*"Once we thought a few hundred corpses
would be enough
Then we said thousands were still too few
And today we can't even count all the dead
everywhere you look."*
– Peter Weiss, Marat/Sade

I arrived by Jeep in Quang Tri, and was pleasantly surprised by the remarkable brick and wood building that was Quang Tri Provincial Hospital. Several of the buildings had been built by the French, in the style of French colonial architecture. A handsome stairway led up to a large, ornate, arched entrance to the hospital. Visitors were greeted by an impressively large foyer about twenty feet square, whose marble floors were kept clean and well-polished at all times. US Naval Commander Robert Hurst, whom I was to assist, was the small hospital's full-time physician-surgeon. Commander Hurst showed me around the eighty-bed provincial hospital, which included two large tents outside which could expand the hospital's capacity to 350 beds. The tents were for overflow cases, but they were empty when I arrived. Commander Hurst introduced me to the staff, including some of the Naval corpsmen and the Vietnamese nurses.

The surgical suite, constructed of brick, had a number of open windows which let in light, and it was a fairly decent space to work in. Neither the surgical suite nor the hospital wards were air-conditioned, and there were no screens on the windows to keep out the flies, but there was a watering system and a sewer system. From the standpoint of the Vietnamese civilians, Commander Hurst assured me, Quang Tri

Provincial Hospital was a first-class facility and the local people's best hope for decent medical care in a jungle war zone.

They didn't provide me with mosquito nets in my small room at the hospital, where I slept after I first arrived, and I was given only a wool blanket to keep the mosquitoes off. Very soon after arriving in Quang Tri I became extremely sick, suffering chills and fever. I came down with what would later be diagnosed as malaria when I got back to the US. Commander Hurst came to visit me in my quarters, I remember, and I told him I had injected myself in the buttocks with big doses of penicillin, trying to speed my recovery. I was able to get back up to speed before too long, probably because, at Commander Hurst's insistence, I resumed taking chloroquine phosphate twice a week as prophylaxis against malaria. I had stopped taking it for a while because of side effects.

Unfortunately, as I began to get well, Commander Hurst came down with a critical case of hepatitis, possibly because he didn't operate wearing rubber gloves. Rubber gloves were not always available, or used, for surgery in Vietnam. Commander Hurst left a few days after I arrived. He was probably taken to the USS *Sanctuary*, a hospital ship anchored off the coast a few miles away. The first civilian doctor in the hospital, assigned as a general practitioner, I was now also the only doctor in the house and I would have to handle the surgery, too. If it came to me, I would have to do it.

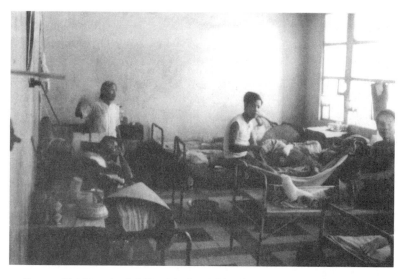

Quang Tri Provincial Hospital, 1968. Photos by Richard Hughes

I would remain the only doctor at Quang Tri Provincial Hospital for much of the next two months. With the exception of occasional drop-in teams of Australian and Canadian doctors, and an American military doctor stationed there for two weeks, for most of my tenure I was the only civilian doctor on duty. As Quang Tri's resident *Bac si*, I was ably assisted by a group of eight Navy corpsmen that rotated in and out, dependable as clockwork, and a group of Vietnamese nurses that were not very dependable at all.

Dr. Allen Hassan at Quang Tri Provincial Hospital, Vietnam, 1968.

Quang Tri was definitely in the jungle, although it was not the densest jungle in Vietnam, which was found in the Mekong Delta. Some of the land around Quang Tri was farmed to rice and other crops. The jungle around Quang Tri and many other Vietnamese cities was honeycombed with deep tunnels, where the North Vietnamese and Viet Cong forces hid until launching their sudden attacks.

Quang Tri city had a population of about 35,000 people when I arrived, but there were many more civilians in the outlying villages and farming areas. Also in the area were up to 87,000 Marines in I-Corps. Around the time I took over my responsibilities at Quang Tri, approximately ninety miles away to the South, in II-Corps, future Secretary of State Colin Powell was serving as information officer during the massacre of 500 civilians that came to be known as My Lai.

Tens of thousands of Marines were based inside and immediately around the city of Quang Tri. We were definitely in a war zone. For our protection, Quang Tri was surrounded with tanks called "dusters," special vehicles carrying twin 40 mm cannons well-adapted to use in the jungle. Tanks and armored personnel carriers rolled through the streets of Quang Tri, carrying American and South Vietnamese soldiers.

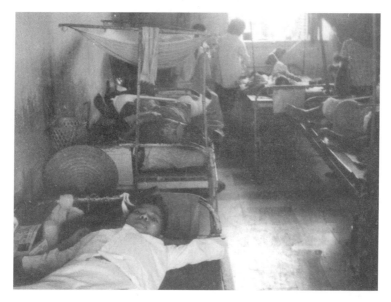

A ward in Quang Tri Provincial Hospital, 1968

Not long after I arrived, I was issued a Jeep and an M16. Quang Tri was also not far from the demilitarized zone, and the fighting ranged around us. Once, when it appeared the city would be overrun, I remember the sudden appearance of military helicopters in the hospital courtyard, ready to evacuate us before the enemy closed in.

The war hadn't really changed much since the French were fighting to retain Indochina. During the Indochina War, French General Pellet had observed: "The enemy is everywhere. No continuous front, no well-dug-in defense where our powerful and modern weapons of war can be used to effect. Each bamboo grove, each hut, may conceal an adversary. What a burden on the minds of our soldiers who have to face an elusive enemy in all places and at all hours of the day and night."

Almost every day, dozens of soldiers and civilians were wounded and dying. The battlefront was fluid, with many casualties and injuries in "free fire zones" where it was open season on anyone, including farmers going back to feed their water buffalo, or women and children gone back home to burn a little incense over the graves of their ancestors. Although most Vietnamese typically never strayed farther than five miles from their place of birth during their entire lifetime, millions were driven from their farms and homes during the war. Americans considered the Vietnamese like long blades of grass in a field, blowing in the wind, their loyalty changing depending on who had control of their region at the time.

The fighting was fierce. The week I arrived in Vietnam, American troops took more casualties than during any single week of the entire war. Some 713 American servicemen were killed in action between May 3-10. Our troops were dying at the rate of more than 100 per day. The Tet Offensive, launched January 31, 1968, had morphed four months later into a second offensive, called Tet II. In the month of May, a total of 2,370 American combat soldiers would die in the jungles of Vietnam. The escalation of the Vietnam war was at its peak, with no end in sight.

After the Tet offensive and the overwhelming American response, arguments began about whether the Viet Cong had been defeated as a capable military force, or if it was the US who was losing patience over mounting and appalling battlefield casualties. And of course, while most Vietnamese and American doctors in Vietnam were assigned to the military, many civilians were killed or wounded every day, along with many who also fell victim to the bewildering arsenal of exotic tropical diseases which had afflicted the Vietnamese for centuries.

I stepped into war-torn Quang Tri as a relatively young, inexperienced medical doctor who had been trained in general medicine, psychiatric medicine, and veterinary medicine. I was thirty-two years old. I had worked a year in hospital emergency rooms in California, and this did give me some experience with trauma patients. My time as a surgical first assistant enabled me to get some feel for the complex surgical problems that would confront me one after another on the operating table at Quang Tri. The ability to work fast and hard, and the self-sufficiency and discipline I learned on the farm and in the Marine Corps would also help me in the trying times ahead, when wounded Vietnamese patients would fly past me like so many blips on a radar screen.

Medicine in a Third World country far away from any sophisticated facility is entirely different than many doctors can imagine. Some doctors who were thrown into this type of primitive medical environment asked to be transferred back to Saigon, or to a hospital in Japan where they had adequate facilities. Before I was sent to Quang Tri, I did not know that a flake of shrapnel the size of a fingernail could kill an adult or child by piercing a vital organ. I had not seen victims with multiple tiny wounds barely visible to the naked eye who would die on my operating table. To work with the endemic population in a situation where there was so much mistrust, where a doctor might be a hero one day and shot for malpractice the next, it was incumbent on any physician to quickly adapt and develop a trust with the personnel with whom he was working and the community in general.

I was soon given quarters in a house in Quang Tri, which I shared with an American missionary family. The house was only a short walk down a dusty trail away from the hospital

Quang Tri was forty-five miles from Hue, and over the next few weeks I would keep in touch with the doctors there as much as I could, occasionally visiting and sometimes assisting them with surgeries. We were always aware we were in a tropical country, with constant sanitation problems. Vietnam had a nearly constant high humidity of seventy-five to eighty percent. The average annual temperature in South Vietnam was eighty-four degrees, but it was warmer than that in Quang Tri.

Vietnamese hospitals even smelled different than the clean, prim hospitals in the US, which often reek of rubbing alcohol and antiseptic. Another volunteer doctor, Dr. Clyde Ralph, remembered the old poorly lighted hospital in Nha Trang as "a hospital of many odors." Dr. Ralph recalled, "A constant fight goes on to prevent the foul ones from taking complete mastery. Feces and urine are deposited freely, anywhere. They seem to live among it, and with it, free of any negative attitudes."

In Quang Tri, the interpreter assigned to me was a young, likeable 17-year-old Vietnamese man named Nguyen. Nguyen, pronounced "n-win" is a common name in Vietnam, but he was not a common young man. Nguyen had bright dark eyes and dark hair, and he was the son of a provincial chief. He had a perpetual smile even though he had seen nothing but war for most of his young life. Cheerfully optimistic, Nguyen obviously admired me. He used to follow me around the hospital with a big smile on his face, observing and trying to learn as much as he could. His greatest quality was a desire to help others around him, and I saw this all the time I was with him. He wanted to be a doctor, he told me, and he asked me almost every day if I could help him get to America and study to be a doctor. He helped me in more ways than I realized in Quang Tri.

Every morning, Nguyen showed up for work in a bright white clean shirt, black trousers, and sandals, smiling cheerfully.

"*Bac si*, what can I do for you today?" he would ask.

With his command of both English and Vietnamese, Nguyen helped me interface with the patients, as well as the Vietnamese nurses and other staff. Along the way, he would teach me not only about the Vietnamese language, but also about the country's history and culture.

Nguyen got sick not long after I arrived, and he trustingly came to me for treatment. He was feverish, with shakes, chills, and dehydration. I diagnosed this as a kidney infection. We had no urine testing to confirm my diagnosis, but I gave him medication and told him to take the medicine and stay home for five days.

Five days later, Nguyen returned and said, "I still have the illness and I'm not able to shake it."

By then, I had learned more about the local medical practices. I knew, for instance, that some Vietnamese put medicine on their wood-burning stoves, a ritual which they believed helped them ward off illness more than actually taking the medicine.

"I don't want you to put your medicine on the stove mantel. I want you to take it," I snapped.

"No, no," Nguyen reassured me. "I'm an educated Vietnamese. I took the medicine."

He told me that when he didn't get better, he visited a local Chinese doctor, and received an herbal medicine for malaria. When I examined him, he was showing signs of a slow, but steady, recovery. Although I missed a disease that could have been fatal, Nguyen never held this mis-diagnosis against me.

I quickly learned that my American medical training didn't teach me everything I need to know in a war-torn tropical country like Vietnam. Nguyen's doctor had given him the Chinese herb sweet wormwood, used for centuries in the Far East to treat malaria. Having seen what this herbal remedy could do, I had him bring some wormwood into the hospital, and we kept it in our medicine chest to help us treat malaria.

In addition to my interpreter Nguyen, eight Navy corpsmen were assigned to the hospital on a rotating basis. These corpsmen were brave, decent people, dedicated to helping the Vietnamese.

Often, when the corpsmen could have taken the day off, they would gas up the Jeep they sometimes used as an ambulance. Then they would load up the Jeep with medical supplies.

"Come on, Doc," they'd call. "Let's go out to the hamlets and treat some people."

Away we'd go, into the jungle villages and hamlets around Quang Tri. We'd examine the inhabitants who wanted to see us, and give them shots and vitamins as needed. We would hop into the Jeep to make quick trips to vaccinate the local children, sometimes even venturing into hostile areas that were under fire.

The corpsmen were extremely dependable. The Navy corpsmen showed up for work at the hospital, whether a Viet Cong attack was rumored or not. They would show up even in the worst of circumstances, but they never stayed at the hospital after six o'clock, because their orders required them to return before nightfall.

In sharp contrast, the Vietnamese nurses would sometimes disappear for days at a time. The nurses were the primary care providers at the hospital, and they took care of the patients at night, but they were not dependable. They were not the professionally trained registered nurses you might find in the United States, but rather para-nurses who learned from each other on the job, with very little formal training. As the war raged, I was dismayed to see that the slightest rumor of an attack would send the nurses scurrying away. This happened several times while I was working at the hospital. Sick and wounded patients were abandoned, not receiving their IVs or life-sustaining medications. Some of our patients died because the nurses weren't on the job.

I asked other doctors what to do about this.

"Just keep doing what you're brought here to do," one doctor advised me.

"Do the best you can," sighed another doctor.

When the nurses vanished, the corpsmen and I would make the rounds the next morning. We'd determine which IVs had run out, and which patients had died during the night. Some mornings, we'd find that several children had died during the night. This was particularly disheartening. But over time, I became more hardened to the death of young patients who should have been saved. Although this situation nearly overwhelmed me at times, I determined to keep doing my best for the people I had volunteered to help.

In Vietnam, I saw rampaging epidemics of diseases I'd never seen before in the cleanliness and comfort of medicine in the United States. Poliomyelitis, nearly eradicated in the US through polio vaccines at that time, was still common in Vietnam. Malaria, dysentery, anthrax, cholera, and typhoid fever were some of the other diseases endemic to Vietnam.

At Quang Tri Provincial Hospital, I don't know how many patients I lost to exotic tropical diseases which could have been prevented or easily treated in the United States. I lost several patients to bubonic plague, and to typhoid fever. In the United States, I would have isolated these patients in a hospital room for six months. In Vietnam, this was impossible; we had to treat them as outpatients. I could only give them a shot, a few pills, and tell them to come back in ten days, always hoping for the best.

We saw several cases of typhoid fever, several cases of bubonic plague, and several cases of polio that came to the hospital. They were treatable, and we won the battle. We had antibiotics available for patients with typhoid fever, who could be transferred to a special ward at the teaching hospital in Hue. Bubonic plague also swept through Vietnam during the rainy season, and I found I was living in an area of Vietnam that was called "the bubonic plague capital of the world." Although I arrived before the rainy season, there were already signs of a rat infestation, rats bearing the fleas that harbored the bacillus of bubonic plague. Bubonic plague was one of our easier "cure or kill" cases – patients were placed on heavy doses of antibiotics, and treated as outpatients. Eighty percent of these, at least, would survive. We knew this was a good ratio because without us, none would have survived. Chloramphenicol and penicillin were all we had available for all of our infectious bacterial diseases such as bubonic plague, but we had patients wait for them and gave them supportive care. We had no treatments for polio except for supportive care.

After seeing several cases of polio, I mentioned to one of the corpsmen that our American vaccines could help prevent some of these crippling outbreaks of disease. Within three days, out of the blue, our hospital received a shipment of polio vaccine. I am certain my loyal corpsmen arranged for this.

I began researching all these diseases whenever I could spare a little time, consulting my medical books, talking to other doctors, and observing what my Vietnamese patients said about their symptoms. With Nguyen interpreting beside me, we were able to save many patients' lives. The Chinese herbs he brought into the hospital came in handy for malaria. Many other medical problems I encountered I would never have seen in the United States.

Other volunteer doctors had experience with these baffling, ubiquitous tropical diseases which sometimes overwhelmed our facilities.

Further south in Bac Lieu, volunteer physician Dr. Tom H. Mitchell recalled, "The presence of so many cases of tuberculosis was shocking, as was the fact that we had little (usually none) medication for these people. The intensity of diarrheas and the resulting dehydration was appalling, especially in the children. You just did the best you could with what you had. One day, I had five deaths on the pediatric ward, which was most depressing. With adequate supplies and earlier access to the patients, most could have been prevented."

Dr. Gilbert Lee remembers: "In traveling about from Saigon to the river delta, I saw the hospitals were all overcrowded. I also noted there was one building with empty wards. With some indignation I asked why they had an empty ward. One of the nurses took me aside and said the monsoon rains would soon be upon us." When Dr. Lee sarcastically thanked her for the weather report, the nurse patiently explained that when the rains came, rats scrambled into the houses, carrying the fleas that carried bubonic plague. Soon, the Vietnamese nurse predicted, every bed in the empty ward would be full of plague patients.

"Seventy-two hours after this conversation, the rains came," Dr. Lee recalled. "Two weeks later I saw plague complications, common in many parts of Vietnam, and neither I nor my textbooks knew anything about it."

"About a week and a half into my tour into Nha Trang, a cholera epidemic broke out and all bedlam broke loose," recalls Dr. William P. Levonian, who left a peaceful medical practice in Santa Cruz, California, to volunteer his services in Vietnam. "Families laid their sick ones all over the floors of the wards, into the hallways and corridors or wherever. The hospital generator was out, as was often the case. No lights, no running water. The water pump was dependent upon the power. There was vomit and diarrhea all over the cots and the floor. The hospital windows were devoid of screens, and outside, dust and flies everywhere. I was writing medication, intravenous fluid, and electrolyte orders as rapidly as I could in French. In the midst of all this crisis, I again pondered how it was that I got into this chaotic foreign world."

One of my first surgeries in Quang Tri was a forty-four-year-old Vietnamese man who'd lain wounded in a field for four days. I knew the man. I'd seen him around town as I walked to the hospital to work. When I took over his care, I saw the man had been wounded by shrapnel. He had also sustained a large burn in the area, from which his backbone actually protruded.

He was so badly wounded I feared he wouldn't live more than a few days. As we operated, of course, the windows were open to help cool the room. Flies were everywhere. Inflammation had filled the wound around his spine with pus, and several vertebrae protruded out of a mass of granulated tissue on his back. I cut the dead tissue out of the wound, a debriding procedure he could not feel, and gently washed his spine, observing his nerves as they disappeared into the muscles around the spinal cord.

Since we treated him immediately with antibiotics, his problem wasn't sepsis. His main problem was tetanus, from the *clostridium tetani* bacilli which were multiplying anaerobically in his wound in the presence of iron from the shrapnel. Tetanus spores form in the soil and in the intestines of animals such as man, and these bacteria can colonize a wound and multiply rapidly at the site of the infection when iron is present.

Since he had not been vaccinated against tetanus, and we had no serum antitoxin to treat it, I knew he was probably going to die. Not many Vietnamese had been vaccinated against tetanus. Because of the tetanus toxin his body was producing, the man was shaking, convulsing, and trembling around the clock. His involuntary jerking movements or paroxysms, typical of tetanus, intensified as the tetanus multiplied and spread. I knew he was in great pain, and I also knew he was aware of what was going on around him.

I visited him every day, to give him the useless anti-tetanus medication, and morphine for the pain. We used continuous lavage as much as possible, with hydrogen peroxide, but nothing worked. I tried to smile and be upbeat when I visited him. I wanted to cheer him up and give him hope. Time after time, I would shoo away the flies, then debride the wounds along his spinal cord, rinsing out the pockets of pus with water that might have been contaminated. As I left, the flies regrouped around his wound.

I had learned a few words of Vietnamese, and I wanted to make him as comfortable as possible. During my visits, I would say, in Vietnamese, "I love you, my dear friend."

He would faintly smile back at me, knowing someone cared.

In Quang Tri provincial hospital, with the open windows letting in the heat and the flies, and the red dust swirling, his wound became like so many others a massive tetanus bog. The man died on the eighth day, after taking every bid of debridement I gave his wound with a gentle smile.

His last words were "*Bac Si, cam on,*" or "Doctor, thank you."

I never found out his political leanings, and I didn't care. It was difficult to tell who was on which side in the war, and we treated everybody who needed medical attention at our hospital. I do know that if he'd been vaccinated against tetanus, or if we'd had the right medications available, he would not have died, even with his serious wounds. After he died, I placed a post mortem tag on his body, writing the words, "wonderful human being of the world."

7

Surgeries in the Jungle

"Many of the greatest tyrants on the records of
history have begun their reigns in the fairest manner.
But this unnatural power corrupts both
the heart and the understanding."
– Edmund Burke

Before I knew it, I was thrown into work not only as a general practitioner, but also as a surgeon, performing emergency surgery on battlefield injuries. Our hospital was the end of the road for civilians around Quang Tri wounded or injured in the war – there was no other place anywhere close to send the worst cases for emergency treatment.

As the fighting ebbed and flowed, the number of wounded civilians fluctuated accordingly. If there was a lull on the nearby battlefields for a day or two, long lines of people would line up at the hospital door, seeking treatment. Word quickly got out that a doctor was there and working full-time on the sick and injured.

"*Bac Si My*," they'd say, greeting me respectfully, or "*Bac Si Number One.*"

Operating conditions in Quang Tri provincial hospital were primitive, security was spotty, sanitation was poor, and drugs and medical supplies we desperately needed were not always available.

The key to saving lives was quickness, quickness, quickness. That was the only key. Prompt operation is an important factor of survival in patients with large wounds accompanied by toxemia from infection or from the products of tissue breakdown. If you didn't have your adrenalin pumping on high for eighteen to twenty-four hours at a time, during times when patients swamped the hospital, you could save no one. Although I didn't keep count, I probably performed more than 200 surgeries over the course of about two months. Some days were slow, but other days we'd be operating in the hospital until midnight.

When necessary the corpsmen, nurses, and I went right to surgery, bypassing the time-consuming bureaucratic procedures that occur in American hospitals prior to emergency surgery. Often we came up with improvisations that could have never been considered in an American hospital. We had no specialists, no neurosurgeons, no vascular surgeons, practically no surgeons – only me, the corpsmen, and an occasional drop-in military doctor.

Like much of Vietnam, Quang Tri was hot and humid during the day, and it didn't cool down much at night. While antibiotics and other useful drugs were often scarce, insects were ubiquitous in the sticky jungle heat. Flies and gnats swarmed all over Quang Tri Provincial Hospital, through the unscreened bay windows we had to leave open because of the heat. In the wards, flies covered every scratch and open wound. Patients not attended by a family member with a fan, keeping off the flies, were covered by dozens if not hundreds of flies. The swarms of flies reminded me of my days on the farm in Iowa. In the hot summer months, flies would swarm all over the heads of our horses and cows, and cover their waste as soon as it hit the ground.

In Quang Tri, even the operation field was not fly-proof. Flies buzzed around open wounds even as we operated, although the nurses would try to shoo them away. At night, while the flies slept, up came the mosquitoes from the ponds, bearing malaria and other diseases. After a while, we were able to round up some DDT to help keep down the insects, but like everything else we needed, DDT was in painfully short supply in Vietnam.

Ironically, my training as a veterinarian back at Iowa State University probably prepared me for what I was doing more than any of the work I did in medical school or in emergency rooms. In vet school, working on cattle, dogs, cats, and smaller animals, I'd performed hundreds of operations and learned intricate surgical techniques that I put to use many times.

In Vietnam, right off the bat, I had to become an anesthesiologist, and I became one in two weeks. True, I was a physician and I understood the levels of consciousness required for the basic surgeries, but I was not a well-trained anesthesiologist. It was hit and miss with the ether and Pentothal we used to put the patients down. In vet school, the only anesthesia we used was Pentothal, and because dogs and cats are smaller than people, they require only tiny doses of medication. With my human patients, I always erred on the side of caution. Fortunately, I never lost a patient from improper anesthesia.

After battles in the countryside, patients came walking and crawling into the hospital from their homes and villages. Some arrived in a Jeep or military transport. Others were carried piggyback by their relatives, on a gurney between two bicycles, or even in a bag on the side of a water buffalo. Injuries came from all the instruments of modern war – bullets, grenades, artillery, mortars, napalm, and bombs.

The first thing you had to do was look over the total patient and see what the hell was going on. The corpsmen and I were forced to evaluate the extent of their injuries using only the most basic tools – blood pressure, pulse rate, and respiratory rate. You used your five senses of seeing, smelling, touching, listening, tasting and that sixth sense – looking for the unexpected. Often it was necessary to improvise.

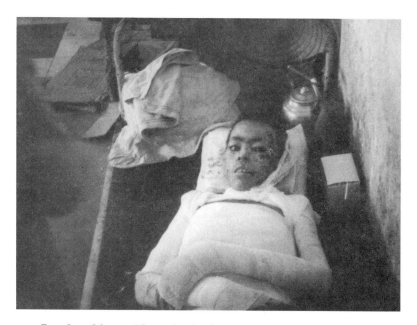

Paralyzed boy with multiple shrapnel wounds at Quang Tri
Provincial Hospital a few hours before his death.

*Vietnamese mother and her children waiting in line
for hospital care, Vietnam 1968.*

Many of the wounded civilians that came to Quang Tri had blast injuries, some from the 2,000-pound bombs dropped by B-52s from high altitudes, which also caused many civilian deaths. These bombs were the size of Volkswagen Beetles when they fell, but the shock of their blast could be felt ten miles away. If you were within five miles of the detonation of one of these bombs, you would feel that your life was coming to an end. The earth would shudder and shake and there would be such a rumble you'd think you were in the center of an earthquake. The first time this happened I thought the bomb had fallen right next to me. Later I realized that despite the noise and the shaking, I was miles away from the blast, and relatively safe except for falling debris.

Those big explosions produced a variety of injuries, depending on how far you were from the blast. Powerful high-pitched blast waves close to the explosion pass through the body, sometimes rupturing a liver, kidney, intestine, or heart. Blast waves can throw a man, woman, or child against a solid wall or object, and kill or injure them. Farther away from the blast, longer wave lengths heard as a low-pitched loud thundering sound could easily rupture your eardrums, since ruptures occur at a pressure of seven pounds per square inch above atmospheric pressure. If you are in contact with any solid object, the blast wave is transmitted through the object and into the body, producing injuries out of proportion to the force of the blast wave. Blast waves from mines under water created even more deaths and injuries, since the blast travels more rapidly and effectively under water, and the human body is about the consistency of water. On the open ground, with the exception of the eardrums, the body can withstand up to thirty pounds per square inch of pressure above atmospheric pressure, if you are protected from debris.

From a medical point of view, blast waves create many chest injuries, including damage to the chest wall, rupture of the pulmonary alveolar network, and hemorrhages in the lungs. These injuries come because the force of the blast pushes the ribs into the lungs. Patients with these injuries may not show objective signs, or maybe they cough up a little blood because of multiple hematomas of the lungs. In Quang Tri, almost everyone with a serious blast injury had to be treated for shock, but often a life-saving surgery had to come first, before the patient was really prepared.

In modern warfare, most wounds are usually caused by primary or secondary missiles such as bullets or bomb fragments, although secondary missiles like rocks can also be kicked into the air and become lethal. Inside the body, of course, a bullet can create a secondary missile by chipping off a piece of bone or fragmenting, taking bizarre paths through the body. As a doctor evaluating these injuries, the first thing to determine is the position of the victim at the time of taking the hit. The trajectory of a bullet or a piece of shrapnel for someone shot lying down would usually be quite different than for someone standing up. The exit wound, if one existed, was always larger than the entrance wound.

For the battlefield surgeon, the nature, size, shape, and stability of the missile or bullet at the time of impact are important considerations, as is the density of the tissues involved. When compared to wounds from knives or bayonets, high-velocity projectiles and bullets produce an enormous amount of tissue damage.

The speed at which bullets and missiles travel has increased almost four times since World War I, and the damage caused by a projectile traveling 2,000-4,000 feet per second is horrific. The kinetic energy of the missile is transmitted to the tissue upon impact, flinging cells and tissue away from the track of the missile at high velocity. This leaves a temporary cavity around the track of the missile which may exceed the volume of the missile itself by as much as thirty times, rupturing blood vessels, nerves, and fracturing bones some distance away. Small wounds from M16 bullets, which tumble end-over-end through the air, were often more serious than wounds from grenade fragments which were larger and appeared more formidable at first. Of course, with any wound, you always assumed contamination from clothing, dirty skin, dirt, and everything else taken into the wound by the bullet. The exit wound, one also assumed, was equally contaminated by feces, urine, bone or bacteria from the intestinal tract.

In addition, we saw many crush injuries in Quang Tri. We frequently saw crush injuries from children falling off their bicycles as they attempted to run away from tragedy, who were then run over by military convoys and left with legs or arms crushed or dead. Any extremity crushed for more than one hour would develop so-called crush compression syndrome, with swelling or edema of the limb as blood spilled out of the crushed capillaries into the body. Crushed, damaged muscle releases potent chemicals including muscle pigment, potassium, creatinine, and acid which together can lead to liver failure, low blood pressure, and death. When patients with crush injuries arrived at the hospital, we would have to determine whether there were other injuries which required more immediate attention, and decide which to treat first. Usually, badly crushed limbs were amputated since infection was the companion of every ragged wound. Sometimes we worked so fast, there was a bucket full of amputated limbs in the surgical suite.

Whenever possible, you try to save a mangled limb. Prompt debridement, early repair of vascular injury, reduction of the metabolic requirements of tissue, antibiotic therapy—every effort should be made to arrest infection and hemorrhage without resorting to amputation. One reason for delaying amputation is the patient's state of mind after the operation. If the patient realizes amputation is a last resort, and every possible effort has been made to preserve the limb, he or she will better accept a necessary amputation.

Once, I remember, when a team of Canadian doctors came to help for a few days, we worked hours and hours to save the crushed arm of a twelve-year-old Vietnamese girl who had been run over by a Jeep. One of her arms had been left dangling by the radial median and ulnar nerves, brachial artery and vein. I never saw such humane doctors trying to save an arm. We were afraid the humidity and the heat and the bugs and the dirt and the dust and the trauma would either kill her or leave her without an arm. We worked for almost six hours trying to sew blood vessels together, amputate the crushed bone, and bring muscle edges together. All the while, the poor little girl bravely withstood this, and tried to smile. After the surgery, we wrapped her arm in some kind of Saran wrap and packed her left elbow in ice. But what a group of doctors. We did everything possible, but the odds were stacked against her as we hovered over her for the next three days. I was more naive than the orthopedic specialist who did most of the work. On day three he looked at the arm and stated, "We got to take it off and throw it in the bucket." This was not a happy moment but there were not many happy moments in Vietnam.

"My second tour was in Quang Ngai, and my ward was for the worst cases, people who were terribly wounded," remembers Dr. Bill Owen, another volunteer physician. "One was a pretty girl of about fifteen years of age with one leg partially shot off and the other leg in terrible shape as well. I told her she needed to have that one done, too. She cried out. I wasn't very good either. The next morning she was gone. The family took her home in the night. She died at home a short time later."

At times, it was painfully obvious that the medicine practiced in Vietnam was medieval. Mothers would bring in children who had stepped on a booby trap, with their foot blown off. Before the mother finally brought in her child, she would often have already tried a Vietnamese folk remedy. Basically, she'd have stuck the stump of the injured limb into a vat of ox manure. The Vietnamese would use the most vile, rotten, maggot-infected manure they could find. Usually, this "cure" would either kill or cure the patient. After being placed in the manure, what remained of the limb would stop bleeding. Then the injured portion of the arm or leg would turn black, and fall off, leaving a stub. After all this, the patients would sometimes muster the will to survive, or sometimes they would die.

In Quang Tri, I tried to catch and round up such kids before anyone tried the folk remedy. Although their families might not have noticed much difference in the results, we had surgery, antibiotics and follow-up care, and I'm sure we saved more patients in the long run.

The Vietnamese would often try traditional Asian medical treatments such as cupping and acupuncture before they tried anything else. In Vinh Binh, Dr. Victor S. Falk recalled, "Quite frequently, before seeing the American doctors, patients had been subjected to Chinese or Cambodian medicine, most consisting of large suction cups over the affected areas, with a lot of needles under the skin. A caustic paste used by the Cambodians was sometimes applied to the forehead if a person had a headache. One could quite often spot the illness by looking at the wounds the doctors had created."

Many times when a person came in with his or her chest blown away, I would quickly operate and repair the damage as best I could. The Navy corpsmen handled the simple wounds, although if I was not busy I would take over repairing the basic injuries. Some of the corpsmen told me I was one of the best surgeons they had ever seen, but I assumed they were trying to pump me up since I was a psychiatrist in training, thrown into the fray as a surgeon. I didn't have a great deal of training as a surgeon, but I was given the opportunity to learn a lot fast.

One time, after opening an abdomen, I flipped a scalpel from my right hand to my left. Unfortunately, I impaled my own wrist. I calmly pulled the scalpel out, laid it on the table. Fortunately, I hadn't hit the radial artery but I came close.

"Corpsman, please wrap this wound," I calmly said.

"My God, Doc, you've stabbed yourself!"

"I'm sorry, man, wrap it," I said. "Let's get on with the surgery."

Later in the day, after we'd completed our work, the corpsmen said they wanted to nominate me for a Purple Heart, a medal given soldiers who are wounded in battle. Forget it, I said, I'm a civilian. We all laughed.

In Vietnam the fighting usually occurred about four o'clock in the afternoon. The wounded civilians who didn't die would lie around in ditches or fields or rice paddies half-buried in water overnight. The wounded would be evacuated at dawn, when the Viet Cong were the least likely to shoot at rescuers.

We saw many patients who had been shot. The most common wounds came from small arms fire, mortar shells, and booby traps. Tending to shrapnel wounds was an everyday occurrence. On rare occasions, we would treat people burned by napalm, which was used frequently in Vietnam. Napalm burns completely through the flesh and bone; it doesn't stop burning, but napalm was so lethal that few survived long enough to get to the hospital.

When patients came in, we didn't know whose sympathies were with the Viet Cong and whose sympathies were with the Americans, or who was neutral and just trying to stay alive. We treated everybody who came to the hospital, but many were horribly wounded and didn't survive. The corpsmen had the duty of removing the bodies of people who died during the night, but sometimes families would take the bodies away. As soon as we finished with one patient, the young enlisted Navy personnel would sometimes tell the nurses to bring in the next patient, and exercise a bit of black humor at the carnage they saw every day.

"Okay," they'd say. "Bring in the next dead soul."

When we had too many patients at one time, the corpsmen would assist me with the operations. If a patient came in with an arm nearly blown off, and I was busy elsewhere, the corpsmen often performed the amputation. If it was necessary to remove a patient's mangled eyeball, I would usually perform the enucleations and have the corpsmen take over from there. Other times, I was so busy the corpsmen had to perform the enucleations.

Operating on multiple wounds at the same time was not unusual. While a corpsman was amputating a leg, I might be doing the belly while another corpsman might be attending to the wound of a buttock or getting the patient ready for an eye enucleation.

It's difficult to estimate the numbers of patients who came in, the variety of their injuries, and the volume of work we were forced to do except to say that, at times, the numbers were almost overwhelming. Once, for four days in a row, I performed five major abdominal surgeries each day. In the United States, a major operation like this is extremely tiring to the surgeon, and most doctors perform no more than two in a day, or perhaps three in an extreme emergency. We performed a series of these operations for several days in a row, contending with poor sanitation, tenuous security, flies, gnats, dust, nurses who sometimes disappeared, and a hospital which was medically unequipped for such complex surgeries and offered generally poor aftercare.

Some of these patients I vividly remember. One day, a Jeep pulled up in front of the hospital.

"Doctor! Doctor! We need your help!" shouted one of two Marines from their Jeep.

I watched the two young Marines carry a wounded older man wearing black pajama bottoms into the hospital, assisted by my corpsmen. The old man had apparently been a part of the bamboo telegraph, a living local news network which passed information from village to village, not unlike the old American Pony Express. This man ran six miles a day to bring news from Quang Tri back to his village, Quang Dien. One of the Marines had shot him in the belly as he was running to deliver the news.

Navy corpsmen help a 96-year-old Vietnamese man into Quang Tri Provincial Hospital before emergency surgery by Dr. Hassan.

The Marines didn't determine if he was Viet Cong first, they just shot him. Their standing orders were to shoot any Vietnamese seen running. This was a gross violation of the rules of engagement, but in Vietnam these rules weren't always followed.

When I looked into the eyes of those two Marines, it told me more than any psychiatric text I'd ever read about the ravages of war. Although their jaws were hardened, their two young faces were riddled with remorse and guilt. Marines are trained to kill, but when they saw what they'd done to a civilian, their priority had become to get the wounded old man out of the free fire zone and into the hospital without inflicting any more pain.

On the operating table, the man appeared to be about sixty years old. He was small and muscular, perhaps five feet three inches tall, and maybe 100 pounds. His legs were all muscle. Before I examined him, I was afraid that the bullet had hit an artery, and I wouldn't be able to save him.

I examined the gunshot entry point. There was no exit hole, meaning the bullet remained in the body. The old man's pulse rate was 140, indicating no major blood vessels had been hit. Otherwise, his pulse would have been in the 180 range. He was writhing with pain, but also alert and aware of what we were doing as he went under the anesthesia. One of the corpsmen administered a little bit of Pentothal and some ether by mask.

We scrubbed him down as best we could, with our various antiseptic solutions. I opened him up from chest to pubic bone with one quick blade thrust through the skin. He had only one-half centimeter of belly fat. The wound itself was central, but slightly to the left side. The bullet had blown away one of the major parts of his colon. Then, to my surprise, I saw that a .45 slug had lodged in one of the man's vertebrae, between major blood vessels. The bullet lay between the abominal aorta and the vena cava, the large artery and vein transporting blood to and from the legs, and into the transverse process of the vertebrae at the T10 level. Fortunately the bullet had missed the aorta. I struggled to stop the bleeding. Feces spilled out of a section of his large intestine into the abdominal cavity, and I furiously washed and rinsed him out as I continued.

"Antibiotics!" I called out.

I cut out the bad bowel, with more washing and rinsing.

Ignoring the slug for a moment, I concentrated on decreasing the contamination as much as possible. I knew I should have repaired the gaping wound in the large descending colon with a colectomy but I dared not do it. There were too many flies, too much contamination, too much heat, and too few antibiotics to stave off infection from still another open wound. I called for clamps, suture material, and stitch sutures. There was no hyfrecator, all we had was the best we could use. I stopped the bleeding, stopped the bleeding, closing bleeding point after bleeding point.

As I did in cat and dog surgery during my years in vet school, I carefully clipped out the bad bowel, about four inches of his colon, then reconnected the healthy bowel ends. I used 3-0 silk, the best I could find, because anything else was too tough to handle in this situation with the delicate intestinal tissue. With his warm intestines in my hands, I looked for more bowel rents, but fortunately there were no more. I closed the wound, and tried to decontaminate once again.

I found no other wounds, although the shell encased in the vertebral column remained. The bullet was in a dangerous position. The swelling around the spinal column would increase if I did not remove the bullet. Some flesh or a contaminant of some sort might have been embedded with it, which would lead to bigger and more dangerous future infections. Lead poisoning was not uncommon from shells left inside the body, and fragments could also migrate and cause trouble elsewhere. I didn't have much time to decide whether to try to remove it or not. If I extracted it, it could cause more damage, and he could bleed even more. These were the thoughts running through my mind as I worked.

I decided to remove the slug. Carefully, I cut around the bullet, then checked his leg functions. Babinski reflex test is down, down. There was no paralysis. Reflexes appeared to be normal; the old runner had no apparent quadriplegia. After removing the slug, I dropped it into a small glass jar nearby. Will somebody want it as a souvenir? Doubtful. Too many slugs around. Looking at the wound one last time, I realized how lucky the old man had been. The bullet was spent when it reached him. God was with him. If he had been just a little closer to the shooter, the bullet would have surely penetrated his spine.

The surgery went well. I had saved his life. Closed, inside out. Drainage? No. Should I have. Yes. Colostomy? Probably should have. Did I? No. Closed peritoneum, fascial layer, muscle tissue, subcutaneous tissue. Skin closed, he looked great, a tough old man. But I knew, too, that surgery was only twenty percent of the battle. Next, he needed to receive the necessary convalescence for the next ten days.

I looked around the surgical suite in Quang Tri and thought about how the Lord had saved this old man. The bullet was spent by the time it hit him. The Marines had shot him, the Marines had brought him in. They realized they had made a mistake; he was not a Viet Cong, even though he was wearing black pajama bottoms. Those two tough Marines had the compassion and the kindness to bring the old man to the hospital so that he could have a chance to live.

The next day I discussed this surgery with Nguyen, my interpreter.

"Do you know how old this man is?" Nguyen asked.

"Maybe sixty or sixty-five," I guessed. That was my first impression. I remember during surgery looking at his blood vessels, the large aorta running down into his legs during surgery. He had no calcium of cholesterol deposits, which gave him the healthy body of a forty- or fifty-year-old man. I remember thinking how healthy he looked.

"He's 94 years old," Nguyen said. Nguyen told me he was the runner between Quang Tri and the village of Quang Dien. He ran six miles a day to deliver news about the war to his village.

"Unbelievable," I said.

The old man had seen a world of change, and survived a lot in his 94 years. He'd seen the French colonial era, the Japanese occupation of Vietnam during World War II, administered by the Vichy regime, the war with the French, and now an army of Americans sweeping over the countryside.

His diet and his lifestyle had kept him in extraordinary physical condition. In a third world country, diets are often superior to what is eaten in so-called developed nations. Fresh fruits and vegetables, fish, and rice were staples of the Vietnamese diet. In addition, the old man was a respected sage of his village, not only a communicator of news and information, but also a wise and respected elder in a country that valued the opinions and wisdom of the old.

I do not know how much longer the old man lived, but I suspect he lasted a few more years. He showed a tremendous zest for life. In our hospital, he mentored other patients, especially the children whose limbs had been amputated and who were trying to learn how to use their artificial limbs. He lived the Vietnamese way – not thinking of himself so much, but trying to ease the pain and fear of the hospital's many vulnerable children. The children adored him, and gave him tremendous respect, and probably a reason for living. He helped give them hope, and love.

In other parts of Vietnam, other Volunteer Physicians were also working hard in equally difficult circumstances.

"As a World War II surgeon I thought I'd seen it all, but in one month in Vietnam I encountered more casualties than I had in all my service in World War II," said Dr. Victor S. Falk, who was stationed on the Mekong Delta, in a seventy-year-old provincial hospital built by the French at Vinh Binh. "The wounds resulted from gunshots, grenades, mines, boobytraps and air strikes. Mangling injuries of the hands and feet resulting in amputations were all too common. Compound fractures of the femur were frequently encountered and treated with skeletal traction. Surgery was usually kept to a minimum because of the extreme prevalence of infection. One of the most pathetic situations was a ten-year-old girl with a four-quarter amputation because her shoulder had been shot away."

"The wounded came in waves, corresponding to attacks from either side," recalls Dr. Frank Van Orden, who was stationed in Mac Hoe during the Tet offensive, three and a half miles from the Cambodian border. "One eighty-five-year-old man with a gunshot wound to his mid-tibia walked fifteen miles to us for treatment. The suffering of the ill and wounded was borne, generally, with quiet dignity. We did 'meatball surgery,' with a circulating nurse turning the pages of a surgery textbook as we went along. We opened abdomens, but sent head and chest wounds to Can Tho. The attitude of the non-medical U.S. military personnel toward the Vietnamese was generally appalling."

Another volunteer physician, Dr. J. Clyde Ralph, recalls, "Not infrequently, a mother arrives with her dead infant in her arms (still warm, but dead). Once I had my stethoscope on an infant's chest when the heart stopped beating. We went through all those heroic measures of external cardiac compression, intra-cardiac adrenalin, Coramine, and immediate IV with plasma expander—even our carefully hoarded oxygen. For a while, it looked like we might pull it off. Three hours later, he died for keeps. Grief comes hard when you've put your all into it. You have to keep reminding yourself, it isn't the US. Don't expect stateside performance. Still, you know it could be better than it is."

8

The People of Vietnam

"When ancient opinions and rules of life are taken away, the loss cannot possibly be estimated; from that moment, we have no compass to govern us, nor can we know distinctly to what port to steer."
- Edmund Burke

*D*uring the short intervals of calm between the battles, the tranquility and beauty of Vietnam emerged. Many soldiers considered Vietnam a hellhole, and it certainly was for most soldiers. But when Quang Tri was not the scene of a battle, it could quickly entrance me with its unmistakable and sometimes hidden beauty. For instance, the houses in and around Quang Tri were rickety and rundown. Most of them looked like shacks from the outside, but inside they were homes, and almost always clean and hospitable.

The landscape in Quang Tri province, farms and jungle cut by streams and rivers, had a sweet, quiet, humid beauty. In the mornings, exotic birds could be heard singing in the large beautiful trees that loomed over the rice paddies, providing partial shade. Outside of town, Vietnamese peasant farmers grew rice in rice paddies much as they had for hundreds of years, intensively farming their land without depleting its natural wealth. Vietnamese farmers and their families worked twelve hours a day during the growing season, planting, weeding, and harvesting rice. They kept the right amount of water on the rice by using a primitive but highly organized, integrated, and very efficient irrigation system that often relied on hand or foot power.

While the Vietnam war raged, Vietnamese men pumped water through primitive irrigation system using foot power.

When spoken, the Vietnamese language sounded at once singsong and like a can of rattling bones. It could go from beautiful to obliquely unnerving and irritating or frightening, depending on the speaker and the circumstances.

The Vietnamese people were not only physically beautiful, they were cooperative and helpful amongst themselves to an extent I had never seen in the United States. I will never forget the sight of small children running to help their parents take care of the house chores, something I saw every day. In Vietnam, children ten years old or younger would assume not only chores, but also the same responsibilities as a mature late teenager might assume in the US. The children always pitched in cheerfully, with a grace and maturity beyond their years. And they cared for each other. Small girls of five or six years of age would lovingly carry eight-month-old babies strapped to their backs. The children would carry their younger brothers and sisters around not because they had to, but because they loved to do it. These small children were in better hands on the backs of their older brothers or sisters than they would have been with most well-trained nannies back in the US.

Vietnamese society seemed to be based not on individualism, but on a cooperative ethic – doing good deeds and genuinely caring for others, especially among the very tight-knit families. I was continually struck by the marked lack of any selfishness or pettiness among Vietnamese families, even though their lives were being ripped apart by the war. Few countries on earth, I'm sure, had more spiritually or psychologically healthier children, especially in the middle of a war.

As I was witnessing the horrible injuries inflicted by the war on Vietnamese civilians, I was also learning something about the people of Vietnam. Like many other Volunteer Physicians, I came to admire and love the warm, simple, appreciative people of Vietnam

"In spite of their sanitary problems, I love these people," wrote Dr. Clyde Ralph, in Nha Trang. "They seem genuinely suited to life, happy-go-lucky in a life situation, which, on the surface, would seem to offer little to be happy about. These kids run around with their bottom halves naked, squat when they need to, no matter where, and keep impish and genuinely happy smiles almost always. Their keen eyes sparkle with a kind of keen awareness of the good of just being alive. Adulthood seems to change this quickly. They become more reserved and less spontaneous, more suspicious and less sure of the goodness of life, but isn't that true of all people?"

Dr. Ralph recalls leaving the hospital in Nha Trang at the end of the day, and seeing a rice farmer plowing his rice paddy with an ox-drawn wooden plow. Nearby, two small boys were pumping water with a primitive device, a bucket suspended between two ropes, pulling up buckets of water, emptying them, and filling them again. "Hard to feel any emotion except wonder at it all," Dr. Ralph recalls. "Wonder at the bright, happy smiles of the Vietnamese children, wonder at the beautiful poise and dignity of their women. Wonder at the senselessness of their war that surrounds them and adds to the painfulness of their lives. Wonder at the inhumanity of man to man and the lopsided unfairness of the distribution of life's wealth and abundance. But does it really matter? These people have a reality in their lives that keeps them happy. I wonder if we can improve on that."

"I always marveled at their ability to be clean, dressed, attractive, and wonderfully slender," recalled Dr. John McBratney, a volunteer physician in Quy Nhon and Phan Rang. "Young people emerging each day from what appeared to be the most primitive conditions, dirt floors and all, with bright smiles and beautiful attire."

Three Vietnamese boys walking beside me and clowning around on my way to work at the hospital in Quang Tri.

In Quang Tri, at times walking a few blocks to the hospital in the morning seemed like a magical experience. At first, I would usually be joined on my walk to work by skipping young children. I felt a little bit like the Pied Piper of Quang Tri as the children followed me, shouting, "*Bac Si* number one! *Bac Si* number one!"

After a while, I realized that this may have been a way to alert the Viet Cong that I was not a direct threat to them. I was an American, of course, but because I was not a soldier, and because I was a medical doctor, I probably had some built-in protection against being a direct target of hostile forces. The Vietnamese word for doctor, *Bac Si*, my interpreter Nguyen told me, not only meant doctor, but it also indicated a kind of respect, indicating a person to be admired, trusted, and honored. For example, many Vietnamese called the Communist revolutionary leader, Ho Chi Minh, *Bac Ho*, or Uncle Ho.

As a group, doctors have a special place in Vietnamese history and culture that is almost spiritual. In the nineteenth century, the learned Vietnamese scholar Hai Thuong Long shunned the career of a noble Mandarin and retired to a small village in Vietnam to devote his life to the study of medicine. He was a skilled observer who set down many important principles of hygiene and disease prevention in a twenty-eight-volume work. "Medicine is a human art which must seek to preserve life, attend to man's illnesses and sorrows and help him, without caring about wealth or honors," Hai Thuong Long wrote. "Rich men do not lack physicians, but poor can rarely afford good ones. One must pay special attention to them. Medicine is a noble art. We must strive to preserve our moral purity."

　　Although most Americans had no interest in it, the cultural mosaic of the former Indochina was fascinating. Vietnam was mostly Buddhist, although other religions including Confucianism, Taoism, and ancestor worship have influenced the culture. As people grew older, in Vietnam they had an increased status in society. The belief in reincarnation created strong family bonds not only with the immediate family but also with family members who were deceased, and required continuing love and attention in family burial plots. The idea of reincarnation helped the Vietnamese view time not as a linear concept, with a beginning and end as we see it in the West, but as something cyclical. And the Vietnamese had an almost ridiculous reverence for life, a world view that allowed them to either ignore a cockroach any American might try to kill, or even to pick it up and carry it outside. Releasing animals into the wild or protecting wild animals earns the Buddhist extra merit in the afterlife, and exotic birds and animals are sometimes released from cages during holidays or special events. While Western people aggressively chased the chimera of happiness, the Vietnamese felt they were born with happiness, and the most important task in life was to protect that happiness so that they would not lose it. In human relations, the Vietnamese did not really show their true feelings, but rather tried to show that life was a happy experience. The Buddhist emphasis on desire as the cause for suffering allowed people to be poor in Vietnam, and enjoy their life without the stigma which would attach to them in the United States.

　　Life in Vietnam could be extraordinarily primitive, compared to life in the United States at that time. During the monsoon season, volunteer physician Dr. B.L. Tom spent time in Dalat, a pretty, mountainous resort area about 100 kilometers north of Saigon. Although the patients lined up in droves and the monsoon rains came in heavy every day, he recalled there was still time for entertainment at night reminiscent of what might have happened a hundred years ago in the United States. "There is no television, radio, or phonograph, but we amuse ourselves with down home entertainment. The dining room has a huge fireplace that makes the room look like a ski lodge. We all gather around in the evening to sing and listen to a couple of our *Montagnard* friends play guitar. Many of the tribes have been converted to Christianity and the missionaries who have been in the area a long time join in singing hymns. The Vietnamese are mostly Buddhists but enjoy listening to the music."

"I remember the crowded orphanages and the intense suffering of the people," recalls Dr. Richard F. Harper, a volunteer physician in the small town of Moc Hoa about sixty miles west of Saigon, on the Plain of Reeds. "I also saw the spirit of the people, who were determined to survive and try to keep their dignity."

"When all is said and done, the most impressive thing about these three months to me was the Vietnamese people themselves," said Dr. Tom H. Mitchell, a volunteer doctor who served in Bac Lieu. "Their individual tolerance and acceptance of adversity and an amazing willingness to persevere was amazing. They had a resilience you rarely see here in the US. Returning home, I had a hard time accepting some of the poor-mouthing encountered in my practice."

My smart young interpreter, Nguyen, taught me a lot about the history and politics of the region, and about Vietnamese culture in general. Although I wasn't in the market for a girlfriend or a wife, Nguyen even made a few attempts to hook me up with one of the local girls.

Young Vietnamese girl pulls her family's water buffalo through the streets. This picture always reminds me of the hymn "Peace in the Valley," where the lion lies down with the lamb.

Nguyen and his family had thrown in their lot with the South Vietnamese government, and the United States. They would probably have been killed if Quang Tri were overrun by the Communist forces. Nguyen's father held the high title of province chief, a powerful position under the South Vietnamese government, since food and supplies sent by the US Agency for International Development were distributed by province chiefs. Nguyen's father, someone later told me, had probably paid $50,000 in bribes to high-ranking South Vietnamese officials to acquire the title of province chief. Most people who did this earned back their investment in about four months time, I was told. I was quite naive when I arrived in Quang Tri, and since Nguyen was so kind and helpful to me, I assumed his father must have been a kindly, intelligent person who would never cheat his countrymen, or deprive the needy.

One night I received an invitation to dine at Nguyen's father's house. Being invited to dinner by a province chief was an honor, I assumed, and I was happy to oblige. Since Nguyen's father didn't speak any English and I spoke only a few words of Vietnamese, Nguyen interpreted for us during the sumptuous, 10-course dinner that was served in his house.

When the province chief learned that I had no wife, he expressed concern.

"We have many pretty and lovely girls who need a husband," he told me in Vietnamese, with Nguyen interpreting. "We will find a nice wife for you."

I politely thanked him, and continued to eat. Although I loved women, I had already decided not to touch the girls of Vietnam, because to do so, I felt, would have been a form of exploitation.

With some ceremony, Nguyen's father passed me a plate of what was a special delicacy, and insisted that I try it. I saw very thin slices of some kind of dark meat, wrapped in fragrant evergreen mint leaves. The little slices of meat looked good. I ate all I was served, and then asked Nguyen the name of the delicacy I was eating.

Nguyen gave me the Vietnamese name of the dish.

"What did you say it was?" I asked.

"Rat," Nguyen explained.

I had heard that rat meat was a staple in parts of Southeast Asia, but I had not expected to sample it myself. I must admit its tastiness surprised me. But when I thought of the trichinosis that might have infected such meat, I politely passed on second helpings.

Although I didn't see much of him personally, I could see the province chief's hand at work in my life from time to time.

A few days after I had dinner at the province chief's house, Nguyen pulled me over to the window of the hospital and asked me to look outside. I was surprised to see perhaps 100 of the most beautiful young women I had ever seen, demurely standing in line. The young ladies ranged in age from their teens to their early twenties. They were all neatly dressed in traditional Vietnamese *ao dias* of flowing white silk, which made them look a bit like a group of visiting angels.

"What are all these girls here for?" I asked Nguyen.

"Acupuncture needles, medicine," he replied.

"I don't *do* acupuncture, Nguyen," I said.

"No, no," he explained. "They already had acupuncture. They have needles in their bodies."

"What am I to do about the needles?" I asked.

"They all know you take bullets out and they want you to take their needles out," Nguyen replied. "Besides, when one comes by who you like, you can make her your girlfriend."

"Doctors aren't supposed to date their patients," I said. I stiffly informed my young interpreter of the Hippocratic oath.

"No problem," Nguyen said. "You don't have to date her. You can just marry the one you like."

Nguyen happily ushered the first girl into the examining room. Removing her silk *ao dai*, I saw three tiny rust marks that looked like broken-off needles under the skin of her young body. Acupuncture is a staple of traditional Oriental medicine, and all the girls waiting to see me had been treated by acupuncture for everything from coughs to colds to urinary infections, and even malaria. The long, thin acupuncture needles are traditionally reused, and some of the needles had broken off during treatment, and were left there by the acupuncturists who treated the girls. The girls were given no further care until the rust marks showed up, or they had felt something under their skin. Someone – perhaps Nguyen's father, the province chief – had rounded them all up for me to deal with a latent problem that resulted in their receiving some scarring from the needles. At the time, it didn't seem odd to me that there were no men standing in the line with broken needles in their skin.

I tried my best to remove the buried, broken-off needles. On the first girl, after sterilizing the area, I made an incision with a tiny blade. But when I tried to pull the needles out, like you would remove a splinter or a bullet, the needles wouldn't budge. The needles were completely encapsulated by fibrous tissue. I worked for three or four hours on the first two patients, while the other girls waited patiently in line, in their flowing white silk garments. After working for a while, I saw how difficult it was to remove the needles, and the scars that would remain after I had finally removed them.

Finally, I asked Nguyen to tell all the waiting ladies that I wished I could help them, but that removing the needles was not possible without causing even deeper scarring than they already had. I told him that I would not see the girls now. There was another line of old people and children that were waiting for me, whom I had to see immediately. Nguyen got rid of the girls in short order, then glided back to me.

"How are you ever going to be a happy person in Vietnam?" Nguyen asked me when he returned. "You are old enough to have a wife here. You need to be a happy person each day. I want to find a good girl for you."

A group of Vietnamese children gathered at the gate to Quang Tri Hospital included my interpreter Nguyen, upper left.

I smiled and winked at him. I knew his intentions were good.

My interpreter's attitude was always to look out for the interest of family, friends, and those most in need. He presumed that I was in need of female companionship, although I didn't feel that way. Although I didn't realize it at the time, the simple charms of the life that he lived everyday, and the life that I was experiencing, were seducing me and changing my point of view in many different ways.

The Vietnamese people, with a culture thousands of years old, had accumulated a great many holidays to celebrate. Often, big holiday dinners were occasions for merrymaking and celebration. Holidays gave the Vietnamese some welcome relief from the war, providing a time to celebrate and relax. A couple of times, I was lucky enough to be invited to participate in these holiday celebrations. I remember the gentle plunking sounds of soft Asian music, and happy children and families sharing food in harmony.

On one of these holiday occasions, I was served a special food that everyone at the table insisted that I eat. This entree looked like some kind of black chocolate custard. Everybody said it was a prized delicacy that I had to try. Looking around me, I saw that everybody at the table was digging into their bowl of this black custard-like substance with great enthusiasm.

When I took a bite, I was aghast at its bitterness, and I impolitely spat it out. Somebody explained to me that this local delicacy was ground raw liver and blood, a mixture that had been left to ferment.

When I indicated that the taste was unpleasant to me, and alien to my American palate, several of the children in attendance tried to make it up to me. They brought me another delicacy - *trung vit lon,* or buried bird eggs.

When I asked, I learned that the eggs the children held out to me were duck eggs that had been buried in the warm earth for several months. Although they were buried, the tiny chicks had continued to grow for a time, developing to the state where they had eyes and even a beak. At that point, the eggs were boiled in water. Since the eggs had become somewhat petrified, the correct state to be eaten, the children offered them to me.

"Please try, you like very much," the kids said.

I thanked the children, but they continued to try to get me to eat the eggs. I could not bring myself to eat any of those eggs. Later I learned that the children had been showing good manners by offering me the eggs first. After I refused, the children were able to eat the *trung vit lon* eggs themselves.

9

Life During Wartime

*"Without freedom of thought, there can be no
such thing as wisdom; and no such thing as public
liberty, without freedom of speech."*
- Benjamin Franklin

*"Character is formed, not by laws, commands,
and decrees, but by quiet influence, unconscious
suggestions and personal guidance."*
- Marvin L. Buston

*A*s my stay in Vietnam continued, my attitude about what I was doing went up and down. I knew too well that there was a brutal war on, with many casualties and many wounded. I knew my life could end any moment. I knew I could catch a stray mortar round or a bullet with my name on it. A few weeks after I arrived In Vietnam, I heard the news that Robert Kennedy had been shot in California. The next day, he died. But despite the gravity of the situation, my mood wasn't always fatalistic. On many days, I felt a tremendous exhilaration, a feeling that I had no problems at all. I was exhilarated to be doing good work and saving the lives of innocent civilians. I had escaped the petty, mundane, boring drudgery of my residency at a state mental hospital back in the US, and I felt light years ahead of where I might have been had I stayed home. I felt that I was accomplishing something worthwhile in Vietnam. I knew what I was doing was more fulfilling, more necessary, more humanitarian, and more humane than anything I could have been doing in psychiatry.

Each time I made a life-saving effort to give some poor person another day on earth, I felt some small joy and great personal satisfaction. At some of these times, working faster than I thought possible, this was exhilarating. Many times I felt like I was making progress, when young Marines would express their appreciation that I was one of them and coming back into the "heart of darkness" to help. But the next moment, I would be paranoid and afraid for my life.

Suddenly, without warning, the war would be right on top of me. The air overhead would be filled with choppers, and crackling bursts of rocket fire and mortar fire. Or without warning, the earth would shake under my feet with the muffled concussions of B-52s dropping bombs in the distance. I would smell the distinctive odor of napalm in the air. Often, when I experienced these reminders of the ongoing war, I would immediately become depressed. I would helplessly wonder how many innocent civilians were being caught in the crossfire, how many were dying at that moment. I wondered how many were suffering horrible wounds and disfigured bodies, and how many would be crawling or carried to my hospital for help within the next few hours.

After a long day of dealing with misery and death, walking home in the humid darkness, I would wonder, what are those shadows by the side of the road? Are there suspicious spooks or people following me? Other times, I would wonder, what is that explosion I just heard? Is that mortar fire? Who was just firing rounds, and why? Which direction did that round come from? Would the next round find me?

But being young and doing good work, for a while I felt that I was bulletproof. Early on, the children of Quang Tri put out the word that I would help local people who were sick or injured, without pay. I sometimes felt no one in Vietnam would ever harm the benevolent *Bac Si,* a Pied Piper followed by children on his way to work. I was a brave doctor who had come in peace to help the Vietnamese. On other days, however, for some reason I never knew, the children who followed me to the hospital would not show up. I began to wonder how much the children knew.

Walking to and from work, or walking around Quang Tri, I sometimes recognized the familiar sound of bullets sailing through the trees near me. I knew the sound of bullets from my days in the Marine Corps, but since I was the town's good *Bac Si,* I could not imagine that the snipers would be shooting at me. For a while, as an American helping any Vietnamese civilian who needed medical help, I thought I was immune from the bullets from either side.

The first few times, I thought the bullets I heard were only stray gunfire. I wasn't too concerned. But as I continued to walk to work, and the sound of passing bullets continued, I eventually realized that the bullets were coming very close to me. After a while, I realized that the Viet Cong were probably firing at any American who happened to be in the area. Sometimes, I thought that perhaps I was never directly targeted, but only warned by shots over my head intended as "calling cards," perhaps because I was treating all comers at my hospital, even Viet Cong.

Other days, when I was more cautious and more on edge, when I heard bullets, I would run back to my quarters in the residential compound, sprinting and dodging. Although I was trained in the use of firearms in the Marine Corps, and I was issued an M16 when I arrived, a super weapon compared to the ancient M1 I used as a Marine, I never carried a weapon in Vietnam. I didn't want to become a target. I was there as a doctor, not a warrior.

But as the battle lines shifted and the war closed in around us, fear was contagious Everyone in Quang Tri was affected. Military convoys rolled through town. People hurried about their business. I vowed to keep going, and to do my necessary job every day, no matter what. There was so much sorrow and chaos around me, I just had to block it out to continue my medical work.

A Vietnamese mother and her children help care for wounded civilians left on stretchers by military transport outside Quang Tri Provincial Hospital, 1968.

Increasingly, I realized I was truly in the middle of a war that both sides were trying to win. Quang Tri lay just thirty-five kilometers south of the 17th parallel, Vietnam's demilitarized zone. The residents of the town had divided sympathies. Some townspeople were Viet Cong sympathizers. Some worked for the US during the day, and when the sun went down they became armed guerrillas, attacking American and South Vietnamese soldiers. I was convinced the Viet Cong had infiltrated the local police force. From day to day, I never knew if the townspeople would be loyal to the South Vietnamese regime, the Viet Cong, or the National Liberation Front backed by the Communist government in Hanoi.

Although it was impossible to accurately estimate, Quang Tri was probably divided, with about twenty-five percent sympathetic to the South Vietnamese government, another twenty-five percent loyal to the Viet Cong, and a majority of fifty percent who could swing either way, depending on the course of the war.   Most Vietnamese liked the Americans, and especially liked their money, but many of them surely knew they might have to kill an American combatant at some point to unite their divided country.

One day the rumors would fly that the North Vietnamese army was winning the war, that the Viet Cong were getting stronger, and that so many Americans had been killed that the Americans were going to leave Vietnam. On these days, the Vietnamese nurses would not show up to work at the hospital. The next day, rumors would fly that the Americans had just won a big battle and that South Vietnam was going to win the war. The nurses would return to work. The morale of the people was continually tested as the conflict surged back and forth, with both sides struggling to get the upper hand. Everything was in play. On the nights when the rumor mills were strongly against the Americans, Nguyen or other Vietnamese warned me to be careful and I took their warnings seriously.

One afternoon, on a visit to Hue, I got a clear picture of Viet Cong stealth, and their ability to penetrate a so-called secure zone. My mentor Dr. Detwiler and I took some time off to visit a religious shrine in Hue, once the capital of imperial Vietnam. At that time, Hue was protected and held by American troops.

As we approached the shrine, we paused to look at what appeared to be a funeral procession was passing by on the street ahead. A group of men carried wooden caskets, while others rode alongside in pedicabs called *cyclos* in Vietnam. At that moment, a Buddhist monk calmly approached us. He warned us not to go near the procession. The monk whispered to us that the caskets were full of grenades and other munitions. He said the men in pedicabs were lookouts, scouting for any possible trouble.

Dr. Detwiler and I thanked the monk. We returned to the hospital sooner than we'd planned. Within a supposedly secure city, more or less occupied by the United States, we'd just seen a caravan of Viet Cong. Things were not always as they seemed in Vietnam.

The feeling of danger intensified as I stayed in Quang Tri. One day I inadvertently walked into a highly dangerous situation. As I walked, from a distance, it looked like several military doctors were talking with one of the Vietnamese interpreters. I stopped to talk to the doctors, not realizing I had stumbled into a hostile situation. I had a camera with me, and I innocently took a picture of the docs. Then I noticed that the interpreter was brandishing a hand grenade.

"You run my country, you tell me I steal your gas, you fire me from my job, now I kill you!" the Vietnamese man shouted hysterically, shaking the grenade.

"Wait, my friend," I said, walking toward him. "Come on, what's this little problem here? We can settle it. Let's talk about it."

"Americans fire me, they call me a thief!" he said.

He said he had been fired by the Americans for stealing some fuel for his motorbike. He said it was only a liter, and I told him it was not worth killing everyone over.

I gently coaxed him out of range of the other doctors, who were apparently innocent bystanders. I talked to the man. I got the man to hand me the hand grenade. I told him he could have all the gas he needed, and promised him I'd help him get his job back. His job paid about $6 a day, much higher than the average wage of less than $1 a day in Vietnam. When he calmed down, I gave him the grenade back and told him to take it out of the area immediately.

When I visited the location the next day, I was told the man was a suspected Viet Cong agent, and that two of the military doctors whose lives I'd saved had reported me as a possible Viet Cong sympathizer! I couldn't believe it! My life-saving intervention, framed as a pro-Communist act? Whatever *noblesse oblige* I exhibited to save all their lives and defuse the situation was viewed with suspicion. As a result of that event, I probably became "a suspect with suspicious motives," at MACV headquarters in Quang Tri. Later, when I saw the movie *Apocalypse Now*, I realized how close to the truth that surreal movie had come.

cannon canoe

Postcard from Vietnam shows North Vietnamese fighters on motorized canoe

Many times we could actually feel the war moving closer. Mortars hit Quang Tri regularly. There was bitter fighting around us. The city was almost overrun on several occasions, and we thought we'd have to evacuate the hospital.

My living quarters were not in a good location. The house I shared with an American missionary family was halfway between the province chief's house and a large South Vietnamese ammunition storage facility located in the citadel. These were both strategic targets for the opposition forces. This made the house an exposed target for stray incoming mortars.

About midnight one evening, I was asleep in my bed when I felt the hard frightening shock of a mortar round exploding in the corner of the courtyard, about ten yards from my bed.

I bolted awake at the orange flash outside my window, and the loud explosion. The blast blew out all the glass in the windows in the house. The bedroom wall began to crumble. Right after the blast, I felt imminent danger. I heard someone scream, breaking the silence that followed the blast.

More mortars were coming in, not far away. I heard small arms fire. I grabbed the M16 rifle that had been assigned to me, but that I'd never used. I made sure there was a clip in the rifle, then crawled under the bed. I spent the night under the bed, hoping that the mattress would at least protect me from incoming mortar rounds or falling debris. Although I had an M16, I realized that if the Viet Cong stormed the house I would be hopelessly outgunned.

I was wide awake. All my Marine training came back to me. I became hyper-vigilant. I was trained in the "art of war," but this was not an old-fashioned war, with clear boundaries between soldiers and civilians. There was really no front line, and no rear line. It was a war of national liberation, played out with cunning, skill, and stealth by the Viet Cong, and with heavy firepower and brute force by the US Armed Forces.

It was a very long night. The thunk, thunk, thunk of mortars continued, seeming to hit almost every minute or so until the sun rose. With the first rays of sun streaming in the smashed open windows of my house, and the steamy heat of the morning, the battle was over. The guns were silent. I heard the sound of a few choppers in the distance.

*A bunker is built outside Dr. Hassan's quarters after a
mortar attack, 1968.*

I took a shower, shaken to the core, but determined to get to the hospital for another day of work. Outside my door, I was surprised to find that my guard's head had been scraped by a piece of shrapnel. He was still standing guard with a long scalp wound where shrapnel had skinned the hair and skin off the top of his head. During the night, he had been partially scalped.

Not long after the mortar attack, Nguyen's father, the province chief, sent over workers to place sandbags and construct a fortified bunker next door to my house. A large secure bunker was built for me, which I used more and more.

When I asked Nguyen why his father did this, he explained, "Father like you, respect you, and hope you never die. He pray for you and pray you find a nice wife, too."

The residential compound where I lived was also home to a Christian missionary family from the US, a husband, wife, and three pre-teen children. As part of their work, the Jehovah's Witness missionaries passed out donated powdered milk and other dairy products to Vietnamese families and children in the area as a part of their "humanitarian crusade." I found this medically questionable, since most Vietnamese children were lactose intolerant, and would react unfavorably to cow's milk. In retrospect, this was an example of Americans wanting to "do good," but not really understanding the cultural and health issues inside Vietnam. But I do remember the pleasant sound of flute music coming from the missionaries' quarters some nights, and Vietnamese sitting around their quarters with their native instruments, and sometimes a guitar, singing songs for peace.

As I remained in Vietnam, I developed a respect for these people, and a concern for their safety. I told the missionaries my new bomb shelter was available to them or anyone else during emergencies. The missionaries did not have a bunker, so some nights they slept in the bunker with me. We all knew well we were in a war zone, and that we might have to huddle together to survive an attack.

10

Visiting a Re-Education Camp

"For if men are to be precluded from offering their sentiments on a matter, which may involve the most serious and alarming consequences, that can invite the consideration of mankind, reason is no use to us; the freedom of Speech may be taken away, and, dumb and silent, we may be led like sheep to the slaughter." – General George Washington, Address to the Officers of the American Army

A few days after the mortar attack, I went to a nearby village with some Navy corpsmen for one of our periodic child care and vaccination clinics. I was to see more of the horror of war. In this village, I saw a "re-education camp" for the first time. Like many other camps of this type built with American money, and brutally manned by the South Vietnamese, the village was filled with a couple of thousand nearly naked men, women, and children, deemed enemy prisoners of war. The so-called "re-education camp" held local people rounded up without hard evidence, and they were treated like animals. These people were forced to confess, jailed without trials, and treated brutally.

This was not the worst treatment the South Vietnamese and the Americans could dish out. People suspected of working against the South Vietnamese regime were put in "tiger cages," which were bamboo enclosures that were literally low cages crowded with human beings. The tiger cages were anchored by bamboo stakes as thick as your fist, which were spaced a few inches apart and driven into the ground all around the outer edge of the cage.

The cages I saw were about four feet high, ten feet wide, and twenty feet long. The top of the cage was so low, prisoners could not stand up. As many as twenty prisoners were placed in one of these cages. Captives were served food through the bamboo slats, and were forced to live with their own excrement. I saw people taunting the prisoners in the cages, and spitting on them.

As I walked past the tiger cages, the prisoners must have noticed that I was an American in civilian clothes. They sat on their knees and silently held out their hands inside the cages, pleading for help. At that moment, I looked into the most sorrowful and pitiful faces I had ever seen in Vietnam.

I was told that the most committed Communist guerillas were kept for long periods of time in the tiger cages. The captives believed to be the worst were left to die "like dirty rats." Usually the cages were built in the open sun. Many prisoners died from dehydration or starvation in the long, crowded cages which would have been considered unsuitable even for farm animals.

Beyond that, the most unapologetic prisoners, I was told, the die-hard revolutionaries who were deemed unlikely to be "rehabilitated," were never even taken to the re-education camps. Later I learned that during the war an estimated 40,000 Vietnamese people were assassinated by South Vietnamese and Americans under the Central Intelligence Agency's Phoenix program, which also set up the re-education camps. According to Stuart Herrington, the unapologetic author of *Stalking the Vietcong: Inside Operation Phoenix: A Personal Account,* Vietnamese civilians who were found to have a picture of Ho Chi Minh in their huts, a radio, or more medication than they could personally use were assumed to be Viet Cong and immediately killed.

The camp I saw was just another facet of the brutal, dehumanizing war. In Vietnam, a military officer once told me that we needed to kill the Viet Cong children, because they were like nits who would grow up to become dangerous enemy lice.

When things slowed down at the hospital, or when I had adequate relief, as an American doctor I was able to travel around Vietnam on military airplanes and helicopters. I was tremendously confident when I was around American troops. Usually these tough young guys reminded me of the way I felt when I wore the uniform and I was a proud Marine.

But sometimes, even in the troops, a ripple of fear or desperation appeared. It sometimes seemed as if the young troops thought or hoped that I, as a doctor, could have some influence on the political leaders back home, and get them home sooner. Because I was a doctor, perhaps, some of these men looked up to me, maybe more than some of their own officers. Out of the blue, a soldier would sometimes confide his fear and apprehension to me. Some soldiers desperately wanted me to hear them out, and help them get "back to the world," as the United States was called in Vietnam, as quickly as possible.

Entrance to Da Nang Military base, Vietnam, 1968.

At one military stop a young Marine blurted, "We're losing the fucking war! The whole damn thing is bullshit! We go out on maneuvers and try to make contact, but we don't know who the goddamn enemy is. If we make contact now, it's usually over fast, since they shoot us up real bad or just wipe out everyone."

Another young soldier told me, "Doc, please tell the public the war is going real bad and for no reason at all. The officers don't lead us into the bush, or even follow us anymore. They're afraid of getting shot or blown up, but they send us in anyway. We're being ordered out on patrols that don't mean shit and we're dying like flies out there."

Hearing this from young US soldiers and Marines was heart-breaking and tragic to me, as a former Marine. The soldiers' comments did not encourage me to support our country's continuing involvement in Vietnam.

Our brave but beaten-up troops occasionally displayed a cynical, frightened, fatalistic attitude. Waiting for flights, I would see guys in their late teens or early twenties who had faces of stern and serious men fifty or sixty years old. Out of the blue, they'd make occasional cryptic remarks.

"I don't think I can make it much longer, Doc," one would said.

"I've already lost a bunch of buddies, and I don't want to be out here and end up like them," another said.

On one airplane hop, to Phu Bai, I hurried to board a military aircraft, but then found myself on the wrong flight. I was trying to get back to Quang Tri, but I had boarded the wrong airplane. I was surprised to find myself on a fully loaded troop transport, headed for An Khe, fully 350 kilometers south of Quang Tri. It was a perilous flight that I have remembered for years.

Over 150 Marines were on board, packing all their combat gear – M16s, ammo belts, machine guns, grenades. Flying over Vietnam in the heavily loaded troop transport, we took fire from below. Some of the Marines were sleeping, some of them frozen with fear. Not many wanted to talk to me, a lost doctor who had stumbled onto the wrong flight.

"What you doing with us grunts, Doc?" a young black Marine of about nineteen asked me. "You going into battle with us?"

I explained I was headed back to Quang Tri. He told me the plane was headed the other direction.

"Hey, doc, tell me this," the young Marine said. "How the hell you get through medical school if you don't know where you're going?"

We laughed. Then the young Marine told me a personal story.

"I was nearly killed about two months ago," he said.

He showed me a six-inch scar on his neck, near his jugular vein. "Piece of shrapnel cut my jugular and I nearly bled to death near Con Thien. They shipped me out and got me to the hospital, then they said I might be brain-damaged because I lost so much blood. Do I look crazy to you, Doc?"

I said I didn't think so.

"There should be some kind of rule says when you've been wounded like this, you get more time off. But they say I'm probably okay, and I know they're short up there so I gotta go back. My brothers need me. But I'm afraid this is my last battle, Doc. I got some strange feeling about this one."

The young Marine leaned back. His eyes rolled back, and he seemed to be in a daze for the rest of the flight.

I found a Marine Corps captain, who laughed when I told him what I'd done. It was the only other laugh I heard on the flight. The captain told me I'd need to take a flight back when one became available.

"I'd give you a chopper lift back up to Quang Tri, Doc," the captain said. "We got enough choppers, but the chance of making it to Q-T in a chopper is only about 50-50. Wait for a fixed-wing aircraft, gives you better odds."

"I'll wait for a plane," I told him.

He nodded, with a slight smile.

When the plane was landing in An Khe, we heard rounds bursting and echoing through the belly of the plane from snipers trying to shoot us down from below. I saw real terror in the eyes of the of the troops. Their bravery was also obvious. Each man knew that perhaps half of the soldiers around him on this combat operation might not survive the firefight into which they were heading. The boys were all just trying to survive another day, living and fighting for their fellow Marines, and doing their combat duty for the United States.

11

Operation Arc Light

*"What difference does it make to the dead,
the orphans, and the homeless, whether the
made destruction is wrought under the name of
totalitarianism or the holy name of liberty or
democracy?" - Gandhi*

*T*ime was flying. Most of the time, I didn't have much time to think about the tragedies I had seen, or to worry about those that I might encounter later in the day. Mornings I would walk down the dirt path from my house to the Quang Tri hospital, or sometimes I would take the Jeep. More often than not, the moment I arrived at the hospital I'd be swamped with work.

I recall two days after a carpet bombing raid very vividly. The military operation was code-named "Operation Arc Light." In Quang Tri, we heard heavy bombs being dropped by B-52s falling and exploding in the distance, perhaps ten miles away, shaking the earth under our feet. The military base at Khe Sanh was under heavy fire. To retaliate, bombs the size of Volkswagens were being dropped every day, the sound and force of their blasts resonating through the hills and valleys. As the earth shook, I could almost hear the cries of the civilian population in the distance as the mighty bomb blasts reverberated all the way to Quang Tri. We were short of help at the hospital. All the technicians and military doctors around who would normally be able to help care for the civilians, and almost all the Navy corpsmen, had been ordered to the battlefield to care for wounded soldiers.

After the bombing raid, lines of injured, traumatized civilian patients lined up at the hospital, many of them children. I was the only doctor in town. The wounded had no place else to go.

Children came to me, wounded by shrapnel from the bombs, and many died in my arms. Severely wounded patients flew past me like blips on a radar screen. I had to work very fast, assisted by only one Navy corpsman. As he amputated the legs of small children and tended to their wounds, I plunged into surgery after surgery next to him.

I remember an old woman presented with a piece of shrapnel in her head. The fragment had missed vital blood vessels in its path to the midbrain. Her headache appeared to be non-life-threatening, so I left the fragment in place, relying on antibiotics to clear any infection.

I remember performing an eye enucleation on a teenage boy, removing his eyeball, but within hours the wound had become badly infected. I did not have the proper equipment to remove the eyeball. I starkly recall the grittiness of the wound. I had given the young man Xylocaine injections to numb the eye area. His good eye was saved, but he would be scarred for life. The brave little boy smiled at me when I gave him medication to clear the infection, and he realized he would be one of the lucky ones and would live, and I took his picture which is included in this book.

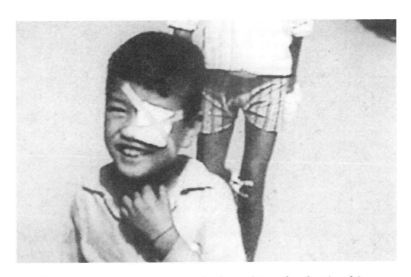

A Vietnamese boy smiles happily three days after having his eye removed in Quang Tri Hospital. He lost his eye, but not his smile.

We became so swamped that we had to activate all our temporary facilities outside the hospital, the two large tents on the hospital grounds. Sanitation was impossible. Our temporary wards were tents with rows of bed on dirt floors. Patients as well as their family members and visitors would urinate and defecate at the end of the row of beds. Someone would come along later and channel the wastes into a ditch that ran directly into a stream that fed the river, but before long the feces would pile up again.

Although I didn't have time to deal with it, the sanitation situation was continually disheartening, and an obvious menace to public health. The drinking water system at the hospital was wretched and unsanitary. Many diseases could have been prevented if the most basic potable water procedures had been instituted. Several times I tried to explain to Nguyen how bacteria affected their water, and how critical it was for him to instruct the staff on how to keep the system clean. Cleanliness is vital for a surgeon, but we had no rubber gloves and I could not really wash my hands because the water was polluted. I could only brush a small amount of antiseptic over my hands periodically, between patients, to try to maintain sanitation.

Meanwhile, the lines of wounded grew longer. Two young girls with belly wounds came into the hospital. When I examined them, I saw that the shrapnel fragments had fortunately not penetrated their larger arteries, although in each girl, portions of the bowel would have to be removed. With the assistance of my one corpsman, I operated on both girls at the same time, opening them up from sternum to pelvic brim. I remember the feel of their warm wet intestines in my fingers, as I searched for life-threatening perforations. In each case, I found the fragments embedded in the soft tissue, and successfully patched them up.

But after a few days of working every waking hour, nearly overwhelmed by what I had seen, I lay in my bed, unable to sleep. There were so many innocent wounded people, old people, women, and children, innocent victims of the massive, ruthless American bombing. After work, the thought of all the dying and wounded left me profoundly shaken, crying silently to myself into the early morning hours.

One case I vividly remember was an eight-year-old boy whose name was Thang. Thang had been struck by shrapnel in his belly, pelvis, legs, arms and trunk. The little boy had been hiding in a ditch with a perforated bowel for two days, before American troops brought him into our hospital by chopper. He was accompanied to the hospital by his mother and several other relatives.

Thang's desperate mother stayed with him night and day. I found out she had lost her three other children near Cam Lo, a Viet Cong stronghold fifteen miles away. Thang was the mother's last living child, and she desperately wanted to protect him and keep him from dying. I felt deep down that if her last child died, she might die, too.

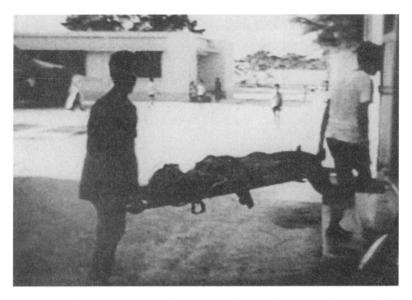

Wounded civilian on stretcher carried into the foyer of Quang Tri Provincial Hospital, Vietnam, 1968.

Thang was running a high fever when he was brought in. Even though he was terribly wounded, he smiled faintly when he saw me. His brown eyes sparkled with hope. I performed a tracheotomy without hesitation because the inability to breathe is the most common cause of sudden death. When we stripped him and laid him on the table, his stomach was hard as a rock. Intubation with nasogastric suction was performed, with an end-line catheter placed on his bladder.

The first thing you have to do in these situations is prevent shock and treat it if it exists. The second thing is to try and prevent infection. When a patient is wounded, you explore the wound, looking for blood clots, debris, and other foreign material, and cleaning the wound out while trying to protect major blood vessels and nerves against damage. The third most important thing is to relieve the patient's anxiety and the fourth is to try to get the wound to heal in as natural a process as possible, while trying to preserve function.

When I opened the boy up, his abdomen was full of pus. I flushed out the abdomen through the peritoneum, using all the antibiotics I could get my hands on, cleaning the wounds and pockets of pus.

Shrapnel and bits and pieces of flesh were scattered around his abdomen, much of it around the aorta and some embedded in the liver. Hunting carefully, I picked out all the bits and pieces of shrapnel and skin I could find. The boy had so much sepsis it was frightening, but fortunately his vital signs were strong. His 103-degree temperature was a good sign; it meant his body was still fighting. No temperature would have meant his resources for fighting infection had closed down.

Leaving the benign pieces of shrapnel in place for later, and flushing with antibiotics, I re-sectioned a twelve-inch area of his bowel, removed the dead tissue, and closed the wound. Since there had been cavitation from the shrapnel, the bowel tissue several inches around the path of the shrapnel had been devitalized and was microscopically dead; this dead tissue had to be removed. Any devitalized tissue would give way, allowing feces to pour into the abdominal cavity, triggering a vicious peritonitis. This had already happened to the young boy, and it was probably going to kill him. The edges of the wound also had to be very carefully placed together. I probably should have done a colostomy, but I felt if I opened another wound it would be a source for more infection and I was trying to keep him alive.

After all this, the boy was still bleeding. I operated a second time eight hours later, looking for the source of his internal bleeding, but I could find nothing except some stress ulcers in his intestinal tract and his gastric mucosa. We had used our one pint of blood we got from another patient, and I gave a pint of my own blood because I was O positive.

Blood transfusion is one of the most important factors in managing shock. If blood pressure drops below 100 mm/Hg after wounding, transfusion should begin as quickly as possible. Below 80 mm/Hg, there should be no delay at all; the patient shouldn't be moved until some blood or intravenous fluids were given, if any were available. Administration of fluids in Quang Tri Provincial Hospital was not always an option, but immediate surgery to stop the bleeding was. A simple trick used in military hospitals was to raise the litter eight inches at the head for about five minutes; if blood pressure, pulse rate and volume, color of the skin and lips remained unchanged, the patient could tolerate anesthesia and surgery with the support of further transfusions or fluids.

*Tanks like these from North Vietnam wreaked
havoc during Vietnam War.*

For a while, Thang seemed to be getting better. But infection is the handmaiden of war wounds characterized by devitalization of tissue, extravasion of blood, disruption of the local blood supply, and introduction of foreign bodies and contamination with a variety of bacteria, and all these factors interact. We fought this with everything we had. We are talking 30 million units of penicillin every four hours, draining the penicillin cabinet daily to try to keep this boy alive. In the United States, one and one-half million units every four hours might seem like a lot. In Vietnam, I had already learned, even to prevent pneumonia, it was 60 million units a day for tiny babies. We placed the boy on IVs, and meticulously instructed the nurses that fluids had to be run into him. We achieved some homeostasis. Then we noticed his hemoglobin was only 8 gm/100 ml, which is approximately half the normal amount, and of course we had no more blood resources. We continued to baby the young boy, hoping for the best.

On the third day, we had no more blood for transfusions, and I operated again. The boy was still bleeding but I could not find a source. His smile got fainter. His mother was becoming delirious with pain and anger. I knew his hope for life was slipping away. His young eyes deadened. Suddenly, he released a pint of thick blood out of his rectum, like a glob of dark purple Jello on the operating table. Then the bright light of hope in his eyes went out forever, released like a mist. That young boy died in my arms after a total of twelve exhausting hours of surgery.

"Americans killed my baby!" His mother shouted, falling to her knees when I told her.

She grabbed my legs and screamed, "Americans killed my baby!"

Before I could console her, she ran into the courtyard outside the hospital, where she screamed and shrieked at the top of her voice for the next hour. Her loud cries were very upsetting. Later, I was told that this display of what psychiatrists refer to as ventilation was a common phenomenon in Vietnam. No amount of consolation could temper the mother's loud, passionate, public display of heart-rending grief.

But later that same day, the mother came back to the hospital, helping to care for the survivors in our outdoor tent hospital. She went about her mission of mercy with a shocked, vacant look.

That particular night, I remember, I went to bed too sad and tired to sleep. I was so exhausted. I had given it everything I had. I would not admit to anyone around me that I wept like a baby. I was a surgeon and I could not let these things affect me, but they did. This was not the first time in Quang Tri I had wept with agony and exhaustion when I went to bed. I had been trying to save lives in a war zone for what seemed like a long, long time.

The endless tragedies of the dead and wounded children were getting to me. A kind of depression creeps into your life in these situations, and it becomes contagious. I so longed for a human connection, out there on a limb in Vietnam, and over my head in blood and urine and feces. I wanted so much to hold a woman in my arms, to kiss her and hold her, but there were always more patients who needed immediate help, and more patients after that. I knew that I needed to keep a professional distance between myself and my patients, to maintain my objectivity and to allow me to focus my abilities as a surgeon.

Still, I couldn't get this one brave little boy out of my mind. The night he died, I thought about him lying alone in a ditch for two days and nights, with shrapnel in his belly. He had even managed to smile at me when he was carried into the hospital. I remembered looking into his eyes, and witnessing that passionate hope for life. I did everything I could, but I could not save him.

As I remembered him dying in my arms, I vowed to try to do something for the betterment of the world, to work for waging peace, rather than waging war. I made an oath to myself that night in my bunker, an oath for the children like him in the world, an oath that said,

"Never again." In the following years, as I remembered this night, I would live a life of giving back in small ways and large, wherever I felt I could have a significant impact on events.

12

The Beautiful Women of Vietnam

*"Throughout history, the world has been laid waste
to ensure the triumph of conceptions that are now as
dead as the men who died for them."*
– Henry de Montherland

*U*sually I never went out of my bunker at night. But one evening, a young man appeared at the door to my bunker and pleaded for my help. It was dark outside. Gunfire was already sounding in the distance. With gestures and halting English, he told me there was a young woman in a village not far away who needed help in having a baby. He said he would take me there. For some reason, I trusted this earnest young man, who so desperately pleaded for my help. I grabbed my medical kit, and we walked outside into the darkness.

As we hurried away from my bunker in Quang Tri and out through the jungle, we heard more sounds of gunfire, and exploding mortars. Eventually we arrived at a hut. We paused for a moment at the doorway to the mud hut. I saw flares above me, illuminating the battlefield, and heard the sound of a firefight close by. We were obviously very close to the fighting.

As I entered the hut, my young guide and the woman's grandmother waited outside. Inside, I found an exhausted young woman who had been in labor for twenty-four hours. The dirt floor was covered with blood, and the air was buzzing with flies. When I examined the young woman in the dim light, I saw a baby's lifeless feet and body dangling from between her legs like a doll.

The hut was quiet and still as I examined her. I quickly determined that the baby was already dead. The baby's head was much larger than normal, which had prevented her from giving birth. If we had been at a hospital, I would have cut the dead baby's head off, and performed an emergency cesarean section, but I had no surgical tools, and I knew the mother would not be able to live long, in her weakened condition, with the lifeless baby's head lodged inside her uterus. Once again, I was forced to improvise. Mortars were falling outside. I couldn't get the woman to the hospital. She probably wouldn't have gone if I'd tried to get her out of the village. I knew I had to get the baby's corpse out of her body, or she would die, too.

I asked her to hold onto the side of her bed, the strongest and most solid structure in the mud hut. The wooden bedposts were buried in the dirt floor. As the young woman held onto the bedpost with both arms, her legs spread open, I braced myself against a wall and yanked the baby's legs as hard as I could. The woman screamed with pain. The baby didn't come out. She cried and screamed some more. Time after time, I pulled the dead baby's legs with all the strength I had.

Finally, after much screaming, the hydrocephalic baby came out, its grotesquely large head crushed and elongated. The dead baby's head was as big as the rest of the baby's body, or bigger. The woman stopped screaming. Now she wept silently. I was exhausted, too. She patted my hand. I picked her up and put her on the bed. The woman weighed only about seventy-five pounds.

By some miracle, she was no longer bleeding, but I feared that she'd bleed to death later. Her uterine inertia could cause fatal bleeding. When I checked her pulse, it was 120. And she had only a low-grade fever.

I had too much work waiting for me the next day at the hospital, and I couldn't stay with her. Calling in my young guide, I fumbled in my medical bag and pulled out a hundred tetracycline tablets. I explained through the guide that she had to take two tablets every four hours, with her meals. I asked the woman if she understood, and she feebly indicated that she understood my directions. As I left, I instructed the guide to have someone check up on her daily. Remaining in that hut, however, I wondered if she would get any follow-up care at all.

Mortars fell around me as I returned. Sometimes I walked, sometimes I sprinted, sometimes I crawled through the jungle countryside. I was now afraid for my life, and I thought only of getting back to the safety of my bunker where I could safely sleep.

The firefight was raging as I ran into three black US Marines. They encountered me in a clearing, with tough, distant stares. They looked rugged and tough, with their rifles and combat gear. They wore camouflage uniforms.

"Son of a bitch!" one said. "What the *fuck* you doing here? You in the middle of a firefight, man!"

"God dammit, what the hell you up to?" another asked me.

I had never been caught in a firefight like this, although I was aware that the war was closing in all around Quang Tri.

"*Parlez-vous francais?*" I blurted, without thinking.

"He's a goddamn *Frenchman!*" one of the black Marines said. "He ain't understanding a word we're saying!"

The soldier turned to me, gesturing.

"Go, go, shoo, *di di mau!*" he said, using the Vietnamese word for "go away."

I smiled, saluted, and hurried back to my bunker as fast as I could safely get there. God bless the Marines, I thought when I got home. They were just doing their duty, on a highly dangerous mission, and I'd gotten in their way. I didn't want to tell them I was some foolish American doctor who had wandered unarmed into a "sensitive zone." I didn't want my leatherneck friends to have to detain me, and maybe cause them trouble later, or even to have me slow them up. I didn't want them to get ambushed trying to protect me.

I breathed a big sigh of relief in my bunker. I was alive. I had gotten through a very insecure area outside of Quang Tri, moving along a long and dangerous battlefront on a night I would long remember.

On most occasions, women gave birth very quietly in Vietnam. Another volunteer doctor, Dr. John McBratney, slept next to the delivery room in Quy Nhon but didn't realize it because Vietnamese women were so quiet when giving birth. "My room was right next to the delivery room and I didn't realize it for the first three weeks. And I'm not deaf either! Fifty milligrams of Demerol for nulliparous ladies and nothing for the rest. What a cultural difference," he marveled.

A Vietnamese woman, left, and Dr. Hassan, Vietnam, 1968.

As many American men observed, the women of Vietnam were quite beautiful, with dark hair and dark eyes, and a particularly Asian grace. Another volunteer physician, Dr. Leonard M. Pickering, was sitting on a veranda in Saigon in 1968, when he wrote the following poem about one of his fellow physician volunteers who had fallen in love with a Vietnamese prostitute.

He was a skinny ... bespectacled ... physician
who fell in love ... with a Saigon streetwalker ...
In his early forties ... enthusiastic ... tickled ...
His excitement was pervasive ...
The air around him ... was impregnated ... with the fragrance ...
Of love ...

He confides to me ...
Though married many years ...
It is the first time ... he has felt warmth from a woman ...

I salute his elation ...
For I know unhappiness awaits him ...
One his age cannot stand the onslaught of initial love ...
Only youth can bear its burden ...
Only the young ... can heal that broad wound ... inflicted gently ...
Yet unwillingly ... upon one's soul

Vietnamese woman recovering from war wounds
at Quang Tri Hospital, Vietnam 1968

In the provincial hospital in Quang Tri, it was always a surprise to witness the sudden appearance of love. This came through to me in the irony, the beauty, the pain, and agony of the strange romance between an American soldier and a Viet Cong female soldier or "Co Cong" named Liu Ygn.

It began when US Army Sergeant Thomas hurried into the hospital, carrying a wounded female enemy soldier in his arms. He was hysterical. I knew Sgt. Thomas because he'd stopped in at the hospital several times before. He was on his second tour of Vietnam. But he was already in a hysterical panic.

"Help! You got to save her, Doc," Sgt. Thomas said. "Please Doc, you've just got to save her!"

The young Vietnamese woman in his arms was beautiful, in her mid-twenties, with long, flowing black hair. She had a badly mangled leg, which dangled from ragged black pajamas by a few threads of tissue and flesh.

"She was coming at me! Shooting at us! I had to shoot her!" Sgt. Thomas confessed. "Now you gotta save her, doc. Whatever I can do, I'll do to save her, but you've got to save her, doc. I just need to know she's going to be okay!"

Sgt. Thomas had strapped a belt just above the woman's knee as a tourniquet to stop the bleeding. But her knee had taken two rounds from an M16, whose deadly bullets spin like twirling batons through the air, and chew up bone and tissue. When I examined her, I immediately feared that I would have to remove her leg above the knee.

One of the military doctors I'd saved from the employee with the grenade miraculously appeared. With that doctor and two corpsmen, we worked on the beautiful young girl for about four hours. She was in shock. Her vitals were a thready pulse, low blood pressure, and she was pale. Her hemoglobin had probably dropped from 12-13 to around 6, meaning that she had lost half her blood volume. Her hands were cold. She was not sweating.

Vietnamese women and children were trained to fight and shoot during Vietnam War.

We had to save every drop of fluid we had, so we kept the tourniquet in place until all the major arteries and veins could be found and ligated. The World War II idea of releasing a tourniquet five minutes every hour had been shown to be unwise, unnecessary, and dangerous to the limb. It was better to accept the risk of possible ischemia gangrene in an already badly injured extremity than to jeopardize life from further hemorrhage by the temporary removal of the tourniquet.

An amputation is always a defeat, since a limb of doubtful viability can be amputated later, but cannot be replaced once it is removed. But as we looked her over, we were amazed at the amount of damage her knee and leg had sustained. Almost all of the meniscus, the anterior and posterior cruciate ligaments, the patella, and the tendons and muscles that secure the upper and lower leg had been blown away. This type of "missile injury" so badly mangled the vital structures that they were very obviously not viable. We removed what was left of her leg. We cushioned the end of the stump with fatty tissue, fascia, tendons, ligaments and everything else we could draw together, to form a soft cushion that could support her weight on an artificial leg, then sewed the skin carefully together over the end of the bone.

As she recovered from the surgery, I saw that the lady Viet Cong soldier was a beauty. Like so many Vietnamese women, she was outrageously beautiful.

We loaded her up with antibiotics, and within a day or two she had regained some of her strength. Although she was in our hospital, she had been in the thick of battle for a while. I noticed that she constantly looked scared, as if afraid to be killed at any minute by either her fellow Viet Cong, the South Vietnamese troops, or the Americans.

But Sgt. Thomas came in to visit her every moment he could. Obsessed by the young woman, he took over the bedside as if he were her personal guardian angel. He refused to leave. He actually went AWOL from the Army. Before too long, his worrying vigil even made him psychotic. I tried to get him to take chlorpromazine or Mellaril, but Sgt. Thomas wouldn't take either one of them. His attention was focused on the beautiful enemy soldier, day and night. He felt responsible for her, perhaps because she was beautiful, perhaps because she was someone he had shot and permanently injured.

"I caused this, and I'm going to marry this woman," Sgt. Thomas told me. "I have to get her back home to the States. I have to take care of her. I'll do anything I can to take care of her. I'm going to take care of her forever."

But the beautiful Viet Cong woman continued to look scared. All the horror of war remained on her face for several days. However, by the fifth or sixth day, caressed by the love-struck American soldier, the look of fear on her face began to fade away.

Sgt. Thomas held Lui. He hovered over her, shooing away the flies with his hand. He brought her food and drink. Sgt. Thomas knew enough Vietnamese to caress her with his words, letting her know that he was sorry, and that he wanted to take care of her.

Vietnam created some strange combinations. I do not know what happened to this strange couple, a Romeo and Juliet who met in the heat of battle. But they had both met the enemy, and seen the face of humanity on the other side.

13

The Horror of War

"Better a thousandfold abuse of speech than a denial of free speech. The abuse dies in a day but the denial slays the life of a people and entombs the hope of the race." – Charles Bradlaugh

In the beginning, I had many moments of exuberance, moments where I felt I was really making a difference in Vietnam and showing the Vietnamese some of the goodness, greatness, and generosity of America. But I questioned this feeling one day. I was at Phu Bai firebase, waiting to catch a short hop over to Da Nang. Entranced by the exotic visual beauty of Vietnam and the shock of war, I had been filming some of the things I saw with my Bell and Howell Super 8 camera. I was filming a helicopter coming down in a hard landing. A US Marine pilot emerged from his chopper. The Marine pilot had been wounded in the foot by a sniper. He was limping across the tarmac. When the pilot saw me panning his way, he pointed to me and ordered the Marines under his command to surround me and to seize my camera and film.

"Blow his fucking brains out unless I get that camera and all the film!" the pilot shouted as the Marines surrounded me.

"Hey!" I protested, lowering the camera. "I'm a former Marine! Give me a break! I'm a doctor! I'm not the enemy here!"

But I neither looked like a Marine nor a doctor in my dusty jeans and my sweat-stained T-shirt. The Marines surrounded me and raised their

M16s, ready to fire. If I had stayed in the Marine Corps, and attended Annapolis, I might have been standing in that lieutenant's shoes, as an officer in Vietnam. Instead, I was here as a volunteer doctor, giving most of my day to treating sick and wounded civilians.

"Who gives a fuck who the fuck you say you are? Hand the camera over *now*, son of a bitch, or your brains gonna get blowed out!" a Marine shouted, holding out his hand.

I was furious at this treatment, and wanted to shout back.

"Go ahead, you goddamned jarheads, blow my head off! You're not getting my film and camera! From one Marine to another – fuck off! You're all full of shit!"

I didn't actually shout at them, but I was upset by the unnecessary confiscation of my movie camera. I felt misunderstood. I docilely gave them my movie camera and my film, nodding to them as I did. Because I was a former Marine, I understood well the gravity of that moment. The Marines would not have raised their weapons if they weren't prepared to fire. I already had more than a taste of the craziness of the Vietnam war. I knew that the stupidity of one hotheaded Marine could have gotten me killed, and no one would have given it a second thought in Vietnam.

I wandered away without my camera. I felt like I'd been mugged. I was upset and angry with the Marine lieutenant who had ordered them to take away my camera, but I wasn't angry at the young Marines who were just following an officer's orders. I quickly shrugged it off. As I looked back, I thought perhaps the young officer just wanted a filmed record of his heroic moment, when he stepped off the chopper with a wounded foot. I told myself that maybe he needed something more than the well-deserved Purple Heart he would receive. As I thought forward, I thought I should be happy that the lieutenant made it back to Phu Bai alive. Less than an hour later, I was on another chopper, headed for Da Nang, and I put this incident out of my mind.

ONE AFTERNOON IN MAY

One afternoon near the end of May, I was working at the hospital when I heard the familiar loud whack-whack-whack sound of the slowing helicopter blades of a Medevac helicopter. An Army or Air Force chopper was landing in the grassy courtyard of the Quang Tri

Provincial Hospital. It was a little unusual for military helicopters to bring in civilians to be treated, but it had happened a few times before.

Three uniformed pilots quietly hurried into the foyer of the hospital, carrying a stretcher. The stretcher was loaded with children. The children's colorful tops, mostly white, appeared to have been freshly washed that morning. I stood there, watching the pilots unload the three or four children who had been piled upon the stretcher, and went out to the helicopter for more.

Then the nurses and I watched dumbfounded as the pilots brought in more children, on stretcher after stretcher. I noticed the hands of the children limply hanging over the side of the stretchers. The dangling hands seemed to ask the question, "Why? What did I do wrong? Why me?"

Wordlessly, the pilots lay the last of the young victims on the floor.

"Here they are, doc," one said.

No one said another word.

I remember the look on one of the pilot's faces as he turned to go, as if he was pleading with me to do something, to stop the holocaust.

And the chopper took off, disappearing over the jungle.

This was Vietnam, and this was war, but I could not believe the grotesque human tableau spread out in the foyer before me. I saw row after row of wounded bodies, totaling perhaps forty very young Vietnamese children. The children ranged in age from infants to around five years of age. The wounded children all wore plastic medical armbands. Some of the children were already dead. Those who were alive tried to move their arms and legs.

Moving closer, I immediately tried to help the children who were still alive. I saw that each beautiful dark-haired little boy or girl had a bullet hole through the head, a small, round, untreated wound. Blood spurted from the holes in their heads. The children had apparently all been shot through the head, execution-style.

This was my hospital. I was the only doctor. These children were dying.

I yelled for Gelfoam, a product used to control bleeding in emergency rooms. Gelfoam forms a seal around the edge of the brain, and temporarily stops fatal bleeding. I desperately stuffed Gelfoam into the bullet holes, trying to help some of the children. Their wounds were completely hopeless. All of the children were dying. I realized after a few desperate minutes of attempted triage that none of these innocent children could possibly survive. Eerily, the two Vietnamese nurses who were there began wrapping up the children who were already dead in blankets, and carrying them out of the foyer.

I experienced moments of heartbreaking despair, those moments every doctor feels after fighting heroically to save a patient who has slipped away. Without any warning, I was losing forty patients at one time.

I noticed medical armbands on the children. I looked at the plastic armbands. The neatly lettered armbands all read, "Interrogated USMC." I had been a Marine, and proud of it. At that instant I was no longer proud to be a Marine. Nobody in the Marine Corps could possibly have interrogated these children, but somebody had rounded them up and executed them all.

I had never completely lost my cool before in Vietnam, but my entire body shook at that moment. A shock wave of nausea swept over me. I felt as if I was personally under fire, as if mortar shells were falling on the roof of my hospital. The sight of several dozen executed babies was imprinted upon my brain. As those children quietly died, weakly waving their arms, gasping for breath, one after the other, I wondered if it would ever be possible to atone for such an extraordinary slaughter.

As a Marine I had been trained to kill the enemy in hand-to-hand combat. I had seen war as disciplined, honorable combat between warriors. In Vietnam, I knew that soldiers were fighting, and thousands of civilians were being injured by napalm, bombs, and stray bullets. Most of those injuries were accidental, the collateral damage of war. But what I saw that afternoon in the foyer was not accidental. The children were not accidentally injured by a bomb that fell on their village. They had not stepped on a land mine. Somewhere around Quang Tri, soldiers who were probably US Marines had rounded up all these children, perhaps pulling them out of the arms of their mothers. There was no way those small children could have fought back, resisted, or even understood what was going on. Yet they had been killed like so many unwanted cockroaches. Even with everything I had already seen in Vietnam, I was unprepared for the execution-style murder of so many innocent babies and children who literally died before my eyes.

Not quite believing what I saw, I snipped off two of the armbands, and slipped them into my pocket as evidence of what I had seen before I went off to other work.

It seemed to take days to scrub the children's blood off the marble floors and walls of the foyer. After I saw the dead babies, it was an understatement to say that I was angry and upset. In the days that followed, I told some of my corpsmen I was appalled by the senseless butchery that I saw, and that I was going "to take it to the top." My words apparently set off warning bells not far away. Unknown to me, the My Lai massacre had occurred only two months before, less than a hundred miles from Quang Tri. Although I had never seen anything like this before, the practice of executing civilians was already going on. The butchery and brutality of war was creating piles of collateral damage in the jungles of South Vietnam.

That day, I had a lot to do at the hospital. Later, I asked the two corpsmen on duty what had happened to the bodies. I wanted to know where the children had been buried.

"The nurses took care of it," they said.

I never found out where the children were buried. Because I had work to do that day, I tried to move on, but I could not forget the dead children.

Vietnam War Veteran Ronald Pelfrey, PTSD patient of Dr. Allen Hassan:

"While I was in Vietnam in 1970, about July of that year, I was in patrol around LZ Baldi. We were ordered to clear a village just outside the perimeter wire. We were told to eliminate everything that moved. This included women and children. Forty-seven people were eliminated and the bodies were taken away in choppers by ROK (Republic of Korea) Marines. The next day we were told the village was a free-fire zone. There was no return fire from that village. No weapons were found. No trap doors to justify what we were told to do.

"Two months later while on patrol I was bitten by a bat when a grenade was thrown into the jungle where movement was heard. I was sent to the USS Sanctuary (an offshore hospital ship) and to this day I don't know why the people in that village were killed.

I talked about it to others at the hospital. In the days following the massacre, I remember, it became eerily quiet in the hospital. Patients stopped lining up outside. The nurses didn't report for work. The hospital was unusually silent. Almost no one talked to me. On top of that, I came down with a fever, possibly a recurrence of the malaria brought on by the additional stress of witnessing the atrocity on top of everything else that the war brought in the door. When my temperature shot up, I pumped myself full of penicillin, continued my malaria medication, and tried to continue with my work.

I felt terribly isolated from everyone now, and broken-hearted, as if I was being rendered impotent by memories of the atrocity I had witnessed. I felt angry and sick over the horror of what I had seen. I was beginning to feel like I was being exploited. I was beginning to feel as if I was simply a pawn for the US war machine, a public relations ploy to make our military occupation look better to the Vietnamese, and to the folks back home. Although I had eagerly volunteered to help "the cause," and I knew I had helped some people and saved many lives, all the excitement and joy at helping out in Vietnam was gone. In place of the exuberance I had sometimes felt, I was now enveloped with a flood of sorrow and disgust.

Somewhere in there, when I was still fighting off the fever, a package arrived. The Super 8 camera that had been confiscated by the Marines at Phu Bai was inside the package, but the film I shot was missing. The Marine lieutenant who confiscated my camera apparently inserted a little note saying, "No hard feelings, best regards." I thought to myself that the better angels of valor in the Marine Corps had come through, and that for the most part, in this incident these Marines had kept the Marine Corps honor intact.

But as I feverishly looked around my living quarters, I noticed that some items I had kept stored while I was away were missing. For one thing, the M16 assigned to me was missing from under my bed. Also missing were some still photographs and exposed rolls of movie film I had taken in Quang Tri, which I left lying on my dresser. Most ominously, the two armbands I'd taken off the children which read "Interrogated USMC" were gone. I had left the armbands next to some other valuables that were not disturbed. Damn, I thought to myself. Now I had no evidence that what I saw ever even happened. Someone or something now is really trying my patience, and adding to the fear and fever that I already feel.

Working to fight off the fever, and increasingly depressed, I fought to keep it all in perspective. But dark clouds were gathering around me. I was apparently being watched from several quarters, most particularly from a nondescript building just down the street.

14

Two Mysterious Strangers

"But we know that freedom cannot be served by the devices of the tyrant. As it is an ancient truth that freedom cannot be legislated into existence, so it is no less obvious that freedom cannot be censored into existence. And any who act as if freedom's defenses are to be found in suppression and suspicion and fear confess a doctrine that is alien to America." – President Dwight D. Eisenhower, Letter on Intellectual Freedom

Two and a half blocks down the street from the hospital was a plain-looking building I at first took to be the Agricultural Pacification Headquarters. On a tour of town, another doctor had told me the Agricultural Pacification Headquarters was housed there. But one day, as Nguyen and I were passing the building, I said something about the Agricultural Pacification Headquarters building. My young interpreter looked at me with amazement.

"You must be kidding, *Bac Si*," Nguyen said. "That's the CIA headquarters in Quang Tri."

"I think you're wrong, Nguyen," I replied.

"No, I am not."

"What does the CIA have to do with this town?"

"The CIA runs this war," my interpreter said.

The first few days of June 1968, after the incident with the babies, my title of "*Bac Si* Number One" was wearing thin with me. I had already seen so many ugly things in Vietnam – untended and curable illnesses that became fatal, devastating bullet and shrapnel wounds that caused unnecessary amputations and unnecessary death, people permanently disfigured from chemicals, bombs, and accidents of war. But almost all of these wounds and deaths seemed horribly impersonal. Most of the deaths I saw, even among the troops, were from shrapnel. Not many injuries that came my way resulted from hand-to-hand combat between fighting men.

In Vietnam, U.S. combat forces almost always received excellent care. For wounded civilians, good medical care was more problematical. Many civilians I saw lost legs from booby traps, but even an amputated leg didn't have to be a death sentence if it was cared for properly. Military medical personnel did often try to save injured civilians wounded in battles, but just as often the wounded civilians would be characterized as "dirty VC" by South Vietnamese or US forces, and not given immediate care. Once, I remember, I was in an area where a battle had been raging for a couple of days. After their village was bombarded and ravaged by the Marines, I assisted in bringing a truckload of wounded civilians back to the hospital, including mothers and children.

Before I witnessed the executed Vietnamese children who were airlifted into my hospital to die, none of the violence I had seen in Quang Tri seemed directed at particular individuals. Rather, it seemed like we had unleashed an overwhelming firepower on a poor Third World nation, a firepower which was far out of proportion to the enemy, largely ineffective, and ultimately counterproductive to winning the hearts and minds of the people.

In the United States, President Lyndon Johnson angrily called Vietnam a "damn little piss-ant country," and ordered the military to win the war. Military and civilian war planners unleashed "surgical strike packages," and sent in more and more troops. If American troops detected what we took to be hostile fire coming from a village, our commanders were allowed to declare it a "free fire zone," and just waste everything that moved. Women and children were not supposed to be targets, but in many cases they were the most likely to be hit. Viet Cong and North Vietnamese forces were often dug in during an attack, or prepared to flee into their tunnels whenever necessary, while civilians were usually quite exposed.

Moving through life in this cynical and disillusioned frame of mind, I received a startling reality check one evening, when my quarters were visited by two total strangers. After the mortar blast that almost killed me not long before, my sleeping quarters had been moved out of the house and into a bunker which was protected by double sandbags. My bunker was quite safe, but I had occasional roommates, which I didn't much mind.

One night after I returned from the hospital, two military men in jungle combat gear came into my bunker and asked if they could spend the night. It was unusual for me to receive military visitors in my quarters. The only other time was early on, when I was feverish, and the military doctor who was supervising me, Commander Hurst, had come by to check on me. The sudden appearance of these men made me a little suspicious. Still, the men wore uniforms, they were obviously Americans, and I couldn't really refuse them shelter for the night.

The mysterious strangers were neat and well-groomed. They had the air of officers, and were maybe twenty-three or twenty-four years of age. They looked like they'd just stepped off a Hollywood movie set. Their camouflage uniforms were perfectly pressed, but neither of their uniforms had insignias identifying them as members of a particular branch of the armed forces. The weapons they carried and the grenades that fit in a special place in their belts were shiny and new, as if they'd just taken them out of the box. Although they wore American military uniforms and carried American weapons, they didn't look like they'd been doing much real fighting inside a dirty, tropical jungle war zone.

Later I realized the men were probably there for what the CIA called "damage assessment," basically to determine just how serious I was about reporting the murder of the small children. According to other writers, the CIA's Phoenix and Phuong Huong programs not only set up "re-education camps" all over Vietnam where people were routinely tortured, they also eliminated people they saw as problems at the time, even killing Americans if that were necessary.

The uniformed men broke open a deck of cards, apparently to relax me. They said they'd come to play cards and chat about the hospital "situation."

We played poker in the bunker, illuminated by flickering candlelight.

After a little small talk, one of the strangers started asking me some probing questions.

"We hear you've had some problem up here, doc," he said. "Something has been going on that's got you worried?"

I felt I was being interrogated. My defenses went up.

"I'm a former Marine," I angrily replied. "And I sure as hell know the Marines are getting their balls blown off all over Quang Tri. They're dying like flies in this goddamn war for no fucking reason. This is a terrible, senseless war, but if there's somebody in the way that gets shot once in a while, innocents that get shot, sometimes that's just part of the fucking price we have to pay for being over here in 'Nam.'"

I answered loudly, on purpose, instinctively using gung-ho Marine language peppered with profanity. That seemed to put the strangers back into their place as a couple of normal guests, just shooting the bull and playing cards. But I was on edge. It was a tense evening. I was not at ease even after the strangers went to sleep in my bunker.

Mortars fell not far away during the night. Most of them were from Viet Cong, a few from the perimeter South Vietnamese army position. Since my bunker was between the ammunition depot and the province chief's house, nobody really wanted to be in my area at night. This also made me wonder about my mysterious guests who had chosen to stay with me rather than finding a safer military location.

In the morning, the strangers put on their uniforms and quietly began hooking up their weapons belts, their matching .45 caliber pistols, and their hand grenades.

Just before they left, one of the young men approached me and held up his hand in front of my face, with his thumb and forefinger spread about a half inch apart.

"You came *this close* to being offed last night," he said.

"Oh, you mean the mortars," I said.

"Not the mortars," he said. "And it's still an option. We'll be watching you for unnecessary talk, or anything else that's suspicious."

And then they left. I didn't quite realize what was occurring at the time. Looking back, I strongly believe I had been visited by a special unit of the CIA's Phoenix Project. They had probably heard about the scene at the hospital, and my reaction. Perhaps I was perceived as a danger, even though I was a former U.S. Marine and an American doctor doing humanitarian work in a war zone. I now believe I was a target of a CIA practice called "counterespionage." In 1988, the *CIA Handbook* defined counterespionage as "to manipulate, deceive, and repress individuals, groups, organizations conducting or suspected of conducting espionage activities and they must be destroyed or neutralized to prevent such activity."

Of course, my paranoia increased. After the two strangers visited me, and gave me that thinly veiled warning to keep my mouth shut, I was certain I was being observed. I knew the CIA headquarters was just down the road from the hospital, and I began to piece things together, and think the whole thing through.

As an act of self-preservation, I stopped talking about the massacre of the babies with anyone. I didn't mention it to the kindly Catholic priest who visited the hospital regularly. I didn't mention it to the Marines I knew well, to the Navy corpsmen who rotated in and out, or even to my loyal interpreter, Nguyen.

Statement of Vietnam War Veteran Christopher Kane, PTSD patient of Dr. Hassan:

"I wake up every morning and the first thoughts I have are of Vietnam. During my time in the 519th Military Intelligence Battalion, I was exposed to four terrorist bombings, two mortarings, one rocket attack, two 'friendly fire' incidents, a bunch of ugly traffic accidents, and one small riot.

"I was ordered to 'locate any/all documents which will give away the geographic location of any/all VC, NVA, hospitals or medical dispensaries.' When I objected to this as a Geneva Convention and UCMJ violation, my sergeant was unmoved. When I said, 'If we do this we'll be no better than a bunch of Nazi war criminals,' he changed his mind and went with me to see the major. That line changed our major's attitude. When he called a two-star general, this line fell on deaf ears. The general's answer was, 'I'm sending this order down the chain of command and the first one to refuse goes to the LBJ [Long Binh Jail].'

"Going to sleep at night and knowing that some of your fellow human beings are working hard to kill you before the morning is sick. Knowing that you and your buddies will spend the next day working hard to set people up to be killed in the 'most efficient, effective manner possible' is equally sick. As part of my job (96B20A Intelligence Analyst) I handled captured enemy documents. These documents were often taken from the pockets of the dead and were therefore soaked in blood. By the time I got them the blood was dry. Writing this [statement], the smell is back. I also helped CIA Phoenix people with document searches. Sometimes they would start 'talking shop.' These guys make US Army Intelligence look like choirboys. The fact that they sometimes killed Americans is still classified and denied by our government. Being only nineteen, I was too stupid to tell them to shut up. Later while on TDY in Da Nang, I got a briefing on which Americans and why. When I tell civilians [nowadays] about these guys, they say they don't believe me, but then they avoid me like the plague."

The horror of war in Vietnam is captured in this photo of wounded Marine Gunnery Sgt. Jeremiah Purdie, in center, and several other fighting Marines. This apparent mud in which they were fighting was created by what is called a "slush bomb," weighing about 20,000 pounds.   The bomb was dropped by parachute from

*a C-130 to clear the jungle for a helicopter landing. Unfortunately, the bomb quite
often pulverized the land to such a degree that it turned the moist ground to slush.
The site of these blasts became a target for enemy rocket fire and often caused
multiple casualties in our troops. Photo by Larry Burroughs/Getty Images*

Trapped in the paranoid insanity of Vietnam, feeling my every move was monitored by the spooks of the CIA, I became extremely wary and fearful. I was afraid that if I talked about the terrible atrocity I had just seen a few days before, I could easily be sequestered and shot in the back of the head, just as the babies I saw had been killed, execution-style.

One of the most decorated soldiers in US military history, Colonel David Hackworth, spent four years in Vietnam. Col. Hackworth became so increasingly fed up by America's losing strategy and heavy troop casualties that he rebelled, and went public in the media about his frustrations. This made him *persona non grata* in the US Army. As he described in his autobiography, *About Face*, Col. Hackworth recalled an incident that left him shaken with a final dose of paranoia as he left Vietnam. The very day he was to leave, during a routine vehicle check, he discovered a grenade lodged under the front seat of his Jeep. The cotter pin had been pulled. The grenade was wedged to explode at the slightest bounce of the Jeep. He was lucky. Fragging incidents like this – officers killed by their own troops – were not an uncommon occurrence in the nightmare world of Vietnam. And Hackworth wrote that the CIA's excesses in Third World countries after World War II rivaled the excesses of the Nazis in their heyday.

Threats, warnings, and intimidation entered my daily thoughts. As the days and nights passed in Quang Tri, my mind began to speculate incessantly about the sadistic killers of the children. In Vietnam, I had already learned, things were often not what they appeared to be. I asked myself what the atrocity was *really* about. Who was *really* involved? Was it really a bunch of US troops gone mad with blood lust? Was it a sinister Viet Cong trick? Was it set up by the ARVN? Was it all part of a diabolical CIA plot, played out at my hospital, that somehow involved me?

I have pondered these events for years. I still do not know with absolute certainty who carried out the despicable atrocity that I witnessed at Quang Tri Provincial Hospital on that afternoon in May. The neatly lettered ID bracelets provided evidence of Marine Corps complicity in those killings, and I have long had suspicions that the perpetrator of those crimes was indeed running riot in I-Corps.

15

The Soldiers Who Couldn't Go Home

"Man is the only animal that deals in that atrocity of atrocities, war."
– Mark Twain

A few days after the spooky interrogation in my bunker, a Marine sergeant I knew came into the hospital and asked me, "Dr. Hassan, sir, would you like to go with me a few kilometers north to see some wounded Marines? They're all in pretty bad shape. They could use a morale boost from someone like you."

Dong Ha was approximately twelve kilometers below the demilitarized zone which was the border between North and South Vietnam. Although I knew the sergeant's proposal was dangerous, I didn't refuse. We weren't that busy at the hospital, so I took my interpreter Nguyen with me. I knew the young Marines he asked me to see had already taken far greater risks than I would take going out to see them.

We were headed into the most dangerous territory in Vietnam. Our destination, Dong Ha, was a thirty-minute sprint due north up the Street Without Joy. Highway 1, the Street Without Joy, was crawling with snipers. Snipers made the journey dangerous during the day, and almost impossible at night. But my driver assured me we'd be traveling too fast for the Viet Cong to get a good shot at us. I climbed into the Jeep, and we barreled away as Nguyen listed to Viet Cong radio broadcasts on his walkie-talkie.

"We don't have to worry about being ambushed, *Bac Si*," Nguyen said, putting down the walkie-talkie after a while. "The Viet Cong say there's a priest in the Jeep."

As we headed north, I remember the beautiful canopies of lush green jungle that lined the road. Occasionally, we passed a sparkling green rice paddy, flooded with shallow water. The countryside appeared tranquil. Aside from the sound of our Jeep, the only noise we heard was the wind whistling past our ears as we hurried north in the humid, open air.

It was a bright, sunny day. As we got closer to Dong Ha, I saw mountains in the distance, shrouded by clouds. I noticed a few puffs of smoke from far-off artillery, rockets, or aerial bombing raids.

The first things I saw at the camp were three large tents, and a sign which said "US Armed Forces Regional Headquarters." My heart skipped a beat as I stepped from the Jeep. If I had gone to Annapolis, I could have easily been commissioned a combat officer. I would have been committed for another eight years of service after Annapolis, and I could have easily have wound up right here, as a combat officer in the most dangerous part of Vietnam.

As the sergeant led me into the first of the tents, I saw horribly wounded men inside. At least two hundred badly mangled Marines were laid out on neat rows of beds. Walking through the tent, and then from one tent to the next, I was struck by the massive scale of the carnage all around me. Most of the wounded soldiers were amputees, and like the United States population, they were a mix of races. The colors of their bodies glistened in a geometrical array of colors, from dark black, to yellow, to bronze, to brown, to pale white. Some of the wounded men moaned uncontrollably in their racks, but most were too traumatized or damaged or disheartened to moan at all.

Most of the wounded men had neither arms nor legs, and were quadruple amputees, although a few had some stumps remaining. Well-muscled young bodies had been reduced to trunks and heads.

I walked past row after row of horrible quadruple amputees. Tubes linked to their heads, chests, and abdomens drained into a maze of tubes and bottles hanging around and below the severely wounded Marines. As I walked through row after row of wounded men, I couldn't help notice the IV tubes running out of their noses, down their throats, into their bellies and chests, and into whatever veins were available.

The main thing that struck me was that the faces and eyes of these men were hopeless and shattered.

I was there as a civilian doctor, to try to lift their morale. Walking through the tents, trying to be supportive, I could see the task was impossible. None of these kids was in any condition to talk, to listen, or even to see me clearly.

Also ministering to their fellow troopers were somber corpsmen and medics, mostly kids in their late teens. Looking at the age of the corpsmen and the troops, it seemed to me like teenagers taking care of teenagers.

"We can do some good for twenty or thirty percent of these guys if we get them home *quick*," I said, feeling a medical urgency in the horrible spectacle I was witnessing. "At least some of these guys can have their last days with their families back in the states. There's plenty of air transport to get them back home."

The corpsmen listened.

"We've got them on maintenance, Doc," one corpsman explained.

"One Medevac plane could get them all out of here immediately," I said. "What's the problem? They'll have great care when they arrive back home."

"We can't send these guys home, Doc," a young medic explained. "We can't airlift them home, unless they go home in a body bag."

"What? Why?"

"They're too grotesque," a medic explained. "They'd stop this war the second they saw the horrors up this close. As soon as that Medevac plane landed back in the world, and everybody saw these guys, they'd riot, and the war would be history."

To me, at that moment, evacuating those men seemed like the right thing to do. I knew all the quadruple amputees had been triaged by military surgeons far more competent than I. They had been evacuated from battle and given excellent care in a makeshift hospital not far from the front. I couldn't believe a calculated decision had been made to leave all the amputees in these somber military hospital tents until they died in the jungles of Dong Ha - out of mind and out of sight - with only the military brass and their young caretakers ever even knowing what happened. At the very least, I said again, these young soldiers should go home to die.

Another corpsman heard our conversation and joined in.

"You must be joking, Doc," he said. "We've got our orders. We can't send these guys home. We gotta fight this war and win it. Don't you get it? They can't handle the truth back in the world."

After this exchange, I walked by the mangled bodies in the last tent, trying to speak to the men and cheer them up. I got only an occasional grunt, or slight eye movement as a response.

A rather depressed-looking young corpsman was emptying bed pans in the last tent as I passed.

"How long have you been here?" I asked the corpsman.

"I've been in Dong Ha for almost a year, sir," he replied. "But I'm not going to make it home, just like these patients. They got us surrounded, and they're circling us in the hills. The more we pound them, the more troops they send down the Ho Chi Minh trail. Our position here could get overrun any day now. I made it through three or four really bad scrapes in the past few months, but I'm nearing the end."

As I listened to his fatalistic words, I realized this corpsman was what was called a "short timer." He was experiencing what was called "30-day syndrome." The closer many soldiers got to going home, the more they feared dying just before they left. It was as if returning home was a dream they expected to be pulled just out of their reach. After weeks and months on the firing line, after seeing many of their buddies die, many soldiers could not believe they would be among the lucky ones to survive, and go home. And this corpsman was not only a short-timer, he was working in an environment of grotesquely crippled soldiers who reminded him every minute of the grim, horrible reality of war.

By the end of my visit to the tents, I wondered if it had been arranged by the strangers who had visited my bunker a few days before. If so, the message was clear enough. Not even wounded heroes of the battlefield would be allowed to disrupt the prosecution of the war, or to provide a grotesque testament to its lack of progress. I realized that the full human cost of the war's savagery to both sides might never be revealed.

After witnessing all this, I was walking down the dusty trail back to our Jeep, where Nguyen was waiting. The sergeant and I saw a young family herding two water buffaloes across a meadow, about a hundred yards away. It was a father, a mother, and three little children. In an armed encampment alongside the trail, an US Army soldier had seen them, and loaded his mortar. He fired mortar round after mortar round at the family and their animals for no reason, as if were all a joke, and he was playing Russian roulette with the Vietnamese civilians.

In the distant meadow, the family had already abandoned their animals, and they were already running for their lives. Bombs already exploded just yards away from them.

"You goddamn idiot!" I yelled. "What the fuck are you doing, man?"

The soldier turned to face me.

"Stop this shit right now!" I shouted.

"Just a little gook target practice," the soldier yelled back.

"You fuckhead!" I shouted. "Stop it! Those are unarmed civilians!"

He paused for a moment, before placing another projectile into the firing tube. Then he shrugged at me, as if it was nothing, and turned around to light a cigarette.

By this time, the family was almost completely out of sight. With some relief, I saw that the family and their working animals were apparently safe, miraculously uninjured by the exploding mortars.

At that moment, approaching the Jeep, all I could think was: This is a horrible war, a war without honor, a war without glory, a war without scruples, a war without end, in which civilians are slaughtered for amusement and soldiers are not allowed to go home to die with dignity. It is a war we will inevitably lose. Every innocent Vietnamese family insanely targeted for amusement or shot without justification in a free fire zone will pass the word. Word will travel along the bamboo telegraph. Eventually, even our South Vietnamese allies will be overwhelmed, and want our military presence and our protection to end.

If Americans only knew what was happening to their children, I thought. Families back home denied the opportunity to be with a dying son would revolt against this medical holding tank for their horribly wounded sons. If they knew the full extent of the senseless brutality that was everywhere, I thought, American families would refuse to offer up their sons for such a meaningless and dishonorable war.

And the military Jeep carrying Nguyen and me hurried south through the jungle, down the Street Without Joy.

16

In the A Shau Valley

"Those of us who shout the loudest about Americanism and making character assassinations are all too frequently those who, by our own words and acts, ignore some of the basic principles of Americanism: 1) the right to criticize; 2) the right to hold unpopular beliefs; 3) the right to protest; 4) the right to independent thought." - Senator Margaret Chase Smith, June 1950

On another trip to Da Nang, not long before I left Vietnam, I met a commanding combat officer. He was a major in the Army who headed up a team of commandos south of Quang Tri. We clicked in an odd, competitive way, I thought. Or maybe he was just trying to size up how much courage the young doctor and former Marine standing beside him might have.

"So you're a pretty tough guy?" he asked me. "But have you seen the war close up yet? And do you think you can take it?"

The major commanded a small observation team of about fifteen South Vietnamese troops, and eight Army commandos whose job was to scout North Vietnamese troop movements at a small perimeter forward observation post, deep in the jungle. I told him I had just been to the military base at An Khe, where a lot of fighting was taking place. He nodded with a knowing glare. Out of the blue, the major invited me to accompany him to a small Army outpost on the edge of the treacherous

A Shau Valley, located in the A Shau Mountains about sixty kilometers southwest of Quang Tri.

"Let's go," I said. I was curious.

Climbing aboard a military helicopter, we headed for the major's camp. Below the helicopter was a green expanse of triple canopy jungle that provided a dense overhead cover to anything below. The thick green jungle extended as far as the eye could see below us and the major said it made discovering the enemy very difficult.

The major told me the North Vietnamese would lie low in miles of underground tunnels that ran all over Vietnam. The tunnels kept the enemy invisible to American troops, until the moment they rose out of the tunnels and chose to fight. The enemy knew the terrain inside and out, and they constantly toyed with the Americans and even their South Vietnamese allies, like cats playing with mice. During the war, the North Vietnamese also used clouds, darkness, and rain to maximum tactical advantage. With their greater numbers and knowledge of the climate and terrain, the enemy seemed to know exactly when to pounce.

The American and South Vietnamese troops lived in tents and bunkers in muddy, squalid conditions. When we arrived, it was humid and already wet. The monsoon season which began in July was almost underway, and some rain had already begun to fall as we landed.

Shortly before we arrived, a South Vietnamese army deserter had been tortured and killed. As we got off the helicopter, his dehydrated corpse was lying under a sandbag not far from the center of camp. The major didn't take much notice of this. The man had tried to run away, he said. He tried to go back to his village, but he was caught by the South Vietnamese troops and punished as a deserter. The South Vietnamese put a heavy pack of sand on the man's back, and forced him to walk and run around a pole for hours without a drink of water until he finally dropped dead of dehydration.

The South Vietnamese troops showed me the pole and the man's body and explained, "This is what we do to cowards."

I questioned the major about this treatment.

"The ARVN have their ways of justice, and we have ours," he said. "If I tried to interfere, they would have laughed at me. They would have thought I was a bad leader. I'd have lost face. So I let them march him. I don't think we'll have any more cowards around here."

The South Vietnamese troops left the soldier lying where he died, under the heavy sandbag, his face contorted by agony. They didn't bury his decomposing body for two days, to make him an example for the other troops. The war brought out brutality and cruelty on both sides.

In the A Shau Valley, the American and South Vietnamese troops were tested around the clock. Camps were constantly harassed by mortar and rocket fire. Occasionally, the perimeter of the camp was penetrated by the enemy, and the camp peppered with bursts of rifle or pistol fire, usually around sunrise or sunset. When least expected, the enemy appeared, probing, taking pot shots, keeping up the pressure, and looking for weak points in the camp's defense.

South of Da Nang, near the Street Without Joy, a memorial service is held for thirteen Marines killed in action in 1968. These services minimized Post Traumatic Stress Disorder in veterans who survived. Photo by Richard Hughes

As rain fell hard on the tents one afternoon, I looked into the faces of several brave and stoic grunts. What I saw in their faces was stark demoralization. Seeing their faces suddenly heightened my awareness of the danger that lurked everywhere in this very insecure perimeter camp. Many units in such lightly defended positions had been completely wiped out, I knew, and all the men in the camp on the perimeter of the A Shau Valley realized they could die at any moment.

While extremely disciplined, the US soldiers were reluctant to go out into the jungle on long-range reconnaissance patrols called LRRPs. They feared being ambushed by the dug-in enemy, who knew the jungle terrain better than they did. The South Vietnamese soldiers were even more reluctant to patrol than the Americans.

It was easy to walk into an enemy ambush, but hard to uncover any significant enemy forces by surprise. Units like this one were sometimes stuck out on a limb in jungle outposts for months at a time. They developed their own ways of doing things, not by the book, and not the way they did things back in Da Nang. The camp resembled a primitive and remote penal colony. My determined friend, the major, made up his own rules as he went along.

I saw the major indoctrinate his troops with a brutal singsong chant, and his troops took it up after him.

"Kill the gooks! Kill the dinks! Kill the slopes! Kill the slant-eyed bastards! Kill or be killed!" he chanted, with his troops chanting in response to each phrase.

"Body counts! General Westmoreland and the brass want higher body counts! Free fire zones! Free killing zones! Killing fields as far as the eye can see, that's the key to victory!" he chanted.

"You understand, soldier, somebody's got to win this war and you have to be that somebody!" the major shouted.

"Yes, sir!" his troops responded.

As gentle rain fell on the major's tent, he and I talked into the night. The major was a staunch believer in the war effort. He was sure the US and South Vietnam would win the war with superior firepower. We would frighten the Vietnamese into submission, he believed. His philosophy was that whoever carried the biggest stick and most horrified the other side would win.

I wondered about the major, who seemed like a reasonable man, under the circumstances. Surely he must have known that he was in an untenable position, directing a small commando team of fewer than two dozen men in a jungle valley crawling with hundreds of dug-in enemy fighters and troops.

The major and I debated the war into the night. I felt the war was an unfortunate extension of French colonial rule. The French debacle had ended with a major defeat at Dien Bien Phu in 1954, I reminded him.

The major enjoyed the debate. He bought into the domino theory, which held that if Vietnam went Communist, all the other Southeast Asian countries would follow suit and also become Communist states. Basically he saw it as a war against Communist aggression.

The major had a degree in economics. He insisted the United States could reap a lot of material benefits if we won the war, and established a capitalist system in Vietnam.

"Remember," he said. "All wars are not fought for political ideology. Wars are fought primarily for economic reasons."

The major forcefully explained that the war was being fought for a strategic mineral, tungsten, which was exported from parts of Vietnam.

"We're here because we need tungsten to make all the light bulbs work. Somebody's got to shine the light for all the world to see!" he smiled.

The major insisted this was true, and at the time I thought he might have been right. But some time later, I found out that although Vietnam did export some tungsten, it wasn't the irreplaceable strategic mineral the major claimed it was.

Still, I could see the major was a true believer, so I didn't argue much more with him about the war. Years later, during the second Iraq War, I would wonder if he was right after all, because it seemed like we had gone to war over a strategic commodity, oil.

Early one morning, two days later, the major took me out of the A Shau Valley by Jeep. As we sped away from the tiny camp, so isolated and vulnerable, I wondered if the major and his troops would survive their lonely, perilous ordeal.

As I traveled around Vietnam, the mantra I heard from many of our troops and officers was: Kill! Kill! Kill! More and more body counts! Win the war! Win the war at all costs! Dehumanizing the enemy into "gooks" and "slopes" was a strategy to depersonalize the killing. But at the same time, many troops were also receiving messages from the outer world that the killing was wrong, triggering internal conflicts in troops who were trying to both obey orders and do the right thing.

One year later, the battle for Hamburger Hill or *Dong Ap Bia* Mountain, a 900-meter hill on the flank of the A Shau Valley, would make headlines back in the US. It began when the Army committed nearly 2,000 combat soldiers and the Air Force contributed massive firepower to conquer Hamburger Hill, which was held by enemy troops.

Certificate of merit from American Medical Association was given to all volunteer physicians for their humanitarian service in Vietnam.

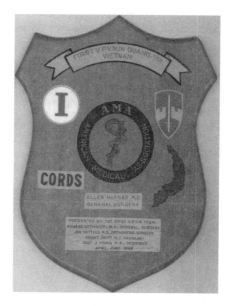

"First VPVN in Quang Tri, Vietnam" plaque was given to Dr. Hassan by fellow volunteer physicians Doctors Howard Detwiler, Grant Raitt, Ralf Young, and Joe Nettles, who were stationed in nearby Hue.

A month after the Army took the hill, they abandoned it, losing 70 soldiers and wounding 372 in 10 days of vicious fighting, according to Samuel Zaffiri, author of *Hamburger Hill*. These heavy losses led the increasingly skeptical US Congress to ask more questions about America's military strategy in Vietnam, according to Guenter Lewy, author of *America in Vietnam*.

That day, I returned to Quang Tri without incident. Within a couple more weeks, my stint as a volunteer doctor would come to an unceremonious end. About ten days before I left, I was told that my Jeep was no longer officially issued to me. I began to feel unwanted. I kept my silence about the things I had seen until I left Vietnam, but I wanted badly to help end the war when I returned home. And I was not the only one.

I had been in Vietnam for only about two months, but it felt like a lifetime. I remember the day the news of Bobby Kennedy's death came over the walkie-talkie as I was riding in a Jeep through Da Nang. Da Nang was already unsafe because of fires and mortar attacks, and at that moment I remember I feared the war might go on forever. Because Robert Kennedy had made it clear he would pull out the troops, he could have done it, but he was dead. Tears came to my eyes because I thought Robert Kennedy was our last hope to end the war quickly and compassionately, given all the competing political interests in Vietnam.

I left Quang Tri Provincial Hospital on July 4, 1968, American Independence Day. Arriving back in Northern California, I felt less like I was returning home than engaging in another contradictory battle over America's role in the war. Things did not go well at the hospital. Without quite realizing it, I had developed a crop of personal demons, horrible memories of Vietnam and the atrocities I had seen. In some ways, at that time, Vietnam already seemed like my real home.

17

A Second Tour of Vietnam

"The contest for ages has been to rescue liberty
from the grasp of executive power."
- Daniel Webster

I returned to my dreary job as a resident psychiatrist at Mendocino State Hospital, which was very close to being closed down. I had already had several conflicts with my immediate superiors at the hospital, and after the excitement of Vietnam I was bored by my job. I had completed the paper on the Vietnamese psychiatric system, which my supervisors assured me would justify my trip to Vietnam. In Vietnam, I had toured the psychiatric wing of the University Hospital in Hue, done some face-to-face interviews of psychiatric patients, and examined medical treatment records. Despite the hospital's primitive, almost prison-like conditions and the Vietnamese doctors' failure to use many modern psychiatric medications, the kindness of the doctors and personnel in the Vietnamese psychiatric hospital was striking to me.

I was less talkative and less trusting when I returned home. Vietnam had changed my personality. I didn't want to discuss all the things I had witnessed in Vietnam. I felt that trying to describe some of the events I had lived through would trivialize them, and trivialize their enormous impact on me.

One of the most interesting people I had met on my first tour of Vietnam was Richard Hughes, who ran a small humanitarian organization called Shoeshine Boys of Vietnam. One day, a gangly long-haired fellow in green fatigues showed up at Quang Tri hospital as I was treating an 80-year-old woman who had been shot in the head. He looked like a war correspondent, with his non-military long, thick, black hair and a camera on a strap around his neck.

As he watched me examine the patient, I saw that a bullet had barely fractured the old woman's skull. The bullet actually protruded from just under the skin. After I pulled it out, I held the extracted bullet in my hand and showed it to him.

"Are all your cases this easy, Doc?" he asked in a soft, non-military voice.

"I wish they were. I wish everyone could be as lucky as she is," I said. I treated her wound with iodine, and put a large bandage on her head. Then the woman stood, bowed gracefully to me, and slowly walked away.

Richard Hughes and I became friends. Although I did not know it at the time, the friendship would last a lifetime.

If Mother Teresa was the saint of Calcutta, Richard Hughes was the saint of Saigon. A conscientious objector, Richard had arrived in Vietnam in early 1968. He helped provide food, a place to sleep, and clothes to wear for poor children whose parents had been killed in the war. His charitable organization, Shoeshine Boys of Vietnam, was head-quartered in Saigon, although it helped young orphans in several cities.

Orphaned boys and girls were corrupted by the American presence, as were many adults in the government of South Vietnam. Although the boys might have approached you on the streets offering to shine your shoes, to survive on the streets without adult protection, young twelve- and thirteen-year-old orphans quickly became petty thieves, drug dealers, gamblers, prostitutes, pimps, or even murderers for hire. Need a nice camera, cheap? The shoeshine boy will steal one, and sell it back to you for about $5. Need a pack of 555 cigarettes, or some potent Vietnamese marijuana? The shoeshine boy will get you it for thirty-cents or so. Need to score some Chinese white heroin? Shoeshine boy will bring it back in the blink of an eye. Want a girl? There's one just around the corner, for only $2, and you'll follow the kid through streets that smell like open sewers, and into a shack where the windows are open and there's no running water, and you'll get what you want in a small cubicle with a girl, a bed, and a dirty towel, and half the money you pay is a kickback to the shoeshine boy. You want somebody killed? Give the shoeshine boy a couple of dollars. The job will get done and nobody will know. Living on the street is not pretty anywhere, and in an occupied Third World country like Vietnam, young children ran a lot of different hustles to survive.

Richard Hughes helped these orphans find a place to sleep, food to eat, and clothes to wear, no questions asked. One day I saw a bunch of them gather around him, jumping up and down, and asking him to share his paycheck.

"Sorry kids, I don't get a paycheck," he said.

"All GI get a paycheck," they replied.

"Sorry, but I am just a poor Cheap Charlie like you. I have no extra money. I live poor like you."

Richard worked to find shelter and honest jobs for the what the Vietnamese called the *bui doi,* or the "dust of life children." The shoeshine boys had a real friend in Richard Hughes, and his humanitarian efforts helped them survive. He never let them down or cheated them. The street-hardened kids saw that even an American could care about each of them, and try to take care of them like a good parent. When I left Vietnam, I gave Richard a donation of $50 to support his organization, and a letter to the editor I wrote describing the Shoeshine Boys to readers of the *San Francisco Chronicle* helped channel many donations his way during the war.

In October 1968, back in California, I was unhappily marking time at the mental hospital when I received a letter from Richard which simply asked, "Allen, would you like to return to Vietnam and help us out? We have an organization called the Committee of Responsibility, under USAID, funded by the State Department. We need a medical doctor familiar with South Vietnam to come back, and do injury assessments of the wounded children."

Although I was almost finished with my residency, I was immediately excited by the prospect of returning to Vietnam, and of making some positive contribution to saving young victims of the horrible ongoing war. But when I asked permission to go back to Vietnam from my superiors at Mendocino State Hospital, they were adamantly against it. They didn't care who was sponsoring the trip, and they weren't swayed by the reasons I gave them for going. I got the idea that my career as a psychiatrist would be in jeopardy if I went, and that

I might even be expelled from the residency program. It didn't quite register that some of the supervising physicians had changed, and that many of my supervisors were hostile to the anti-war movement. I didn't quite realize all the political consequences I would face when I took a second leave of absence that year. As I prepared to return to Vietnam, I thought my supervisors might see the light when I returned, and let me finish the last few months of my residency at Mendocino.

My second trip to Vietnam was different than my first. Because I wasn't assigned to regular medical duty, I didn't feel the pressure and responsibility of caring for the daily wounded. I didn't have the same daily struggle to save lives with inadequate supplies and outdated equipment, although I knew from personal experience that many hospitals in Vietnam were badly in need such things and I thought I could be of service to other doctors in some way.

The Committee of Responsibility, begun in late 1966, was composed of doctors, scientists, clergymen, and other concerned citizens who wanted to help civilians injured by the Vietnam war. Dr. Herbert Needleman, an associate professor at Temple University's School of Medicine, was the chairman of the board throughout the organization's existence, from 1966-1974. In April 1967, before I went to Vietnam, American medical doctors Dr. Henry Mayer, Dr. Theodore Tapper and Dr. John Constable first toured thirty-five provincial hospitals in Vietnam. They estimated that sixty percent of the civilians injured by the war were children under the age of sixteen. However, because Vietnamese hospitals were so overcrowded and care so limited, children were often the last to receive treatment. Children were dying like flies from napalm burns and other serious wounds and rampant infections. Many children had lost arms, legs, eyes, and more, and could benefit by coming to the United States for rehabilitation, nursing, foster care, physical therapy, and other treatment. At the time I was contacted, the main mission of the Committee of Responsibility was to bring children who needed medical care to the United States, but there were several layers of government bureaucracy to contend with, many personnel changes, and a constant need to re-establish the actual medical needs of children in Vietnam.

The Committee for Responsibility was keenly interested in airlifting any severely injured children who needed immediate medical treatment out of Vietnam, and transporting them to a modern fully staffed hospital in the United States. When I returned to Vietnam on January 18, 1969, I was the Committee's representative, charged with assessing the needs of Vietnamese children injured in the war.

THE CULTURES OF EAST AND WEST

EAST	WEST
We live in time	You live in space
We are always at rest	You are always on the move
We are passive	You are aggressive
We like to contemplate	You like to act
We accept the world as it is	You try to change it according to your blueprint
We live in peace with nature	You try to impose your will on her
Religion is our first love	Technology is your passion
We delight to think about the meaning of life	You delight in physics
We believe in freedom of silence	You believe in freedom of speech
We lapse into meditation	You strive for articulation
We marry first, then love	You love first, then marry
Our marriage is the beginning of a love affair	Yours is the happy end of a romance
Our love is mute	Your love is vocal
We try to conceal it from others	You delight in showing it to others
We are taught to want less	You are urged everyday to want more
We glorify austerity and renunciation	You emphasize gracious living and enjoyment
Poverty is a badge of spiritual elevation	It is to you a sign of degradation
In the sunset of life, we renounce the world	You retire to the fruits of your labor preparing for the hereafter

Source: Dr. Mai Van Trang

Arriving in Saigon for my second tour as a doctor, I quickly fell in with a group of journalists and humanitarian workers who were eager to assist me in my new assignments. Richard Hughes had arranged for me to live at a Vietnamese family's home, sharing it with Don Luce, a journalist, human rights and humanitarian worker who had been in

Vietnam since 1958 with International Volunteer Services. In Saigon, I met and became friends with John Steinbeck IV and Sean Flynn, the sons of novelist John Steinbeck and actor Errol Flynn, as well as Stephen Erhart and his beautiful wife Crystal, all journalists and foreign correspondents. I came to believe that these journalists were the true patriots of that era, searching out the truths that were so hidden and elusive in Vietnam, and risking their lives to do it. On my first tour of Vietnam, I hadn't gotten very friendly with anybody except my Vietnamese interpreter, Nguyen, so I was pleasantly surprised that the young journalists I met in Saigon became my fast friends.

Steve Erhart, a savvy war correspondent, advised me he'd travel with me to document information on wounded children at hospitals from the Mekong Delta, Central Highlands, and all the way north to my old hospital at Quang Tri. Over the next several weeks, Steve and I traveled from hospital to hospital by helicopter, occasionally being shot at from the ground. I remember a lot of hurrying from chopper to chopper, gathering information about medical conditions at many of the hospitals serving South Vietnam.

Steve Erhart was one of the most articulate and insightful people I have ever met. A correspondent for the Dispatch News Service, he was an expert on the internal situation in Vietnam. He confided to me that, as a good journalist, he always hid his emotions when interviewing American generals and other officers about the war. What he heard and saw he carefully wrote down each evening, using his portable typewriter, and what he felt often found its way into his dispatches.

On the road, I marveled at how Steve could peel away layers of folly from a military commander's statements and get through the bravado to the nitty-gritty that showed the war was being lost. These were first-rate officers he interviewed, but they needed tunnel vision to win on the battlefield. Military careers were made and lost in Vietnam, and an officer's career sometimes hinged on exactly what was said and reported in the press. Despite taking the party line about winning hearts and minds in Vietnam, a few brave officers would sometimes express contrary opinions, hinting that we were wasting men unnecessarily, or that the war might be a lost cause.

Steve and I traveled to more than a dozen hospitals in South Vietnam. These included civilian hospitals, military hospitals, and even a hospital aboard ship. Conditions at these hospitals ranged from excellent to poor. I filed reports on hospitals in Saigon, Dong Ha, Hue, Da Nang,

Quang Ngai, Chu Lai, Nha Trang, Can Tho, Rach Gia, and even my old hospital in Quang Tri.

In Quang Tri, the hospital I knew best, conditions had definitely improved. Screens had been put on the windows to keep out flies and mosquitos, sanitation had been improved, and a burn ward and intensive care unit established, with war casualties falling off from an average of thirty a day to fewer than four per day. At the old university hospital in Hue, where I assisted in my first and only open heart surgery, the Volunteer Physicians had been gone for several months because of poor public relations, but were expected to return. The *Medecin Chef* at Hue University Hospital stated that war casualties were markedly down, and that they had a capable plastic surgeon, although Hue had the problem I saw everywhere, of poor care for paraplegics.

In Dong Ha, where I had before seen all the tents full of quadruple amputee soldiers, we found a team of four to six military doctors working efficiently in the newly constructed Marine Memorial Hospital, where sanitation was high. Although doctors in Dong Ha told me they saw 130 patients per day, only a few war casualties were present when we arrived.

Farther south in Da Nang, there was a large contingent of Volunteer Physicians, but they were poorly utilized. There were two patients per bed in a burn ward said the to be the largest burn ward in Vietnam. The ward had poor hygiene, and an American nurse not trained in burn care was trying to care for seventy burn patients in a ward with forty beds. When asked about the treatment of paraplegics, one neurosurgeon told me, "We might as well send them home to die. We can't give them any special treatment here." When I asked if the hospital could use a shipment of dried milk products, I was told, "We could use potable water first of all."

On the *Heligoland*, a Swedish hospital ship, I found excellent patient care, equal to an American hospital. I called it "a model for what can be done medically and surgically for the Vietnamese people." In Nha Trang, we found eight American doctors and a civilian population largely removed from combat, requiring minimal plastic surgery restorative work.

There was an excellent provincial hospital in Rach Gia, staffed by military and Volunteer Physicians. But in Can Tho Provincial Hospital, my report to the Committee stated: "The hospital has poor plant, poor sanitation, and poor nursing care. An American nurse states that she can't understand why Vietnamese nurses are so lazy and lacking in compassion. There is again an apparent lack of both meaningful dialogue and the establishment of ground rules so that the two teams can pull together, instead of resenting each other's presence. The physician load is adequate, but there is no teaching. In a period of increased military activity in the delta, there is no corresponding increase in casualties. A tour of the post-surgical wards reveals a light patient load, with none suitable for CONUS. The *Medecin Chef* states that the Swiss are having difficulty finding suitable patients."

SONG OF THE CORPSES

After the battle of Hue, Trinh Cong Son, a famous twenty-eight-year-old Vietnamese folksinger and composer, wrote one of his most moving songs, "The Song For Corpses."

As reported by Crystal Erhart, during part of the battle of Hue, he sat in his house and watched North Vietnamese Army soldiers move through his garden, and after living with other refugees in a dark dank room for a month, watching the discovery of mass graves, the bombing of the citadel, the dying of the dead, he wrote this song out of a depth of emotion comparable only to that of the slave songs from the South.

THE SONG FOR CORPSES

Corpses in rivers
In paddies shiver
On all roofs they lie
On streets turned awry

Corpses side by side
Under bridges hide
At corners they climb
Beneath row of pines,

Corpses' bony signs,
Bushes design,
On pavement they shine,
On roads ripped by mines.

Crystal Erhart, for Dispatch News Service, 1968.

In Can Tho, I talked for several hours with the Chief of Public Health for the Marines IV-Corps. He told me that, at first, they were not going to confirm my transport into Can Tho, because the last representative of the Committee left an unfavorable impression with the staff. The Chief was quite openly a Marine first and a doctor second, but many of the points he raised were well taken. There was definitely a need for better medical care for Vietnamese civilians, he noted, but he didn't feel the thirty-seven volunteer organizations in Vietnam were tackling the most basic public health problems first. He said that civilian hospitals in Vietnam were better staffed than hospitals that cared for South Vietnamese Army troops.

Steve and I were beginning to note a pattern as we traveled. We would arrive at many destinations to find the hospitals had unusually few civilian war casualties. There would be only a few children, and fewer grotesque injuries than were reported by journalists who had previously traveled the same route. Since our route was known in advance to the Air America transport wing, which was run by the CIA, it's possible the generals and strategists of Vietnam didn't want us to find anything much at the hospitals we toured. The Committee of Responsibility may have been seen as "a hippie peace group," and I may have been labeled "a suspicious civilian doctor." I still wonder if some of the wounded children weren't removed before we arrived to tour the hospitals.

In a report I sent to the Committee of Responsibility from Saigon on February 8, 1969, I noted "There is little need at present to send patients to the US." I added, "The level of care is low, but to pick one or two patients from a mass of post-surgical infections, paraplegics, and civilian burn cases would be deceiving myself as to the priority of medical attention."

In my summary to the Committee, I reported that casualty rates appeared to be down approximately eighty percent compared to a comparable time period the previous year. Generally, there appeared to be adequate specialists available, although good orthopedic men, dentists, and internists were in short supply in some areas. Although some hospitals were beginning to institute minimal sanitation, I noted that most hospitals still had 100 percent post-operative infection rates, with high morbidity and mortality. US and Vietnamese personnel were not working in tandem, I observed, and not facing the question of responsibility for patient care in the event of an Allied withdrawal. I added, "Although the USAID program has expended millions for medical care, it has failed in a basic regard: that of financial aid to the Vietnamese medical personnel so that they may live in an environment which is conducive to providing leadership within their own ranks."

Somewhere in there, after we had toured a lot of hospitals, and desperately needed a break, Steve and I decided to take a day off in the resort town of Nha Trang. I definitely needed a respite from looking at hospitals full of war wounded. Steve's excuse for going to Nha Trang was to interview some of the Marine officers about how the war was going.

Like any good correspondent of the time, Steve always carried a portable typewriter in his backpack, and a notebook in his pocket. He was an extremely observant person. He also had an eye for pretty Vietnamese women, and Nha Trang was known for its beautiful Vietnamese party girls. On the shore of the South China Sea, Nha Trang was relatively peaceful, and it hadn't been mortared much at all during the war.

We hopped aboard a little plane called "The Otter." The Otter was an unusual little plane, perfectly suited to conditions in Vietnam. It could take off in a steep climb, dive quickly down from a height of 4,000 feet, and land on a runway shorter than a football field in a matter of seconds. In Vietnam, anything flying below 4,000 feet automatically became a target for small arms fire, and artillery. After a quick landing in Nha Trang, we stepped out of the Otter and felt a warm sweet breeze blowing off the South China Sea.

Steve and I walked down the pathway from the airport to the white sandy beach of Nha Trang. Both of us immediately noticed an area of the beach that was covered with a wide circle of bare-chested young Marines. The circle of Marines in bathing suits, perhaps fifty feet in diameter, was so perfectly round it could have been drawn by a compass, forming a sort of human doughnut around a circle of sand and some sort of beach umbrella.

Walking closer, we saw that the Marines were looking at a beautiful American girl. Alone in the center of this circle of sand, a lovely girl in a bathing suit sat under a beach umbrella. All around her were gawking Marines, some with binoculars, others simply admiring this shapely, gorgeous American girl, sitting by herself as if on a pedestal in the sand. None of the Marines was closer than twenty-five feet to her. The girl in the bathing suit ignored them.

For a moment, Steve and I thought we had stepped into a mirage, or a scene from a Fellini movie. The girl had long red hair, and a beautiful face and figure. She was definitely not Vietnamese. Well-tanned and strikingly beautiful, she had a beautiful, lightly freckled complexion. The beautiful girl sat quietly on the sand, writing pensively in a notebook.

Steve and I could not believe what we saw. We stepped over and around the Marines to reach the mirage. Suave, sophisticated Steve asked her what she was writing. She was writing her memoirs. She said her name was Marilyn, and that she was a dancer at a local club. She told us she was writing a book about her experiences in Vietnam. She said she had already saved $150,000 from her work at the club.

I couldn't understand why none of the soldiers so obviously admiring her hadn't put a move on her. Marilyn breezily explained that she was "off limits." As soon as the grunts arrived in Nha Trang for a little R&R, she explained, they were warned by their officers not to go within twenty-five feet of her. There didn't appear to be any officers on the beach, although plenty of enlisted men were now watching the three of us, I noticed.

Marilyn asked us where we were staying.

"We don't know," Steve said.

"Well, you can stay with me tonight," she volunteered.

This was an amazing response. I was thrilled at the idea of being in the same room with this woman. Early on, I had made an oath to myself not to exploit Vietnamese women, but here was an American girl inviting us to spend the night with her. I was a red-blooded American boy, and smiling at us was a beautiful, scantily clad woman. Unlike the grunts staring at us from the beach, we hadn't been told Marilyn was "off limits."

Steve and I accompanied Marilyn back to her quarters, in a little Quonset hut. As we entered the gate to her compound, a Marine guard saluted us. Apparently, I reasoned, only officers were allowed entrance to her compound, since officers were saluted by enlisted men. Steve and I saluted back. Everywhere we went in Nha Trang with Marilyn, we were saluted. Marilyn didn't acknowledge these salutes, but she also didn't seem surprised.

Marilyn's Quonset hut was a small place by American standards. Her quarters consisted of a small bedroom and a kitchen, separated by a little bathroom. We relaxed, took a quick shower, and dressed for dinner. Marilyn put on a tiny little black miniskirt dress that was almost see-through. She had beautiful legs. It was so hot and humid in Vietnam that most Vietnamese girls didn't wear underwear, and it didn't surprise either of us that she didn't wear a bra, or panties either. However, the shapely body she put into that little black dress got our attention right away.

We ate dinner together at a restaurant in Nha Trang. We all ordered wine. Marilyn and I ate shrimp, fruit salad, and rice. Steve ordered a large bowl of rice, perhaps a full quart of rice, and he ate it all. After he finished the rice, the cagey reporter leaned across the table, and hungrily looked Marilyn in the eye.

"If I can eat another bowl of rice this size, will you make love to me tonight?" he asked.

To my surprise, Marilyn said she would.

Steve had an ability to talk. This arrangement rolled off his tongue quickly and smoothly. I was now merely sad. A deal had been struck for the favors of this girl in such a novel manner that I had already lost out, and dinner wasn't even over.

We all ordered more wine. Steve ordered and ploughed into a second large bowl of rice, which he ate in the Vietnamese manner, using chopsticks. Steve slowed down about two-thirds of the way into the second bowl, but I egged him on, insisting that he finish what he had started, every single grain. Steve was extremely competitive. As he soldiered on, finishing the rice, I noticed a peculiar look come across his face, an expression I'd never seen before. He also began sweating, but I could see that he wasn't going to let a little discomfort get in the way of taking the lovely Marilyn to bed. He looked pretty uncomfortable, but I ruefully thought that his torture would be handsomely rewarded.

Steve finished the rice, stood up, and suggested that we go. On the way out, I noticed that Steve was moving slowly, and somewhat sluggishly. He wasn't saluting back at the men who saluted us. With my medical training, I quickly estimated the size of his stomach, and the amount of rice he'd eaten, in addition to two glasses of wine. As Steve began to hiccup and rub his stomach, I quietly calculated that he was going to have a problem keeping down the rice as we entered the lady's home.

The windows of Marilyn's Quonset hut were already blacked out with black tape, and after we entered, she taped the edge of the door with black masking tape, too. Then she turned to Steve, who had begun to look green around the gills.

"You're not doing well, are you?" she asked.

"Al is going to be yours tonight," Steve groaned, hurrying toward the small bathroom between the bedroom and the kitchenette. Marilyn and I could hear Steve vomiting and moaning.

I knocked on the door, politely offering medical assistance.

Steve refused the offer and moaned, "I'll be all right."

The weather that night was typical of Vietnam, about ninety-five degrees, night and day, with seventy-five to eighty percent humidity. The rich lush smell of the jungle had drifted in, mixing with the warm breezes off the South China Sea. Nha Trang that night smelled different than most Vietnamese towns, which often reeked of soot, charcoal, and kerosene. The sweet gentle breeze that wafted through the Quonset hut seemed to purify my soul.

Marilyn spread a blanket on the floor, for us. Steve was given the bed, although he didn't use it much. The rice-eating reporter stumbled back and forth to the bathroom all through the night, moaning and getting rid of the rice. His usual light-hearted bravado was gone, along with his considerable charm. He tried to be inconspicuous and quiet, too.

I lay down on the blanket with the beautiful Marilyn. Just the touch of her body next to mine was electric. All the tension and horror of Vietnam temporarily left me. Marilyn and I kissed each other tenderly, kissing each other's eyes, mouth, and breasts. I was thrilled at the touch of another human being, so unexpected, so fine, so sweet, and so lovely that night.

Suddenly the beautiful redhead sat up on the blanket.

"I'm sorry," she whispered. "I can't go any further."

"What's wrong?" I whispered.

"We can't make love," she whispered.

"What's the matter?"

"I have a sore down there," she whispered. "I think I've got a venereal disease."

"Let me look at it," I whispered. "I'm a doctor, you know."

She found me a kitchen match, then lay on the blanket with her legs and arms wide apart. I lit the match and examined her in the flickering light. To my doctor's eye, Marilyn had what appeared to be a small mole on her labia. I asked her whether she had any problems with urination, or vaginal pain. When she said no, the bright green light of love came on. She did not have syphilis, or any other venereal disease.

"You don't have anything," I whispered, unable to slow my passion and she was mine.

The happiness and joy I experienced in her arms clung to me for many weeks.

By the next morning, my friend Steve had recovered. After we left Nha Trang, we never talked about this lady again. Both of us wrote her thank-you notes. I always hoped that she finished her book, and that she had the good, full life that her generous nature deserved.

While I was in Saigon, I got a taste of working within the Vietnamese bureaucracy. Touring hospitals, I became convinced that a neurological center would be of enormous benefit to the Vietnamese people, and that Saigon would be the ideal location for such a center. At the NRI hospital in Saigon, the hospital administrator, Mr. Cung, estimated that there were 1,600 paraplegic patients in Vietnam hospitals, and that they were not receiving any special care. Mortality among paraplegic

---

DON LUCE TESTIFIES TO CONGRESS

As a representative of International Voluntary Services and the World Council of Churches, Don Luce spent twelve years in Vietnam. In 1971, he testified to Congressman Chet Holifield's Subcommittee on Government Operations about the graft, corruption, and widespread torture of Vietnamese people.

On U.S. participation in torture: "It is the general opinion of Vietnamese, and I have talked with people who have been in interrogation centers and later released, and talked with just in general hundreds of people about this general question, that almost every Vietnamese who is picked up is immediately tortured, and then goes to an interrogation center, or a police station, and is tortured again. Then the question of American involvement in this, the people say that in many cases, Americans are here, so that Vietnamese generally feel that Americans are often watching the torture and are sometimes involved in the torture."

On graft: "Our aid is siphoned off by corrupt officials. A district chief that had bought his job explained that in order to get his money back, he did three things. He sold the bulgar wheat and cooking oil that had been given for free distribution to the refugees; he taxed local bars and brothels and put the money in his pocket; and he sold the identification cards that the refugees needed in order to get jobs on the air base."

On venereal disease: "The incidence of venereal disease has been growing very rapidly...At the national VD center, where the bar girls and prostitutes are brought, when a bar doesn't pay its bribes and people get arrested, the incidence is running

patients was high, he and *Medecin Chef* Mr. Vi told me, because there were no urologists available to treat their infections, which were often fatal. He estimated there were another 5,000 Vietnamese paraplegics who were not even in hospitals. The two men had tentative plans for such a hospital, but no money. The idea was that the hospital should originally service paraplegics, and then expand into a neurology center offering research, education, and civilian patient care to Vietnam.

The Committee of Responsibility gave me an assurance that I could offer up to $2 million of their funds to the South Vietnamese government to help build a new hospital in Saigon. I was advised to meet with the prime minister of South Vietnam, Tran Van Huong. When I contacted his staff, they told me I could meet with the prime minister at his residence. When I met with him, and we spoke through our interpreters, I presented the idea of the neurological hospital to him. The prime minister seemed impressed with the idea. He asked if it could also care for polio victims. I pledged $1 million to start construction on the hospital.

---

about fifty percent. This is a problem which we have created through our military involvement and yet, for political reasons, our government has not provided any medical help in lowering the incidence of VD."

On Amer-Asian children: "My estimates, based upon studies for the World Council of Churches, in terms of the numbers of bar girls, temporary wives, and prostitutes, and interviews with them in terms of children which they have who are Amer-Asian, is that there are at least 400,000 children who are half American and half Vietnamese... When the war is over, this is going to be a terrific problem because the girls now are earning a great deal of money, but at the end of the war they will be without jobs and these children then all will go into the orphanages and the orphanages will have far less money than they have now."

On forced relocation: "Beginning in 1965 we began refugeeing the population; that is, we moved a third of the people from their farm homes, we put them in the cities, around the air bases, and we paid them well to sleep with the soldiers, and wash the clothes and this sort of thing. Now jobs are getting more scarce and this urban unrest, I think, is a natural consequence of what we began back in 1965 when we forced the farm people out of their homes....It has torn apart the most important part of Vietnamese society, that is, the family life. The men are with one army or the other. The women are washing clothes for the American soldiers, the daughters are working in the bars and brothels, and the children are shining shoes and watching cars, washing cars, and stealing. It is a breakdown of the whole societal structure."

"Your idea shows much understanding for the future needs of our country," he told me, through his interpreter. But he made one other comment which I have always remembered. He said, "Please do not ignore our history."

The prime minister offered to schedule a meeting with me with the minister of health, whom he described as a young, dedicated, and ambitious man. On February 13, I met with Nguyen Van Thieu, the assistant minister of health for international aid, to discuss the hospital idea. This government official seemed cautiously enthusiastic, too, and we all left our meetings with smiles.

During my last days in Saigon, I was also surprised to find out that the Viet Cong weren't the only people living in tunnels in Vietnam. Steve Erhart asked me to come as a doctor with him to an area where there were American GIs who had deserted or gone AWOL. American GIs who had deserted the army were literally living underground in Vietnam. In the company of a network television camera crew - I am not sure which network, but I believe it was NBC — we found American deserters living in tunnels under the streets of Saigon. Like the tunnels used in rural areas for military purposes, the Vietnamese had dug a network of tunnels under Saigon during their war against the French. Far below Saigon, in the candle- and lantern-lit darkness, I gave medical exams and ministered to American servicemen who had deserted the military. These were young men, mostly in good health, hiding out until they could find a way to go home — whites, blacks, Latinos, and even one Native American soldier, as I recall. When I watched them being interviewed by the network camera crew, the deserters all said they didn't want to kill any more Vietnamese people for no reason.

This underground warren of deserters under the streets of Saigon was one of the most bizarre places I have ever visited. When I mentioned where I had been to my roommate, Don Luce, he was amazed. We talked about this and agreed it was best to keep quiet to protect the GIs. For some reason, the segment filmed by the TV crew never aired, possibly to protect the deserters from reprisals, or to avoid embarrassing the U.S. government. At the end of the Vietnam War, the US government officially estimated that fewer than fifty men serving in Vietnam were still classified as deserters. However, some MIA investigators unofficially put the total at between several hundred and a thousand. Some of these disenchanted American soldiers surely remained in Vietnam, rising from the tunnels and learning the language and raising families with Vietnamese women after the fall of Saigon.

When I left Vietnam not long afterwards, I wondered if the badly needed neurological hospital I proposed would ever get off the ground. Corruption, payoffs, bribes, and shakedowns were rampant inside the South Vietnamese government, I had learned. It would surely be a job to shepherd such a project through the bureaucracy without having the funds siphoned off. At least, as I boarded the plane to leave Saigon, I knew I had left several good friends in Vietnam.

As the war progressed, my good friends in Saigon met their separate fates. My friend Don Luce led US Congressmen William Anderson and Augustus Hawkins to Con Son Island prison, where they saw the infamous "tiger cages," beginning an uproar that caused the South Vietnamese government to expel Don from Vietnam in May 1971. Crystal Erhart tired of her husband Steve's philandering, and eventually left him. A crack journalist in her own right, she became part of a traveling motorcycle team made up of Sean Flynn and John Steinbeck IV. They lived on the edge, journalistic commandoes covering the Vietnam War. Crystal married John Steinbeck IV, and they eventually moved back to the United States. Sean Flynn disappeared from the face of the earth when covering a story in Cambodia in 1970, with war photographer Dana Stone. What was left of his body was recovered many years later through the efforts of war photographer Tim Page. In looking over the forensic evidence available, Sean was most probably captured and executed by the Khmer Rouge guerrillas after he crossed the border into Cambodia. My friend Richard Hughes was one of the last Americans to leave Vietnam, in August 1976, sixteen months after Vietnam reunited, after trying to help the poor Shoeshine Boys of Vietnam for eight years. Around the same time, Steve Erhart was diagnosed with incurable stomach cancer, and he died in India in 1976, looking for a cure.

18

Back in the World

"Against war it may be said that it makes the victor stupid and the vanquished revengeful."
– Nietzsche

A French soldier named Henri Martin went to Indochina near the end of World War II, prepared to fight the Japanese Imperial Army. But when the young soldier realized what was actually going on in French Indochina, he refused to fight and became a conscientious objector. Henri Martin made a ringing statement at his court-martial that could also have applied to America's later involvement in Vietnam, which used tactics just as brutal and ineffective as those used earlier by the French.

"In Indochina, French troops have acted as the German fascists did in France," Martin told his accusers at his court-martial. "I am disgusted by their actions. Why do our planes daily strafe defenseless fishermen? Why do our soldiers plunder, burn, and kill? Is it to civilize the country? Is it not a handful of rebels we are facing, but a people resolved to defend their freedom! Here, everybody is Viet-Minh. Whatever happens, you cannot destroy a whole people."

The legendary Vietnamese general Vo Nguyen Giap, who had already defeated the French at Dien Bien Phu, said after American forces withdrew that his side was prepared to lose ten people for every American sacrificed in the jungles and rice paddies of Vietnam. In his strategy of a long, slow guerilla war he was essentially right, as America's brilliant military strategists killed millions of Vietnamese soldiers and civilians with vastly superior firepower, but lost the war.

Soldiers called the return from Vietnam to America "back in the world." Many doctors who went to Vietnam also experienced a profound culture shock when they returned to the United States, and some were haunted by memories of Vietnam. Dr. Ralf Young, a pediatrician who helped train me when I arrived in Hue, committed suicide some time after he returned to this country. Personally, I was changed in a way I could not immediately understand by my first and second tours in Vietnam.

When I returned to Mendocino State Hospital, Dr. Wally Cook and Dr. Hewlett Ryan, the doctors who supervised me, refused to allow me to finish my residency. They said I had gone AWOL from my work. I was firmly against the war, and it didn't help that my supervisors supported it. When I tried to show my twenty-eight-minute movie demonstrating man's inhumanity to man in Vietnam to the other residents in psychiatry at Mendocino, I was not allowed to do so. My superiors didn't want to hear about the atrocities I had witnessed in Vietnam. I was shaken to the core by what I had seen, and I talked to several people about the massacre of the babies. At Mount Zion, I wrote to Dr. Weinshol about the atrocities I had seen, but he never replied to my letter. Dr. Wallerstein told me, after a conference with Dr. Ryan and Dr. Cook, that I was distorting reality, and that I should no longer practice psychiatry, but find another job.

"But I only have three months left out of three years," I said.

"Well, you seem to be able to improvise, Hassan," he replied. "I'm sure you'll find a way to earn a living."

Then my supervisors made a proposal to me. They told me they'd let me finish the last three months of my residency if I apologized in writing for leaving, and promised never to do any such thing again. I could not do this in good conscience. I thought I'd done more good in Vietnam than I would have remaining in California.

So we parted company. Mendocino State Hospital was permanently closed a short time later. Unknown to me, Dr. Ryan, a former Marine who strongly disapproved of my anti-war beliefs, wrote that I had a distorted perception of reality, and stated, "If he had not resigned, I would have fired him." And Dr. Cook put a critical letter in my file which said I "identified too closely with the poor, the misfortunate, the underdogs of the world, especially Arabs." He recommended I not be put on any committees. Years later, when I finally saw these letters, I was puzzled by the mention of Arabs in Dr. Cook's letter, since I had only one friend at that time who could be considered an Arab, and he only visited me once in Mendocino. Also in my file, Phyllis Kemper, the chief of psychology at Mount Zion, stated in another memo that I could never become a psychiatrist because I was an Arab, and Arabs held women as chattel. Altogether, several critical letters and memos had been placed in my file. Unknown to me, many of these letters lay dormant in my file at the California Medical Board, quietly poisoning my career. After 9/11 (September 11, 2001), some of these old documents would actually be used to question my patriotism.

At that time, however, I was a lonely and somewhat disenchanted young man. It was 1969. I had been asked to leave psychiatry in a rather unceremonious way. I had no real exit strategy. As a resident psychiatrist, I was in the top ten percent of my class prior to going to Vietnam, but how could I explain not finishing my residency to the medical board? For a while, I survived by working as an emergency room doctor in the Sacramento area on weekends, rotating between several hospitals on an as-needed basis, including Folsom, Twin Lakes, Mercy San Juan, Carmichael, and Arcade Hospital. But memories of Vietnam haunted me. I received 19 speeding tickets, driving back and forth to my work that first year after returning from Vietnam. One night I was working in the emergency room with Dr. Gerald Flick, a doctor who was one of the most energetic individuals I've ever met. Dr. Flick was studying a book for law school.

"Jerry, you must be crazy," I said. "Isn't being an MD enough?"

"Al, I have so many problems with the rules at Kaiser Hospital that I decided to become a lawyer," Dr. Flick replied. This impressed me. I realized at that moment that either I was underachieving, or Dr. Flick was overachieving. Before too long, I decided to go to law school myself.

When I began writing this book some years ago, I wrote my fellow Volunteer Physicians in Vietnam, soliciting their thoughts on the Vietnam experience. More than two dozen doctors responded with the heartfelt letters excerpted in this book, and reprinted in full in an appendix. I found that many Volunteer Physicians in Vietnam felt as I did, that the experience as a volunteer doctor in Vietnam changed their outlook on politics and on life.

"I feel my Vietnam experience meant more to me personally than perhaps any of the patients I treated, although hopefully I did do a service," said Dr. Joe Nettles, who served two tours as a volunteer doctor, in both Hue and Da Nang. "I went over as a hawk, but came back as a confirmed pacifist after witnessing the horror war causes to the innocent civilian population," Dr. Nettles stated.

"The Vietnam period between February and August 1972 indoctrinated me from a physician green behind the ears into a physician more aware of world suffering and misfortune," recalled Dr. David F. Goldstone, who served in Quang Tri and Quy Nhon. "Compassion and fortitude were then ill-defined in my psyche. My conclusion is that the round eye and the slanted eye are no different, only the window upon which the soul shines forth."

Dr. Thomas Felix Oram volunteered to serve in Vietnam in 1967. Dr. Oram was an Englishman whose father was a medical officer in the Royal Army Medical Corps. Dr. Oram himself served in Malaysia as a medical officer for five years, then moved to the United States, where he volunteered to serve in Vietnam.

"I went to Vietnam somewhat skeptical as to what we were doing," Dr. Oram wrote. "I came away convinced we had made the wrong move. I felt the following:

1. The US in its determination to put down Communism would back ANY anti-Communist regime anywhere.

2. The US decided to back a series of governments in Vietnam which were corrupt and had NO following among the vast majority of Vietnamese in general.

3. In backing the South Vietnamese Army, it was an army with little backbone and little well-articulated plans for fighting the Viet Cong.

4. Advisors had been replaced by an ever-increasing number of American troops with an ever-increasing number of weapons and air power – with an ever-decreasing clear directive of what was to be done.

5. Fighting a war with a hand behind the back. The air power could have almost wiped out North Vietnam from the map but North Vietnam was off limits.

6. Most importantly – it should have been clear that the Vietnamese people neither respected nor feared the Viet Cong more than their own forces.

7. The South Vietnamese people showed no hate of Communism.

8. The amount of sheer corruption that Americans were involved in probably will never be known. There were Americans who wished that the war would continue, otherwise some of their sources of money would dry up.

9. 50,000 American lives were lost in a war that was ignominiously lost for no clear cause.

10. Many South Vietnamese almost looked on America as another colonial power only interested in their own ideas."

Dr. Stanley M. Garstka, a volunteer physician in Nha Trang and Ban Ma Thout, analyzed American medical efforts on June 24, 1968, in comments which were included in the *U.S. Congressional Record.* While the Vietnamese appreciated our help, Dr. Garstka observed, problems included doctors who were arrogant and inexperienced, and doctors who performed complicated surgeries without appropriate post-operative care, particularly orthopedic, neurosurgical, and urological cases where continuous supervision is mandatory. US doctors had not eradicated diphtheria, polio, smallpox, pertussis, or tetanus in Vietnam, although we had the vaccines to eradicate them all. US doctors had not diminished the incidence of venereal disease, cholera, typhoid, malaria, bubonic plague, intestinal infestations, and other diseases. High mortality rates of civilians wounded in the war, and subject to surgical intervention, were related not to the quality of the surgeries, but to inadequate follow-up care.

Dr. Garstka continued: "There is an urgent need to recognize we have failed, dismally, in Vietnam, not because we lacked capability or motivation, but because the Department of State and its agencies have been instrumental to create confusion, corruption, and frustration among the Vietnamese and Americans alike. This is the basic cause of our bankruptcy in Vietnam."

Dr. B.L. Tom was inspired by the writings of Dr. Tom Dooley, a selfless physician who spent much of his life in Vietnam. Stationed about 100 kilometers north of Saigon in Dalat, with no television, radio, or phonograph available, he was struck by Dr. Dooley's words: "Dedicate some of your life to others. Your dedication will not be sacrifice. It will be an exhilarating experience because it is intense effort applied toward a meaningful end ... and you will know the happiness that comes of serving others who have nothing."

In 1970 I joined the Sacramento, California, medical practice of Dr. James Cavanaugh, an old buddy from my first tour of Vietnam. I liked the town of Sacramento, which is the capital of California. Surrounded by rice paddies, tree fruit orchards, and many other agricultural crops, and not far from the Sierra Mountains, Sacramento is fairly isolated from California's large coastal cities, and retains something of a small-town feel. However, as I was getting settled in Sacramento, Jim and his wife divorced and Jim left the practice to me.

I kept up with my friends in Vietnam as well as I could, but as time flew by, the Vietnam war became history. I continued working as a doctor in Sacramento, settling into a family practice, performing many surgeries and delivering many babies.

In 1975, I was named chairman of the Department of Family Practice at Community Memorial Hospital in Sacramento. I was honored as "Doctor of the Year" by the *Sacramento Bee* in 1976. Within three years, I was president of the American Academy of Family Practitioners, and a delegate to the California Medical Association. I was even nominated for president of the California Medical Association, but my name was mysteriously withdrawn from consideration at the last minute for reasons I didn't understand at the time. About the same time, I had begun studying a subject which had interested me ever since my days aboard the USS *Toledo*, the law.

I attended Lincoln University School of Law in Sacramento. I met my future wife Sherry Nix at a boxing match between two lawyers. I was the attending physician at the match. She held up the numbers to signal the beginning of each round. A former Miss Arizona who became a lawyer and then a judge, Sherry was perhaps the most beautiful woman I had ever known, in addition to being intellectually challenging. We hit it off right away. We both enjoyed studying law and living our lives together for a while. Law school was about eighty percent reading and twenty percent listening to professors, and it slowly but surely changed the way I looked at the world.

Unfortunately, I could not forget Vietnam. On our honeymoon to Rome and Majorca in 1974, my wife gave me a book entitled *Home from the War*, by Robert J. Lipton. The book triggered memories of my Vietnam experience, which hit me like a scream in the dark. "The witnessing of children's and old people's deaths wrote an indelible script into my psyche. Shot in the head, why?" I wrote in the margins as I was reading the book. "I can never let this be forgotten."

"THE WAR IS NOT OVER"

When Richard Hughes returned to America, on November 7, 1976, he talked to reporter William V. Dunlop of The New York Times. Here are some of Richard's thoughts at that time:

"The War in Vietnam is over in Vietnam, but it is not over in America. It still festers inside us, not just for Vietnam itself, the country, but for what Vietnam meant to us here in America. Until that is resolved, we are spinning our wheels a bit and treading water, because it was psychologically, as well as physically, an enormous issue.

"One of the reasons we put Vietnam into the background is because — and this applies to many things now in American life that I sense in the few months I've been back — people don't feel that they can make a difference in what they do, and they don't want to get involved in something they can't do anything about. If they thought that their life and their action could really do something to help the Vietnamese people, I have no doubt all that they would become immediately involved.

"The American people are not angry with the Vietnamese people. The American people are angry with leaders in our country who developed the Vietnam policy without really telling us what it was. And that's where part of the feeling of repressing Vietnam comes from.

"There is so much that we can learn from the Vietnamese. Amid a society where death was so pervasive, people were so much alive. Amid so much violence, people were still courageous. And I think that what they learned about life, if transmitted here, could answer a lot of our questions.

"I think there will be a normalization of relations...There is talk of responsibility, and whether we have a responsibility. We have a capability, and where we have a capability, I think we have a responsibility. We were there, we were there in great size. And there is so much we can do. We can solve some of the physical problems by giving them resources, and they can solve some of our human problems of the spirit."

Although it lasted several years, my marriage went on the rocks with the strain of supporting two people through law school, maintaining a sizable medical practice, being a clinical instructor in family practice medicine at the University of California at Davis's medical school, studying for the bar, and trying to hold up my end of a marriage, especially when memories and nightmares of Vietnam were thrown into the mix. Some nights, I would wake up in a cold sweat, after dreaming of Vietnam. I pressed through law school like demons were after me. Sherry asked me what was wrong.

"There's something in my background that pushes me," I replied.

"What is that?"

"Fear," I said.

Instead of facing the problems that surfaced in my marriage, I just worked harder. As my marriage began to dissolve, I went into a depression, still fighting my demons. There were documents in my medical file that were causing me problems as a doctor, my wife had insisted. She urged me to investigate, she begged me to investigate and fight, but I was too busy to pursue it and take on the medical board. My practice was successful, and I was also pressing to finish law school.

Around this time, in 1980, driving to assist in a surgery one morning, I was flagged through an intersection, but then hit by a Pacific Gas and Electric Company bulldozer. The collision gave me the equivalent of a broken neck, paralyzing my left arm for a time and forever ending my days as a surgeon. After surgery by my friend Dr. Ed Gamel, I regained at least seventy percent of my strength in the arm. But the tremor that remained finished me as a surgeon and also as an obstetrician, although I'd delivered more than 400 babies by that time. I passed the California bar in 1981, after taking it for the fourth time, the same year my wife and I divorced. By chance, we sat next to each other. As we hovered over our Bar Examination questions for three days, she playfully brushing my knee under the table, as if I hadn't suffered enough studying for the bar four times.

Early on in my practice, I was appointed by the Veterans Administration as a psychiatrist to treat veterans with Vietnam Post Traumatic Stress Disorder, and I have continued to work with veterans as a doctor and an attorney who understands the kinds of physical and mental damage war can inflict on soldiers. Like many of the war-damaged veterans that I still see, at the rate of about one per week, I have never been able to forget Vietnam.

If you have never been to war, any war, and seen action, you may not understand what I am saying. A torment clings to your soul. As a doctor, I never want to forget what I saw. It wasn't because I relished the spectacle of death and dismemberment, or had some sense of accomplishment in witnessing atrocities, or even because I felt good that I had survived it all. I want to remember the disturbing feeling of the warm blood of a child whose arm has been blown off, when I'm trying to stop the bleeding. I want to remember surgery to open up the bellies of children, looking for shrapnel and bullets, trying to save their lives, remembering the horrible moment I notice that a child's spinal cord has also been severed, that the child will never walk again, won't be able to control their bowels, won't ever have sexual feelings, and won't have any ability to navigate the future on their own in a Third World country that cannot support what we call rehabilitation. Because after I experienced all this, the feeling I had when I got back to civil society was: Don't try to put one over on me. Don't try to tell me how heroic war is. Don't even expect me to reply to that, or to give you a long dissertation on how it felt. Don't talk blandly about "collateral damage." Those who have experienced war have seen suffering and sorrow and death and destruction. Advocates of more and more war have not seen the dead children, or the buckets of arms and legs as you amputate feverishly, trying to save lives. A torment sticks in your soul when you have witnessed the wholesale destruction of human beings.

How can a powerful country that has destroyed more than two million human beings in Southeast Asia lecture the rest of the world about savage behavior? The ripples of misery from the lives we have taken and the bodies we have broken spread out like waves of karma throughout the world, touching everyone involved. Somehow, I have long felt, we must atone for what we have done, and stop instigating this endless cycle of death and misery.

In 1988, I joined the Flying Samaritans, a team of doctors and healthcare workers who travel to Third World countries like Mexico to provide medical care for the poor. Visiting the little villages in Baja, Mexico, reminded me of Vietnam. Preventive medicine was unknown in the area, and Mexican *campesinos* or farm workers received no medical care at all. When I would see a sick child, I would pray that the medicine I gave him would work, because I wouldn't see him again for months and he would have no other medical care. As in Vietnam, I could only do my best with what I had, in the short time that I was there.

Some things I saw in Mexico touched me deeply, as had certain things in Vietnam. I remember we once flew into a village, during the rainy season in Mexico. Looking out the window of our makeshift little clinic one rainy day, I saw some people walking across a muddy field toward us, at least a mile away. When they finally arrived, probably exhausted from walking through the mud, I saw that one of them was a young mother, and she had her baby wrapped up in a cloth. I learned that the mother had walked eight miles to see the American doctor at the free clinic. Hearing her story, and seeing her gratitude, reminded me why I had become a doctor in the first place. Since then, I have returned to Mexico every six months, which I feel is part of my personal atonement for what the United States did to the people of Vietnam. Several years ago, I put in a stint as a doctor/psychiatrist at Pelican Bay State Prison in Crescent City, California, ministering to 2,000 hardened inmates serving life sentences.

I see a number of veterans in my practice, and I have assisted many veterans obtain medical treatment and other benefits they certainly deserve. I've come to love the enlisted men and women America produces, and to despise the bureaucrats who make up reasons to send

---

Statement of Vietnam War Veteran Pedro Hernandez, PTSD patient of Dr. Allen Hassan:

"You know, I have been honored by two Presidents, attorney general, two governors of the state of California for my work with gangs and their problems with drugs. I was in Vietnam. When you are writing, just tell them you're crazy, this is true, the war is crazy, and tell them Pedro, me who has been honored by all these people, I am crazy too. I almost killed myself after the war, and my son came up to me and told me, 'Even though you don't love yourself, Dad, I love you.' And then I decided not to kill myself.

"We ferried the CIA. I was intimately involved with them. When I came back to America, I thought about all the killing and death and I went to see a counselor because I was so fucked up. I said this is the way it was and she said to me, 'I am tired of counseling you, you are crazy. I don't want to see you anymore. I don't want to hear what you have to say. I don't believe that what you say could happen.'

"You ask me questions about what we did. Did we kill our own POWs? Of course we did! Did the government deny it? Of course they did! Am I suffering from post trauma stress disorder? Well, I almost killed myself. But now I devote my life to helping kids and helping people.

"When I was over there, in my unit, my unit, three hundred dead, eight were left alive. Yeah, yeah, am I crazy? Maybe so."

---

these young men and women charging forward into the unbelievable horror of war so they can burnish their political resume as "war president." After witnessing the atrocities I saw in Vietnam, I can state unequivocally that doctors owe more than a mere three-minute office visit to a suffering veteran who has been injured or traumatized by war. Many veterans of World War II, Korea, Vietnam, Iraq, and other wars suffer continuing psychological trauma from their wartime experiences, including Post Traumatic Stress Syndrome, and increased incidences of cancer and diabetes from exposure to carcinogenic herbicides like Agent Orange. With both my law degree and my medical experience, I have been able to help many of these men and women get the veteran's benefits to which they are entitled. Over the years, my sympathy for enlisted men and women has grown, while I have less and less sympathy for the generals and politicians who send our young soldiers into senseless wars. And listening to the stories of these veterans reminded me, oftentimes, of my days in Vietnam.

They say you can't cure the guilt of Post Traumatic Stress Disorder, you can only cover it over a little bit. They say those who are involved in violent death and feel they didn't do enough, who find that the violence was caused by the hands of man, that it is unforgettable. It is like schizophrenia; you hear the voices and cries and see the visions of death. It is estimated that 500,000 of the 2.5 million men who served in Vietnam had a firsthand involvement in the death and killing of Vietnamese, and suffer from Post Traumatic Stress Disorder. Most of the 500,000 went through drugs or alcohol, multiple marriages, attempted and actual suicides, and more, leaving a trail of tears through their lives. I have seen that the trauma of war extracts a terrible toll from the living survivors. These veterans are my living heroes and I have treated many of them over the past several years. When they walk into my office, I can see their pain before they say a word.

In her book *Trauma and Recovery*, author Judith Herman wrote, "The violation of the human connection, and consequently the risk of Post Traumatic Stress Disorder, is highest of all when the survivor has not been merely a passive witness, but also an active participant in violent death or atrocity. The trauma of combat exposure takes on added force when violent deaths can no longer be rationalized in terms of some higher value or meaning. In the Vietnam War, soldiers became profoundly demoralized when victory in battle was an impossible objective and the standard of success became the killing itself, as exemplified by the body count. Under these circumstances it was not merely the exposure to death but rather the participation in meaningless acts of malicious destruction that rendered men most vulnerable to the lasting psychological damage."

Although I continued to build a successful medical and legal practice, I was plagued with constant nightmares about Vietnam. Months and years after I returned to the United States, my sleep was broken with images of horror. Often, I dreamed of the dead babies brought into the hospital in Vietnam, who died before my eyes. I dreamed of lifting the neatly lettered armband and reading "Interrogated USMC."

Another recurring dream begins with a mortar exploding, and screams of fear and pain erupting all around me. I sit up in bed, sweat dripping down my forehead. I can barely see the children through the smoke. Are there three, four Vietnamese children? They are gazing up at me, their Bac si.

I think, We've got to evacuate this hospital or we'll all die.

I grab the two smallest children, and pull them up into my arms. I gesture to the others.

Come with me, I shout in the dream.

We run down the hospital corridor. Just as I reach the exit, I collapse. I look down and see blood soaking my shirt, and dripping to the ground. Oddly at peace, I relax into unconsciousness....

Although these dreams of Vietnam did not stop, I continued to practice medicine in Sacramento, which by then had become my home. At one point, Dick Hughes sent me a picture of a pile of bricks that he thought was all that was left of my old hospital in Quang Tri, which had been bombed into rubble during the war.

Over the years, I have made several attempts to tell the story of the children I saw murdered in Vietnam. I told at least a dozen other doctors. In 1987, I wrote a letter to the Department of Defense, and asked them to investigate the murder of the children that I saw. They replied with a three-inch brochure telling me that the rules of engagement wouldn't have allowed such a thing as the murder of children to happen. In 1989, I wrote to General Colin Powell, chairman of the Joint Chiefs of Staff, who was of no help either. General Powell had a subordinate write me back, suggesting that I give any additional information I had on the massacre to the Marine Corps' Inspection Division in Washington, DC. In 1990, I was actually investigated by the Office of Naval Intelligence because of the complaints I had made. In

1991, I wrote to Senator John McCain, who forwarded a report from Naval Intelligence saying there was no evidence that the murder of the babies I saw actually occurred. Every official agency who might have known about these murders had no record of it, or else denied that it had ever happened.

In 1991, I decided to write my great-uncle, Mortimer Marks, a hero of World War II. At that time he was more than ninety years old. As a young boy, I'd heard my family speak of his heroism as a Marine during World War II, where he survived the Bataan Death March, and three years in a Japanese prison camp. I put down some of my thoughts on paper, and he responded with a letter which contains the following remarks:

Dear Allen:

Your three-page letter had to be read several times to absorb it all. The general conclusion I came to was that we are very much alike.

Similarly, we are both half-breeds. You are half Swede and half Arab. I am half Swede and half Hebrew. Because of this mixture we have both been subject to unpleasant innuendoes. I was appalled to learn that a Navy Captain suspected your loyalty as a Marine because of your Arab background. If I had the authority, I would court martial that officer for debasing your character. I, too, have encountered slurs about Jews from those who were unaware of my Jewish ancestry. Racial prejudice has always been a nasty reality for me. It is so ignorant and destructive to society. The best we can do to fight it is to openly stand up to it whenever it raises its ugly head.

I thought you expressed the principle of universality of man beautifully and succinctly when you said, "I am hopeful that the earth will become the United States of the world and that we may give thanks to the diversity of culture everywhere instead of trying to make the entire world just like us."

One of the imponderables of all times is the ancient animosity that exists between the Arabs and the Jews in the Middle East. History tells us that both ethnic groups originated from the same father, Abraham. How and why did they grow so far apart? Perhaps, it is politics, the power to rule. Then it could be religion. The three great faiths: Judaism, Christianity, and Islam have all a common bond. Moses influenced Jesus who influenced Mohammed. Jerusalem is the religious capital of all three. There seems to be far more common ground between Jews and Arabs to live peaceably together than for incessant wrangling. Here again, that nasty, human prejudice appears on the scene to beget misery.

–Mortimer Marks

February 4, 1992

In the years after I returned from Vietnam, I wondered if my experiences in Vietnam had affected my ability to form long-term relationships. My memories and dreams sometimes intruded into my daily life. I wondered if my marriage might have survived, if I hadn't been so frequently awakened in the middle of the night, bathed in sweat, horrified by my dreams of squirming, dying babies. After thirty years, I realized, I still dream of lifting up the limp arm of a baby killed by a single shot to the head, and read the neatly lettered words on the armband, "Interrogated USMC." I could not shake the memory of the blood-spattered hospital foyer, the horror, and the shock of all I had seen.

I have spent about an hour a day for the past thirty years keeping up with world news. I have read more than 200 books on Vietnam, and as more come out, I read them, too. Like many of the other people who spent time in Vietnam, I have continued to be interested in information that continues to emerge about our involvement in the Vietnam War. And over the years, I have often wondered what happened to the people I knew who remained there.

19

Return to Vietnam

*"Throughout history the world has been laid
waste to ensure the triumph of conceptions that
are now as dead as the men who died for them."*
- Henry de Montherland

*I*n 1998, after the United States
had established diplomatic relations with the Communist government
of the reunited country of Vietnam, I made a fateful decision to
return. Vietnam still haunted me. Although thirty years had passed, I still
vividly remembered many of the things I had experienced in Vietnam.
As a tourist rather than a doctor, I made plans to revisit Saigon, the
former capital of South Vietnam, Hue, my old hospital in Quang Tri, and
venture into some of the beautiful mountainous country and former
battlefields beyond.

I was certainly not the only American who was still interested in
Vietnam. Senators John Kerry and John McCain, both Vietnam veterans,
had worked hard to normalize America's diplomatic relations with
Vietnam. Other veterans had formed organizations such as the Veterans
Viet Nam Restoration Project, and became active in rebuilding schools
and undertaking other humanitarian projects in Vietnam. I retained a tie
to Vietnam, too.

On the flight over, I began wondering about how the country
had changed. I wondered about my little hospital in Quang Tri, all the
people I had treated there, my interpreter Nguyen. I wondered if the Viet

Cong soldiers who had fired warning shots at me on my way to work would remember the American *Bac Si*. I wondered if the family being used for target practice by the American GI with the mortar would remember the man who had stopped the pointless attempt to kill them. I wondered if any of the beautiful girls who had stood waiting in line for me would remember the *Bac Si* who tried to remove the broken acupuncture needles from their backs. I wondered if the children at the feast who had brought me the buried duck eggs would remember the expression on my face when I declined. I wondered if the lush jungles of Vietnam would be forever blighted with bomb craters, unexploded land mines, and the defoliating, biochemical effects of Agent Orange.

My plane landed peacefully in what was once Saigon. After the fall of South Vietnam, Saigon was re-named Ho Chi Minh City. The city's name was different, but many things about the city had not changed. I saw the same Quonset huts I remembered at the airport, even the same doors and windows, although some of the tiles had been patched.

The heat and humidity struck me as I stepped off the plane. It was 105 degrees, with eighty-five percent humidity. On my way to the hotel, I saw the same French colonial buildings, the same doors and windowpanes and entrances I remembered from years before. Vietnam was still obviously a Third World country, but a few modern skyscrapers had been built, and I saw some evidence of imported electronic high tech.

The streets of Ho Chi Minh City teemed with rickshaws, vendors, pedestrians, and people on bicycles wearing the distinctive Vietnamese cone-shaped straw hats to shield them from the sun. When automobiles and trucks were added to the mix, the combined traffic was ferocious. Clean-cut young Communist men and women in crisp tan People's Republic uniforms, complete with gold star and red insignia, patrolled Ho Chi Minh City's crowded streets by foot or on motorbikes. When I looked into the smiling, curious faces of some of these young Communists, I realized they didn't know very much about Americans.

What had once been the grand capitol of South Vietnam was now merely a Third World city continuing to decay. Pollution poured directly into the Bay of Saigon, spoiling its quiet beauty. Rusting fishing ships trolled the bay, catching fish to supply the city's open-air fish and produce markets which still remained.

I stayed in the Hanoi Hotel, in the central part of the city, which cost only $30 per night, cheaper than the American hotels which cost a hundred dollars a night or more. Although not many guests spoke English, I was treated like a king at the Hanoi Hotel. I found a newspaper waiting for me every day, and rather than focusing on crime or war, the papers here focused on caring for the poor, rebuilding the infrastructure of Vietnam, and taking care of children. It was International Children's Day in Vietnam, I read. I learned that five million Vietnamese children were to be given Vitamin A, a vitamin in short supply in the Vietnamese diet. A total of 100 million Vitamin A tablets had been donated by UNICEF. That old problem of cleft palates, a problem when I was in Vietnam, remained a problem due to lack of certain trace minerals in the diet.

In contrast to my days in Vietnam, I found there were plenty of doctors available to help civilians in the cities. According to Dr. Nguyen Tai Man and other doctors I met in Saigon, most doctors in Vietnam earn government salaries. The main surgeons earn also small supplemental payments of about $5 US for major operations such as craniotomies. There were 3,400 doctors in Saigon alone, including about 500 working without pay. Vietnamese medical school graduates were willing to work without pay in hospitals because positions in big hospitals were hard to find. Hospital experience was necessary before moving into private clinics where doctors could earn good money selling medications to patients at high prices, which was profitable because doctors didn't pay the same taxes paid by pharmacies. While the cities were full of doctors, however, rural areas in Vietnam continued to have shortages because young doctors didn't want to work where they were unpaid or poorly paid, with poor study and working conditions. Dr. Nguyen Tai Man told me that government policies were at that moment being re-written to force new medical school graduates to work in remote areas, and receive preferential treatment for that work.

A skinny little rickshaw driver appointed himself my guide the minute I stepped out of the hotel. Ironically, his name was Nguyen, the same name as my old interpreter. Every day Nguyen would wait for me to leave the hotel, then take me in his rickshaw to visit his friends who owned restaurants, newspaper stands, and trinket shops. Despite the heavy street traffic, Nguyen would bravely navigate one-way streets the wrong way in his rickshaw, ignoring an onslaught of trucks, buses, taxicabs, and motorcycles heading the other direction. Although he was a thin little fellow, rickshaw driver Nguyen pulled me through the streets of Ho Chi Minh City with a kind of verve and abandon. He had the leg muscles of a horse, and nerves of steel. When we passed groups of small children, they smiled and waved at our rickshaw.

Mothers with children, begging for money, approached my rickshaw many times. The first day, I gave one a few dong. Suddenly, I was swamped by thirty to forty mothers with their babies, all wanting money. Rickshaw driver Nguyen came to my assistance. In a kindly fashion, he let the mothers know that I had come there to help them, and not to give them money. Several times, Nguyen got me out of this type of situation, with most of my money intact.

After thirty years, Ho Chi Minh City seemed drab, compared to the city of billowing silk and bright colors I remembered as wartime Saigon. Many of the shops were filled with boots, medals, uniforms, and other leftovers from the war years. In one shop, when I asked about Western clothes, I was led to a back room where they showed me a polyester shirt with a very large collar in the 1970s style, of the type Sonny Bono might have worn on *The Sonny & Cher Show*, a shirt probably left over from the war years. I bought it for $7, and back in the hotel, I found it fit me perfectly.

At the Hanoi Hotel, I was talking with some of the guests I met about what I hoped to see in Vietnam, when a tiny Vietnamese man pulled me aside and spoke to me privately. I towered over the man, who was about five feet tall, and weighed about eighty pounds. He looked up at me earnestly.

"You must be careful. Do not say some things," he whispered. "People are always watching, and always listening. I am afraid even to talk to you right now." He smiled tentatively, a small smile, and continued. He told me his own father had been put in a prison camp several times for saying the wrong things. As he spoke, his eyes darted around the room as if to assess who was watching. His voice wavered. This exchange made me uneasy, and brought back a little of the old paranoia of wartime Vietnam.

The next morning I flew to Phu Bai, the former military airport that served Hue. I was the only American on the plane. As we dropped below 4,000 feet to land, hundreds of bomb craters left by American bombing raids were plainly visible in the jungle floor.

Two pretty young Vietnamese women, Linh and Tu, met me at the airport. They picked me out of a crowd, a lost American waiting for transportation, and introduced themselves. Linh was twenty-seven, and

Tu was twenty-four. The two pretty young Vietnamese women ran a small transportation service consisting of a minivan that took visitors from the airport into Hue. Linh and Tu were fluent in English, French, and Vietnamese, and they took over as my translators and my tour guides for the next 10 days. It was like two angels had flown down from heaven to welcome me to beautiful, humid, dusty, tropical Vietnam. The girls kept track of everything we spent on handheld computers, and their driver roared through the streets as if he owned the road.

I suggested a certain hotel for dinner in Hue, but the girls warned me away, saying the hotel would charge us an additional $15 because of the air-conditioning. Instead, Linh and Tu took me to a small Vietnamese restaurant next to the River of Perfumes, and helped me plan my stay. There was a cool breeze off the river, and the food was good.

Dr. Hassan's return to Vietnam in 1999 is celebrated by driver Tan, left, and interpreters Tu and Linh on the right.

I thought these girls could have run corporate America. They asked me a few pertinent questions, then more or less took care of arranging the things I needed for my stay, such as lodgings, transportation, and a camera. They said they would take care of my travel, my hotel, find places for me to eat, draw my bath water, clean my room, and have my clothes cleaned, my shoes polished, and they would help me find the roads and trails to my destinations. They put me up at their favorite hotel, the Red Star Hotel, and made arrangements for me to travel to Quang Tri in their air-conditioned minivan. I was relieved to have arrangements made so easily. Linh and Tu found out where I wanted to go, scheduled it, and said they would make sure I was awake by 7 a.m. But when I mentioned the murder of the babies that I had seen, and told them that I wanted to find their graves, the two girls did not seem interested, and looked the other way.

After the squalor and decay of Ho Chi Minh City, the beauty and cleanliness of Hue was stunning. The streets of the old imperial capital showed few obvious signs of war. The shops and markets of Hue appeared intact. Many of the old homes and palatial estates of Hue appeared untouched and well-kept. The Forbidden City citadel remained mostly intact, some of it reconstructed, some of it untouched by the war except for a few bullet holes left by attacking soldiers. Beautiful healthy children played along the banks of the quietly flowing River of Perfumes. There was not much evidence of the destruction wrought by the fiercely competitive armies that took over and abandoned the town. However, an old man with no legs did hobble toward us as we were eating lunch, and ask us to buy lottery tickets. The legless man on crutches was an obvious victim of the war.

The old Hue teaching hospital looked just as it had looked 30 years before, when as a young surgeon I had been thrown into my first open heart surgery, assisting Dr. Detwiler. Walking into the hospital, I felt as if I had just stepped far back in time.

The next day, Linh and our driver picked me up early at the hotel in their minivan. Our driver barreled up the stately old streets of Hue, and we headed north, on Highway 1, the former Street Without Joy. I had forgotten that Highway 1 ran through the city of Hue, and out through the jungle. In our air-conditioned vehicle, we traveled past beautiful green rice paddies. We saw squalid houses and huts behind lush jungle flowers and trees. We passed huts in what appeared to be a swamp. As we traveled north, children and adults passed us, headed the other way on foot, on bicycles, and in rickshaws. I noticed a bombed-out school that had not been rebuilt, a relic of the war. We passed the idyllic waterfalls, luxuriant vegetation, and clear-running streams and ponds of central Vietnam.

I wondered about all the young soldiers, Americans and Vietnamese, whose blood had fallen into these clear-running waters. I compared the Vietnamese people I had known thirty years before, the wounded and war-weary adults and children, with the businesslike young Vietnamese in the car with me, who no longer feared or lived with death. As more memories returned, I felt powerful surges of regret and sadness.

U.S. Senator John McCain on Vietnam:

On October 16, 1999, Senator John McCain, a former prisoner of war, reflected on America's role in Vietnam with television host Larry King:

"We went to Vietnam with good intentions. The Vietnamese people liked us. They never liked the French because they were a colonial power, trying to hold on to their Indochina Empire. The Russians were never liked because they came in after we left and were seen as a dominant imperialist colonial power. The Americans are liked to this day. When you go back to Vietnam, the Vietnamese always say, "America Number One." Yet they still despise the Russians and the French. So to this day Americans are still liked.

"The reason for this is they felt the Americans came there to help their country, unlike the French and Russians who were trying to exploit their country. This shows the innate intelligence of the Vietnamese, understanding the difference, but knowing it was still important to unite their country."

During the Vietnamese War, the United States suffered more military casualties in Quang Tri than in any other province in Viet Nam. American soldiers who protected my hospital and fought within a 100-mile radius of Quang Tri were awarded twenty-six Medals of Honor, many of them posthumously. Quang Tri had been heavily bombed in 1972. American bombers had made a series of air strikes on the town, and that had been followed by a relentless shelling from South Vietnamese army artillery that almost completely leveled what was left of the town. Altogether, more bombs were dropped on the 400-square-mile province of Quang Tri than had been dropped on all of Europe during World War II. An estimated 700,000 water buffalo and other farm animals had been killed during the war, many killed for sport by our troops.

In the new reunited Vietnam, Quang Tri was no longer even a provincial capitol. The province had a new capitol, Dong Ha.

When we arrived in Quang Tri, my old city didn't look familiar to me since much of it had been rebuilt after the massive bombings.

The citadel had been completely rebuilt; it was now surrounded by concertina barbed wire. I tried to orient myself using the citadel, which had been used by the South Vietnamese Army as an ammunition dump during the war years. I took some pictures and used it to try to get my bearings as to where things I remembered might have been. The first thing I discovered was that my old house and bunker were gone from the face of the earth. Some unfamiliar-looking new hutches had been rebuilt nearby. Searching for the site of my old hospital, we stopped at the home of a family I remembered. They lived in a modest home I remembered passing every day, on my walks to the hospital after my Jeep privileges had been taken away, followed by children like the Pied Piper of Quang Tri.

An old woman who must have been eighty years old met us at the door. She looked like everybody's grandmother, a woman you want to be kind to, and take care of. To my surprise, the old woman immediately recognized me, as the former *Bac Si*. As her children and grandchildren gathered around, she told us the old hospital had been bombed, and no longer existed. She thought a house had been built on the site. She said she remembered My Lai, which was several miles from Quang Tri, but she remembered nothing of the atrocity that I witnessed, involving the executed children.

I could not believe that my old hospital had been completely destroyed. Much of downtown Quang Tri appeared to be intact. We did find a completely destroyed former school, which had apparently been left in rubble as a reminder of what the Vietnamese call "the American War." My interpreters and I continued searching the streets of Quang Tri, until we finally found what was left of Quang Tri Provincial Hospital. Two parts of the old hospital still stood, but the rest had been reduced to pieces of broken concrete, cinder blocks, bricks, and rubble. The courtyard area, a grassy plot where helicopters landed with dead and wounded civilians, was already overgrown with trees. Stray dogs wandered through what had been the corridors of the former hospital, sniffing through the former marble foyer and the rest of the building at will.

The sun was broiling, and midday humidity was high. I was dripping with sweat. As I looked at the battle-scarred hospital ruins, at the bullet holes and shell holes in what was left of the outer walls of my old hospital, I was deep within myself. Then we found a caretaker, who took me to a part of the building that was closed. To my amazement, he opened the door to my old surgical suite, which was lit by sunlight filtering in through a broken wall. Even through the heavy rains of the monsoon season, the doors and windows had been fastened so securely that this one room was preserved as if it had not been touched for thirty years.

Walking inside, I was amazed to see that the old surgical suite, where I had worked so hard to save lives, still remained. My operating table remained. Bottles in the corner still held surgical instruments. Each tool and utensil that I had used was still in its accustomed place, stacked neatly against the wall, as if had been frozen in time for thirty years. Emotional memories washed over me in waves.

I thought of the battles that must have taken place after I left, the compounding spiral of death and destruction. And suddenly I suffered a flashback. All at once, I remembered the horrible wounds, the lines of patients, and felt death all around me. For a split second I heard the cries of babies, the whoosh of chopper blades, the sounds of gunfire and mortars. Tears rose from my heart to my eyes. Suddenly I fell to my knees and yelled out, overwhelmed by hysterical frustration and panic. Surely the ghosts of the war dead understood, but my new Vietnamese friends looked away in embarrassment as I spent what seemed like a long time in a fit of angry, remorseful, sorrowful rage.

"Al, are you all right?" Linh finally asked.

She was looking at me sadly and sympathetically. If my young guides had seen me as a wise, stoic, humble American, for a moment they saw me instead as the fragile human being that I truly was.

After a few minutes, I was able to rest under a shade tree. When I asked about the nurses and other employees who had taken care of my patients 30 years before, the caretaker suggested we talk to an old lady named Nang. He gave my translator directions to her home. We walked down a dusty street in Quang Tri, and found her home.

A Vietnamese woman, Nang, pictured here with a relative, remembered Dr. Hassan when he returned to Vietnam in 1999.

Nang had worked at the hospital, as a nurse. She remembered nothing of the massacre, but through my translator Nang told me there was another lady who would be able to give me evidence of the forty babies who were killed. I was thrilled to hear this. Nang said the lady lived a short distance away, down a dusty road.

It was getting late and I was tired, but Linh told me this might be the last chance to find someone who might know about the babies, or what happened to my translator, Nguyen, whose father was a province chief in Quang Tri. We searched for her house in the heat.

Walking down another dusty road, coming in the distance, I saw a middle-aged woman coming up the road. She appeared anxious to see me. She was running to see me. We met. She bowed, and invited us into her house.

We sat in her back yard, on stark wooden furniture, next to a stream, and sipped tea. The woman was a nurse at the hospital in 1968 and 1969, but like the other nurses she was not always at the hospital, and she may have not been present the day the forty murdered babies were brought in. Although I could see the woman was struggling to remember more across the fog of time, to my disappointment, she remembered nothing of the babies being brought into the hospital that one sweltering afternoon in May.

"So many died, so many babies, so many children," she said in Vietnamese, her words translated back to me. "I cannot remember which day so many died, but I know some Americans came to try to help us. The Americans helped us, but the Americans killed us."

At that moment, I could not stop my tears. I cried for the sadness of it all, for all the unnecessary deaths and injuries, and I wept for the continuing tragedy of Vietnam. My translator, Linh, quietly put her hand on my arm as I cried.

For three days, my translators and I traveled back to Quang Tri, with our driver, whose name was Tan. We searched for people who might have remembered the incident. We met people who might have been there, people who should have known, but memories had faded. There was no trace of my interpreter, Nguyen, who would have grown into a middle-aged man by now. I wondered what happened to him and his father, the province chief, in the aftermath of the war.

Later that first day, in Dong Ha, where I had seen the tents full of young amputees, I walked into a school administration building. It was a special holiday for children, I learned. I was approached by a lovely, dignified female teacher. She was in her early thirties, and wore a traditional long and flowing *ao dai*. She was probably only a small baby at the time I was in Vietnam, but she spoke English well. She asked my name, and why I came there.

"I came because of the children that I witnessed die during the war, the mothers, the fathers, the grandparents, because I saw the slaughter of so many innocent people," I began, as she listened intently. I told her of what I had seen, of my deep desire to find answers to questions I had regarding the war. I told her of my journey back to look for answers, and my desire to atone in some way for all that had happened to their people.

"You cared enough to come back to our poor, small town from America?" she quietly asked.

The calm, direct, sincere way she asked this question pierced my heart. For so many years, nobody had really wanted to hear me talk about the suffering and horror I had seen in Vietnam. My career as a psychiatrist had been broken, I had lost my marriage, I had lost my ability to do surgery, and high officials in my own government brushed aside my efforts to tell the truth. Tears welled up in my eyes. I turned away from the woman for a moment, to regain my composure. After thirty years, I thought, finally here was someone who had a sense of the atonement I sought, and its deep emotional truth.

Suddenly, we both broke into tears.

"You are so kind to come back after what happened to us," she said. "Thank you."

On the way back to Hue, we passed a large, well-tended graveyard outside of town, and I asked my driver to stop. The graveyard was impressively well-kept, but full of anonymous graves. Each grave had a simple, black tombstone. One headstone caught my eye. It was next to a rosebush, with one single stem and red bloom trailing over the simple black tombstone. I squatted down next to the tombstone, and read the inscription. The tombstone contained two words of Vietnamese, *Liet Si*, and a date of birth and date of death. I looked around. All the headstones around me were marked with the inscription *Liet si*. According to the dates on the headstones I saw, most of *Liet si* died in the American War.

Back at the Red Star Hotel, I sat down at the bar. A pretty English-speaking Vietnamese bartender in a black silk *ao dai* brought me a beer. She was very attractive, and I asked her what religion she was. She proudly replied "Ho Chi Minh." Then I asked about the Vietnamese words, *liet si*, that I had seen on the tombstones in the neat little country graveyard.

"*Liet si*," she said, "means 'hero of the war'."

It struck me like a thunderbolt that, although I might never find the graves of those babies who were executed, I had received an explanation that would help calm my anxiety about not being able to find where those innocent children were buried. The children had been buried as war heroes. I was certain at that moment that I would write a book in honor of all of the children, old men, and young women who had been killed in what the Vietnamese called the American War.

Liet Si, on Vietnamese tombstones, mark graves of children killed during Vietnam War

Another morning we journeyed to Khe Sanh, farther north up Highway 1. It was a mild, sweet-smelling morning. Jungle flowers were blooming. We passed the new provincial capital of Dong Ha, and turned west at the junction of Route 9, to begin a long, steep climb into the hills toward the historic battlefield of Khe Sanh, once the site of a sprawling Marine Corps base.

It was a long and winding road to Khe Sanh, through the A Shau Mountains. The highway was narrow, rough, and badly in need of repair. We passed the small village of Cam Lo, former headquarters of the National Liberation Front and Viet Cong. We passed Camp Carroll, a former command center of US military operations in this sector of I-Corps, which was now swallowed in thick jungle. The old Hamburger Hill battlefield was also swallowed by the triple-canopy jungle. We passed The Rockpile, once a key US observation point, and many other strategic hills and paths, intertwined with the Ho Chi Minh Trail along the Laotian border.

That afternoon, surrounded by the dense jungle, we continued to climb into the shadowy hills and lush green mountains. For an eerie moment, I thought I heard the clicking sounds of distant chopper blades, echoing against the black canyon walls. Then it was utterly silent.

Many graves of Liet Si in a well-tended cemetery in Vietnam

Below us near the Dakrong River Bridge we saw a peaceful and beautiful little village, the home of a hill tribe, the *Bru Van Kieu*. There are 54 different tribal groups in Vietnam, all called *montagnards* or mountaineers by the French and later by the Americans. Many fought on the American side during the war, and some were still fighting against the current government of Vietnam. As our minivan approached the jungle village, we received shy, welcoming smiles from the Bru Van Kieu villagers, peeping out at us from their houses.

The Bru Van Kieu lived in houses raised up on long wooden stilts, with thatched roofs. They had no running water, sewer, electricity, telephone, or any other amenities. A poor, poverty-stricken people, with some of the lowest incomes on earth, they nonetheless appeared to be happy and their village appeared to be a happy place.

The villagers had just killed a wild boar, and they invited us to lunch with them. The boar was made into a tangy, bubbling stew. The villagers invited us to share, and we accepted. As we ate, we were surrounded by old people, young women, and children, who gawked at us with great curiosity. An old woman at the center of the clan lit up a long carved bone pipe, puffing and filling the air with the aroma of a peculiar, sweet-smelling resin. There were few young men around, but perhaps they were away, hunting, fishing, or working in their fields. I knew that some of the *montagnards* had begun a low-intensity guerrilla war against the Communist government of a reunited Vietnam.

When we finally arrived at Khe Sanh, the historic battleground was desolate and deserted. I had not visited Khe Sanh during my tours of Vietnam, but it was a hot spot during the war. The military base sat in a sort of a natural soup bowl, with the Marine encampment in the middle of the bowl, often taking fire from the surrounding hills. The Marines scorched the surrounding jungle with bombs and Agent Orange, but the Viet Cong were dug into tunnels, and rose up to kill many Marines.

There was little evidence of the huge Marine firebase that once existed. Thousands of US Marines had been tied down at Khe Sanh for many desperate months, until in a surprise maneuver, the Tet offensive was launched during the 1968 lunar new year. The Tet offensive simultaneously targeted hundreds of cities and towns throughout South Vietnam, including a coordinated attack into the heart of Saigon. When the US military finally determined that the siege of Khe Sanh was only a diversionary tactic, they blew up the airstrip and the buildings and went on to fight elsewhere.

Only a tiny museum about the size of a boxcar remained to tell the story. There were only a few interesting artifacts in the small museum. A guest book was available for signing. A trickle of tourists and a few ex-soldiers had made the adventurous trek through the jungle to Khe Sanh. The guest book contained a couple of hundred signatures, and assorted written memories, salutations and salutes, mostly written in English by Americans.

Over the entrance to Khe Sanh was a small billboard which read, "The area of Tacon Point base built by U.S. and Saigon Puppet." A persistent young vendor near the museum entrance hawked the usual

Vietnamese war souvenirs, like fake and maybe real dog tags, frayed patches from uniforms, battle-scarred war helmets, and so forth.

Outside the museum, children scrambled over piles of unexploded ordnance. Beyond the children, farmers with their water buffaloes cultivated a grove of coffee trees.

Another twenty kilometers up the road, we reached the remote frontier border town, Lao Bao, on the border of Vietnam and The Laos People's Democratic Republic, and near the border of Thailand. Lao Bao is a smuggler's paradise of sorts, teeming with all manner of legal and illegal goods, including narcotics and guns. It was a welcome break for us to see this strange little town, before the long return trip back down the mountains to Hue.

Over the years, I would return to Vietnam again and again. But after my first trip, I understood that my experiences there had been the most profound and defining of my life. During my two tours of war-torn Vietnam, for medical and humanitarian service, I grew to love the country and its people. I missed Vietnam. I missed its wonderful people. I had somehow become lost, and then found myself again in tragically beautiful Vietnam.

20

The Lessons of War

"The central question is whether the wonderfully diverse and gifted assemblage of human beings on this earth knows how to run a civilization."
- Adlai E. Stevenson

"For national leaders, it is sometimes easier to fight than to talk. Impatient cries for total victory are usually more popular than the patient tolerance required of a people whose leaders are seeking peaceful change down the intricate paths of democracy." - Harland Cleveland

"The awareness that we are all human beings together has become lost in world war and through politics." - Dr. Albert Schweitzer, last appeal for peace, Oslo, Norway, 1958

*I*n Vietnam, we fought a war to stop Communism but war did not stop it. We inflicted enormous damage on the people of Vietnam and on ourselves. In Vietnam our military emphasized body count, but in subsequent wars like Iraq, our military leaders no longer even counted the bodies of civilian dead. It was Pascal who said, "Men never do evil so completely and cheerfully as when they do it from a religious conviction." It's time to consider the Asian concept of karma, that what we put out into the world will come back to us. What will return to us from America's last 50 years of aggression?

This book is a cry of protest against man's violence to himself, and to the other inhabitants of the earth. Knowledge humanizes mankind, and reason inclines us to mildness, but prejudice eradicates every tender disposition and lead us again and again to war. If we do not reverse course and become what we once were as a nation – a gentle, generous, caring, thoughtful, and peaceful country – we will continue to up the ante and destroy ourselves and our planet with nuclear weapons, dirty bombs, poisoned water, poisoned food, and biochemical war and biological horror.

We have not yet atoned for the damage our bullets, our bombs, and our chemicals have wrought to Vietnam. I hope that we can someday help rid that beautiful country of toxins, unexploded ordnance, and land mines, and then atone to the Vietnamese people for all we have wrought. I hope we are not too proud, too arrogant, or too ignorant to utter the words, *Toi rat sin loi,* which in Vietnamese means, "I am sorry."

As a former Marine I was impressed on a trip to Tunisia by a sculptor's homage to a warrior killed in action 3,000 years ago – a warrior's torso molded in pure gold. Is there any better example of the honor and glory of the warrior killed in battle than to have his torso transformed into gold? Warriors once clashed in hand-to-hand combat, killing only enemy warriors from the other side. But technology has changed war. Powerful chemicals and explosives create mental and physical injuries that are more terrible and long-lasting than ever before. Most of the war dead and wounded are now old people, women, and children, too young, helpless, vulnerable, or frail to flee from the death that falls from the sky.

"War is no longer the battlefield but rather towns and cities populated by civilians with playgrounds full of children and market-places full of mothers," stated an important paper, "War and Children," published in 1998. Authors Michael C.B. Plunket and David P. Southall, of Child Advocacy International and the Academic Department of Pediatrics, North Staffordshire Hospital, United Kingdom note that as recently as World War I, only an estimated five to nineteen percent of all casualties were civilians. However, the percentage of civilian casualties is climbing. Civilian casualties in Vietnam were approximately sixty percent of the total, and in Iraq perhaps eighty percent. In some recent wars, civilians now account for ninety percent of fatalities, the two doctors estimate, and a significant percentage of the wounded are also children.

Children are protected by law against abuse by adults in most civilized countries, but no such protections are in place in wartime. An attempt is underway to spell out the human rights of children. The United States is the only major country which has not ratified the United Nations' Convention on the Rights of the Child, "recognizing that the child for full and harmonious development of his/her personality should grow up in a family environment, an atmosphere of happiness, love and understanding." During wartime, a child's right to this type of nurturing family environment is almost impossible to achieve, since many families are ripped apart in various ways by war.

From a public health point of view, very young children have suffered malnutrition after war has destroyed crops, or minefields laid in agricultural land. Children and adults weakened by the trauma of war have been prey to illnesses and epidemics in countries where doctors are scarce, or where health systems have been impoverished or destroyed. Medical programs to immunize children, disrupted by war, have placed whole generations of children at risk for epidemics of diseases which should and could have been eradicated.

Although children are too young to influence the political systems of their countries, children now bear much of the true cost of making aggressive war. The naive trust of an innocent child can be easily and horribly betrayed. In conflicts all over the globe, children have been conscripted into militias and exposed to many forms of violence and depravity. Children have been tortured to punish communities, to extract information, or even as entertainment.

Children suffer severe and sinister psychological effects that may make them more likely to engage in violence and other antisocial activity, perpetuating a cycle of brutality even after war's end. Children suffer post traumatic stress disorder. Children can experience guilt in a war-ravaged country, and even if they survive, anxiety and depressive disorders in children are common long after the war is gone.

In the past ten years, according to "War and Children," an estimated two million children have been killed in war zones. Another four million children have been permanently disabled. A million children have been orphaned. An estimated twelve million children have been displaced from the security of their homes, and one-third of these have spent time in camps for refugees or displaced persons. Some are still incarcerated in concentration camps, and some children have been tortured. How can we atone for the treatment of these innocent children?

What legacy did America leave, exiting Vietnam? Our mighty war machine did not atone for the destruction of those little children who could not run away from the napalm which rolled out of the sky like a tumbling barrel and burned completely through any flesh it touched. Our generals and military strategists did not atone to the families in the villages who could not dig a hole fast enough to avoid deadly artillery and machine gun fire, or bombs released from B-52s. We did not atone to the mama-san pregnant and laden with child, who could not avoid the soldiers who entered her hut and took her away to a relocation camp, or to those little boys and girls carrying around their little brothers and sisters who could not know where the next surgical strike package would fall from the sky.

At a cost of between $200-400 billion, the United States made war on a country about three times the size of Massachusetts. Altogether, the U.S. released over 15 million tons of bombs and ground munitions onto Vietnam, more than four times the tonnage used in all theaters of war during World War II, and the equivalent to 600 Hiroshima-type atom bombs. An estimated twenty percent of the explosives dropped or planted by the United States are still not yet detonated. Mine fields laid during the war remain. These unexploded time bombs can be set off at any time by a farmer's plow, or the footsteps of a curious child. To this day, according to various estimates, there are also between twenty-six and thirty-five million bomb craters remaining in Vietnam, craters which fill with water during the rainy season and spread malaria throughout the countryside.

Agent Orange, a powerful chemical defoliant, was released by the ton all over Vietnam. Our planes released fifteen million gallons of Agent Orange on Vietnam, which completely defoliated an area the size of Massachusetts. Agent Orange turned five million acres of lush forest and crop land into sticks and straw, denuding a verdant country of food for beautiful exotic animals such as elephants, tigers, and barking deer. Agent Orange affected US soldiers even briefly exposed to its horrible effects, and caused a great deal of lasting damage to the plants and people who must live with the effects and residue of Agent Orange in Vietnam.

For many South Vietnamese, the American War goes on and on. Many Vietnamese lucky enough to have survived the war live on despite horrible injuries, in broken or deformed bodies.

In our arrogant march to control the future, are we sowing the seeds of our own destruction? We have not atoned for what we did to the civilians of Vietnam. There has been no atonement for the well-publicized butchery of My Lai to the Vietnamese people. There has been no atonement for all the other My Lais, like the one I personally witnessed, whose victims lay buried in the ground. We have not atoned for the dead parents and disfigured children, for the grandparents missing arms and legs, or for the emotional trauma and suffering in families that is difficult to calculate and impossible to forget.

Doctors can assess the medical damage, but it takes the law to look long term, to look back and to look at the present, to commiserate and flagellate and to torture oneself to the truth. Unlike the miraculous short-term results changes can achieve, the law is a grinding, slow process. It takes years for the law to resolve particular issues. But by torturing oneself and one's ideas and contesting those ideas in the press and the courtroom, then somehow a strange phenomenon occurs. The truthfulness of the assertions is developed, mistakes and lies are discredited, and a plan can be laid out for the re-emergence of greatness – greatness not based on gross national product, but greatness based on moral values. Morality, ethical behavior, and fairness can all be legislated to some degree, but the possibilities really dwell deep within the individual human soul to take action on a broad and long-term scale.

As a doctor-lawyer, let me begin an attempt to calculate rational financial damages for what we have done in Vietnam. We can begin with an award of $1,000 for each of the 2.7-3.7 million civilians killed in Vietnam by the US. This is only one percent of the average wrongful death award of $100,000 awarded in the US in 1968, but even that small compensation totals about $30 billion. To that we would add another $30 billion, a figure the US State Department has tossed around for the destruction of Vietnamese villages and hamlets. If we calculate $1,000 for every one of the approximately thirty million bomb craters too big to fill, that's another $30 billion. What if we placed a ridiculously low price of just $50 per head for the estimated 700,000 water buffalo and other working farm animals our bombs destroyed, and then included all the other decimated wild animal populations of Vietnam? We are already looking at real money, and we have not calculated damages for the estimated 300,000 orphans, the 83,000 amputees, the 181,000 disabled, the 40,000 blind or deaf, and the 8,000 paraplegic South Vietnamese who lost the use of all four limbs because of the American War.

THE HUMAN COSTS OF WAR IN INDOCHINA, 1961-1975*

Between 1965 and 1973 approximately one out of thirty Indochinese was killed, one in twelve wounded, and one in five made a refugee. Here are the results of what the Vietnamese call the American War:

Deaths

2,284,000 Total War Dead

1,921,000 Vietnamese dead including:
   450,000 South Vietnamese civilians (1961-1975)
   40,000 South Vietnamese civilians Project Phoenix
   176,000 ARVN soldiers (1961-1972)
   900,000 NLF and NVA enemy soldiers (1961-1972)
   155,000 soldiers both sides (1973-1975)
   200,000 North Vietnamese civilians (1961-1975)

200,000 Cambodians, civilian and military
100,000 Laotians dead
58,151 American soldiers
5,000 US ally soldiers

Casualties

3,200,000 wounded Vietnamese, Cambodians, Laotians
14,305,000 refugees by the end of the war
   10,472,000 refugees in South Vietnam
    3,083,000 in Cambodia
      750,000 in Laos

In South Vietnam:
   300,000 orphans
   800,000 children who lost one or both parents
   83,000 amputees
   181,000 disabled
   40,000 blind or deaf
   8,000 paraplegic

In Cambodia:
   480,000 civilians killed and wounded
   260,000 orphans and half-orphans

In Laos:
   350,000 civilians killed and wounded

In North Vietnam:
   hundreds of thousands killed and wounded

For the United States:
    2,500,000 soldiers served in Indochina
    58,151 dead from the war
    303,616 wounded in Indochina
    13,171 soldiers 100 percent disabled
    55,000 former soldiers dead of suicide, addictions, accidents, etc
    500,000 soldiers attempted suicide since return home

PHYSICAL DESTRUCTION CAUSED BY WAR:
15,500,000 total tons of firepower used by US forces, including:
    7,800,000 tons of bombs dropped by the US on Indochina
    7,500 tons of ground munitions used by US forces
    200,000 tons of munitions fired by US naval forces from ships

12,000,000 tons of firepower used on South Vietnam alone
Comparison: U.S. used 6,000,000 tons of firepower in WW II
26,000,000 bomb craters in Indochina
21,000,000 bomb craters in South Vietnam alone
18,000,000 gallons of poisonous chemical herbicides sprayed over six million acres
of forest and croplands in South Vietnam
    1,200 square miles of South Vietnam leveled by US helicopters
1,000 square miles of South Vietnam leveled by incendiary and high explosives
150,000-300,000 tons of unexploded ordnance strewn about Indochina
700,000 fewer water buffalo, oxen, and cows in South Vietnam

FINANCIAL COSTS OF WAR TO THE U.S.
The U.S. spent approximately $168,000 to kill each "enemy" soldier. If veterans'
benefits, interest on the debt, and other indirect costs are included, the total cost of
the war has been estimated at between $350 - 900 billion. Here are the direct finan-
cial costs of the war:
$132.7 billion budgeted war costs 1965-1972
$28.5 billion military and economic aid to South Vietnam
$2.4 billion military and economic aid to Laos
$2.2 billion military and economic aid to Cambodia
$0.3 billion aid to French war effort
$2 billion cost of the war Fiscal Year 1975
$168.1 billion - total direct funding costs of war

* Statistics compiled by Richard W. Smith

The United States government gave an $80 million legal settlement to US veterans permanently damaged by Agent Orange, but our government has never appropriated one penny for the horrible damage Agent Orange has done to Vietnam. The people of Vietnam have had to live with the residual effects of Agent Orange sprayed on their fields and forests long after the war was over. What has been the cost to the ravaged Vietnamese countryside, which could have contained exotic plants which could have been the basis for some new life-saving drug, a countryside which has still not completely returned to normal? We doctors who treat veterans know that American soldiers exposed to Agent Orange suffer high rates of sterility, prostate cancer, lymphoma, leukemia, diabetes, and more – but what about the Vietnamese who suffer from the same diseases as a result of the American War? As one more concrete example, if we look only at the 300 deformed Vietnamese babies secondary to the carcinogenesis of Agent Orange, and add $10,000 apiece for each baby's lifetime medical care, that's another $3 million.

The financial damage we inflicted on the people, the animals, and the farms and forests of Vietnam during the war was tremendous. And we have not addressed the emotional damage to people who suffer and continue to suffer, or even the disfiguring wounds and amputations resulting from unexploded ordnance which remains in Vietnam. A just legal settlement could easily produce a financial atonement figure even greater than what it cost us to make the war in the first place.

We must admit that we did wrong, and that we should not have brought the Vietnam War. Instead of a holocaust we created but cannot face, we need a Marshall Plan approach to Vietnam. And the companies and individuals that President Eisenhower identified as the military-industrial complex, the companies which financially profited from the Vietnam war, should be made to foot the bill for a just financial atonement.

Dr. Hassan addresses Veterans of Foreign Wars,
Sacramento, California, in 2005.

CAUSE AND EFFECT

In medical school, we learned that there is always a cause and an effect. We call the cause the etiology, and we call the development of the disease the pathogenesis. What we doctors diagnose is the disease.

Man is an aggressive animal, and that etiology manifests in a pathogenesis called war. War can be diagnosed as government-sanctified killing of other human beings. The only means by which war can be stopped or contained to some degree is to deflect man's aggressive tendencies. Somehow, this aggressive human energy must be converted into civic or community duties, to the common good, or worthwhile activities on a broad scale. We can battle against disease, we can wage a war against ignorance, we can battle natural disasters and all the forms of pollution we have created before it destroys all the earth's beautiful and abundant plant and animal life. But we must change course.

Physicians are morally well-intended, but we doctors are often too short-sighted to get the big picture. There are just too many things that interfere with a physician's ability to reason through or accept a wider responsibility. Physicians want to act now. We want results now. If a person messes up one day, we want to answer to the mess-up the next day. Doctors have no time to look back or feel guilty about anything, because they are too busy being a hero each day by curing someone, fixing someone, making someone better, knocking out disease, developing vaccines against polio and AIDS – all the glorious and wonderful things we have done in medicine.

As physicians, when we treat epidemics, endemics, or individual illnesses, we must know the cause of the illness. If we don't know the cause of the illness, we can't cure it. We can't place a Band-Aid over a skin lesion of leprosy and expect it to heal. We must look at the modern new medicine that is now a cure for leprosy, but first we must know it is leprosy. Otherwise, the individual will spread the disease to everyone he touches and he will eventually die of the disease, losing first his fingers, then his hands, and then his toes, feet, and then his entire nose in a terrible death.

War is like leprosy; it contaminates all of us and takes our humanity away. The real enemies of the people of the world are bigotry, ignorance, natural disasters, and illness. We have the resources and talent to defeat these enemies, but we need men and women of goodwill who are willing to face these challenges.

As the astronauts sailed from the earth to the moon and looked back, they all suddenly realized we were from one world. As is well recognized in psychiatry, until this concept is deeply internalized, described so that the subconscious truly believes and truly feels the pain of the world, then we will have eternal conflict on our planet.

The danger facing America today is in our own moral corruption, in the arrogance and aggressive militarism that kills indiscriminately in the name of freedom. We will not win over the sympathy of the world if we continue to try to throw a little freedom here, a little there, and in the process kill hundreds of thousands of men, women, and children. It was the great Swiss psychiatrist Carl Jung who observed, "It is honor, reputation, and integrity that permits man to survive permeated by joy, but that cannot be taken from him, for if it is, it permits his very life to be taken."

AFTER 9/11

In the days after 9/11, I had occasion to reflect on Carl Jung's words when my own honor, reputation, and integrity – and even my patriotism – were questioned, probably because I was critical of our national policy, and I happen to be of Palestinian descent.

Shortly after September 11, an unfortunate cascade of events began when I was stopped by a California Highway Patrolman who made sarcastic and insulting remarks about my last name, and in a stream of profanity also called me a foreigner. When I indignantly asked for his badge number, the patrolman overreacted. He handcuffed me, put me in a choke hold, threw me to the ground, and fractured several of my ribs. When I was convicted of assaulting a police officer whose uniform was not even wrinkled, the verdict seemed patently unfair to me, so I appealed my conviction and this process took more than three years.

Next came an investigation by the California State Medical Board, who had been after me for years. After I had been asked to leave psychiatry during the Vietnam War, I had been asking the board for years to release my complete records and files to me, but they had given me various excuses and never released them. Then, one day in 2003, two investigators from the Medical Board came into my office, and asked me what religion I was.

"Well, what does that have to do with my complaints to the Medical Board?" I asked.

"Well, are you a Muslim or not?" one asked.

"What does that have to do with anything?" I asked.

"Okay," they said in effect. "Go see a psychiatrist. We are taking your license away for two months."

My license to practice medicine was suspended for two months, choking off my income and disrupting my relationship with my patients. I was ordered to have a psychiatric evaluation, and also tested for Alzheimer's disease, since the medical board thought this might have been the reason for the incident with the patrolman, and, if so, they could have pulled my license for medical reasons. The evaluations found me sane, with an IQ of 139, and doctors found me free of Alzheimer's. But this rather arbitrary suspension of my license to practice medicine disrupted my practice, and I was enraged by this action. In this process, my friends and colleagues were deposed. Judges and lawyers who are personal friends advised me to lay low and keep my mouth shut, but I am not inclined to remain silent about things I strongly believe are wrong.

A few years before, at great personal expense to myself, I had already won a legal battle against the California medical board, forcing them to disclose information in every doctor's file to the doctor involved. My case against the California Medical Board set a precedent, since it was decided by the California Supreme Court. Several other doctors wrote and thanked me for this action. When I was finally allowed to view my own file, in 1998, I found the medical board had accumulated a three-inch stack of information on me, including letters and memos placed in my file from doctors at Mendocino State Hospital and Mount Zion during the Vietnam war. These documents had lain in my file for thirty years, like so many career-killing racist grenades, and in retrospect I could see why my nomination to be president of the California Medical Association was withdrawn. Finally, I had found the documents that had been the source of rumors and harassment I'd been vaguely aware of for years. The medical board refused to remove the letter from Mendocino which claimed I identified too closely with underdogs, and other misfits, especially Arabs, from my file, because they claimed the letter was a reflection of a character defect. I filed another lawsuit against them, charging them with a conspiracy, and seeking to allow doctors to contest malicious and untruthful letters, and to have them removed from their files.

Then, in December 2004, two US Secret Service men came to visit me in my office and told me I was being investigated as a suspected terrorist. They said an anonymous informant had turned me in, and claimed I'd made three statements. First, that I had rich relatives in the Middle East, which is false since my relatives come to me for money. Second, that I might be related to Saddam Hussein. My father had told me I came from the line of Saladin, the twelfth-century Egyptian sultan and warrior who captured Jerusalem during the Crusades, and Saddam Hussein has a dubious claim to descent from that lineage, too. And third, I'd stated that President Bush would be sorry for the war he'd started in Iraq. The third statement attributed to me was true, although it is not now clear that President Bush will ever sincerely regret anything he has done.

As an American, I thought I had a right to freedom of speech, but the two Secret Service men standing in my office made me question if that was still true. They took my mug shot in my office, and had me sign for the release of my medical and psychiatric records, which I knew they could legally acquire under the Patriot Act. After I answered their questions, I was furious when they told me I'd be on lifetime surveillance. After all, I risked my life for this country as a US Marine and a doctor in Vietnam. I'd spent my life being a good patriotic citizen, working hard and paying taxes in this country. That these men would question my patriotism was infuriating to me.

In 2005, when I had exhausted the appeals for my assault case, I was given an electronic surveillance device and sentenced to confine my activities to home and my medical practice work for a few weeks.

I was strictly obeying the rules, but the electronic device misfired several times. I was called into the probation office, handcuffed, placed in a car in 125-degree heat for about twenty minutes, transferred to a crowded holding cell containing sixty people for eighteen hours and referred to as "Pig Shit Hassan." I was held for 15 days in jail before being allowed to explain that the surveillance device I was given had malfunctioned. When I finally had a hearing, the hearing judge listened to the facts and said, "Ridiculous. Let him out immediately."

As my Irish grandfather taught me to do, each time a roadblock has been put in my way, I learned how to get over it. Overcoming obstacles allowed me to develop a deeper sense of myself, and to recognize the dignity and humanity in every patient who came into my office. Sometimes I feel I have failed, that I haven't done enough for my patients, and I could have done more. Although I work hard and try to live an ethical life, sometimes I feel I will never be able to atone for all the horrible things I witnessed in Vietnam.

THE LEGACY OF WAR

In the past thirty-five years, I have ministered to old men and young boys who served their country in World War II, Korea, Vietnam, Panama, Grenada, and the two Gulf Wars. Some of these veterans have been horribly marked by their experiences. I find great compassion in most doctors, but I find the leadership in the medical societies and associations lacking in compassion, and lacking the courage and tenacity to speak out against evil. The California Medical Board and the California attorney general's office, allegedly the watchdogs of medicine in this state, are good examples of this because even when given eyewitness accounts of criminal behavior in Vietnam, and thirty-five years later in Guantanamo and Abu Ghraib, they did absolutely nothing. As a practical matter, we doctors can do more to assist the veterans who actually experienced the evil of war, and who suffer from exposure to its horror. As a profession, we physicians must do more in speaking out against the atrocities we have seen.

Every death or permanent injury of a soldier or a civilian is a tragedy, and a defeat for civilization. In Vietnam, I do not blame the eighteen to twenty-one-year-old American soldiers, who were just following orders in an environment where they were being shot at, wounded, and killed. Many of them were heroes. Many extraordinarily brave and trusting young men died and never had a chance to tell their stories about how rotten the war was. After the war, when Vietnam veterans came back and tried to tell their stories, they were ignored, locked up, denied benefits, put in cuckoo houses, and told they must be irrational. As happened to me, many veterans were told that the things they saw and did could not have occurred, because America would not allow things like that to happen. People didn't want to hear of these horrors. In my case, the massacre of babies and children I witnessed could not be deleted from my mind. What I saw disturbed me over many years because of my inability to rationalize a means to forget about it.

War is an ugly, inhuman thing. Too well I remember those cold American eyes looking at me that sultry morning in Quang Tri, Vietnam, a few days after the massacre of the children. Stepping out of the bunker into the morning light, an individual who was probably from the CIA put his thumb and forefinger about a half inch apart in front of my face and told me, "You came this close to being offed last night." How often do I think of that warning, and those murdered children, when I try to explain my feelings about the war, and the way it was conducted?

The atrocities against mankind have not stopped, and more and more, they directly involve doctors. When Senator John McCain introduced legislation to forbid torture by any American soldier, the administration sought an exemption for the CIA which Senator McCain rightly observed would have the effect of "legitimizing torture." Recent news reports from Afghanistan and Iraq have revealed that American military doctors and psychiatrists may have witnessed or even participated in the torture of detainees, and reported nothing. As a profession, where are our ethics, our compassion, our honor, and where is our courage? These news reports are a shameful and humiliating disgrace for a profession whose first tenent is, "Do no harm."

In a recent editorial, the editors of the prestigious British medical journal, *The Lancet*, recently reminded doctors that the World Medical Association has adopted a strong stance regarding doctors' participation in or acquiescence to torture, stating, "Doctors shall not countenance, condone or participate in torture or other forms of degrading procedures...in all situations, including armed conflict and civil strife." *The Lancet*'s editors added, "Health care workers should now break their silence." *The Lancet* sounded a call for doctors and others who had witnessed torture or other abuses in Abu Ghraib prison, Guantanamo Bay or elsewhere to step forward and give a full and accurate account of events.

It is possible that tensions springing from a half century of aggression all over the world, in Asia, Central America and the Mideast, rose to a sort of climax in the horror of 9/11, creating a reaction that is in effect a continuing cycle of the same. The chickens we throw out into the world keep coming home to roost.

A HOPE FOR PEACE

I have written this book from the heart and I have authorized its distribution so that everyone may understand that, although I am but a grain of sand upon the beach, there are millions of voices that speak out for humanity, love, and kindness, and that all the grains of sand make a beautiful beach.

There are times, after work, driving home to my farm outside Sacramento, when I marvel at my patients who never seem to give up on me, even when I'm tired and somewhat goofy, and occasionally upset. I marvel at how all this great universe works in such great harmony, generally speaking. I marvel at the human spirit that so often rises to the occasion, giving hope to all mankind. I marvel at the majesty of man and his creations to fight disease, poverty, and ignorance in all their forms. I marvel at the little guys who bear the burden of keeping America beautiful, the craftsmen, carpenters, cooks, ditch diggers and plumbers and the bigger-than-life guys, firefighters, policemen and rescue workers, always there putting their lives on the line, to separate good from evil.

Traditionally, Americans have been in favor of wars of liberation, or wars to promote democracy. After all, we were the New World's first democracy, and our power and influence is stronger than ever before in history. But those hysterical with aggression and conquest should be sobered by revelations of casual atrocities and revolted by heinous civilian massacres committed in the name of the United States. Lies about an attack in the Gulf of Tonkin carried our citizens into Vietnam, and lies about weapons of mass destruction carried us into Iraq. There is no doubt that the arrogant attitude of the United States towards Third World countries is carrying us into a perpetual cycle of aggressive war that has no end. If we cannot identify the etiology or cause of a disease, we cannot treat the pathogenesis or course of the disease, and we certainly cannot cure it.

Terrorism will gradually dissipate from the face of the earth when rich, powerful countries treat Third World countries and their leaders with true dignity and respect, and work with them to achieve their goals. Taking into account each country's beliefs and their history, we can help embed into their society doctors, lawyers, architects, agriculturalists, humanitarians of every stripe, and teachers who do not go to their country to make money but go there because Americans are paragons of instinctive nobility. American nobility is not that of an emperor or an admiral, but a broad democratic nobility that by its nature makes most of our citizens especially fond of doing good.

We are all one human race. There are times when the status quo must be challenged. I believe that wars of aggression are always wrong. The question is, why create more war, when the world is filled with so much majesty and nobility, and so many good causes?

"You bring me the deepest joy that can be felt by man ..." said the great French scientist Louis Pasteur in a speech on December 27, 1892. "The belief is that Science and Peace will triumph over Ignorance and War, that nations will unite, not to destroy, but to build, and that the future will belong to those who will have done most for suffering humanity."

If there is anything I have learned in my voyage through war and peace it is that the individual will triumph. The individual will triumph over the inhumanity of a government gone awry. I saw it in the hospitals of Vietnam, in the cheerful smiles of little boys and girls, hopping around on one leg. I saw it in the smile of a young boy's face, whose eye had been removed without adequate anesthesia and bandaged over at Quang Tri Hospital. I saw this in the eyes of grateful Vietnamese peasants as I tried to mend their wounds during the war, and I saw it again when I returned to Vietnam years later.

I have tried to live my life in a manner consistent with my own beliefs as a doctor, a lawyer, a veterinarian, and a former US Marine. I have done my best to speak out regarding the abuses I have witnessed. This book is a final attempt to set the record straight regarding the atrocities I saw in Vietnam, and to express my hopes for the country of my birth, which still has the potential to be truly great. It is disheartening to see brutal, inhuman behavior still continuing in the name of my country that I love so much, the country where I was born, and the country which has given so much to me. But something magnificently human is challenging man's ancient rites of conquest and enslavement. As long as we can envision a better and more humane future, and work to make it happen, there is hope for peace in the world.

21

Volunteer Doctors Remember Vietnam

*I*n 1998, I wrote an open letter to my fellow Volunteer Physicians for Viet Nam, requesting a favor. I asked for them to write of events in Vietnam that have remained in their minds over the years. As their responses indicate, many volunteer physicians saw instances of extraordinary courage, or extraordinary inhumanity to man. About two dozen doctors responded with the thoughtful, heartfelt letters which are included here in their entirety.

Bill Owen, MD
Bac Lieu and Quang Ngai, Vietnam

Bac Lieu, southeast part of Vietnam. There was no running water and pigs and sheep wandered through the empty wards. I saw 120 children in the first outpatient clinic I had. A mother came in and handed me a baby who died in my arms. A Vietnamese nurse's aide came to me and said, "*Bac Si*, hospital water not good, smell." I went with him to the food preparation building and they had fished a little boy out of the cistern which was the source of water for all cooking. The child was laid out on a slab and was covered with flies.

Once, I was called in the middle of the night to come and help Dr. Vinh with a C-section. The Army area was closed and I drove the Jeep around through the town. When I got there, the tiny baby was on the floor of the OR. I cleaned out his throat and got him to breathing. I drove home and met an enormous water buffalo standing in the middle of the street. I didn't bother him and took a different road!

I always went over to the hospital to make the rounds on Sunday. On Sunday a man came to me and asked if I would look at his wife who had a severe bloody diarrhea and looked terminal. The little technician came and took her blood type (A positive). I told her to take a pint from me and we gave it to the sick woman. The next day she was better and I think her husband took her home.

My second tour was in Quang Ngai. My ward was for the worst cases – wounded terribly. One was a pretty girl of about fifteen years of age with one leg partially shot off and the other leg in terrible shape as well. I told her she needed to have that one done too. She cried out and I wasn't very good either. The next morning she was gone. The family took her home in the night. She died at home a short time later. I had a small group of my Vietnamese help take me out to the airport to see me off, but my experience was *never to be forgotten.*

Joe Nettles, MD
Hue and Da Nang, Vietnam

I was the senior resident of orthopedic surgery at the Mayo Clinic at the time one of my mentors, Norm Hoover, had been instrumental in setting up the volunteer program. After the Tet offensive in January 1968, I persuaded my chief, Mark Coventry, and my super chief (my wife Sarah) to allow me to participate in the program.

I was initially assigned to Da Nang. After being there one night, a request for volunteers to be dropped into the old French University teaching hospital at Hue was issued. I volunteered along with three others: Grant Raitt from Montana, Ralf Young from California, and Howard Detwiler from Michigan.

At a French 1,000-bed teaching hospital and after Dien Bien Phu when the French left, the Vietnamese contracted with four German doctors to take over the teaching responsibilities along with the Vietnamese doctors. This compound had been overrun along with the ancient city of Hue by the NVA during the Tet offensive and they were not driven out until a few weeks before we arrived. The German doctors were found in shallow graves, having been mutilated and shot. The Vietnamese doctors had mostly fled. There were literally two to three patients per bed in this thousand-bed hospital. Included in this was a chronic leprosy wing.

The hospital was secured by day. Incoming mortar rounds came in several times at night. We were advised to sleep in the pediatric ward with our M-16s and hand grenades close by in case of a repeat overrun. Each morning at daybreak, new casualties from the B-52 bombings during the night would be lined up at the compound gate. It was all we could do to keep up with the acutely wounded. A professor from Alabama, the chief of surgery, once stated, "You will never be a surgeon until you have been a wartime surgeon." The horrific wounds were sometimes hard to describe and certainly harder to treat. I was busy from dawn to dusk each day and remember that when the weather got real hot one late afternoon I went across the road in front of the hospital and jumped into the Perfume River in my scrubs to cool off. I was swimming along quite refreshed until I hit a warm current and realized I was swimming through the effluent from the hospital sewage.

I feel my Vietnam experience meant more to me personally than perhaps any of the patients I treated, although hopefully I did do a service. I went over as a hawk, but came back a confirmed pacifist after witnessing the horror war causes to the innocent civilian population.

Navy corpsmen help a wounded woman into
Quang Tri Provincial Hospital.

Tom H. Mitchell, MD
Bac Lieu, Vietnam

The presence of so many cases of tuberculosis was shocking, as was the fact that we had little (usually none) medication for these people. The intensity of diarrheas and the resulting dehydration was appalling, especially in the children. You just did the best you could with what you had. One day I had five deaths on the pediatric ward, which was most depressing. With adequate supplies and earlier access to the patients, most could have been prevented.

When all is said and done, the most impressive thing about these three months to me was the Vietnamese people themselves. Their individual tolerance and acceptance of adversity and an amazing willingness to preserve was amazing. They had a resilience you rarely see here in the US. Returning home, I had a hard time accepting some of the poor-mouthing encountered in my practice.

Gilbert Lee, MD
Quang Ngai, Vietnam

I wrote home from Saigon, October 5, 1967:

Vietnamese language, a chopstick language and the words are bite-sized with sharp edges from which all the fat has been pared. Once joined in speech they rattle like old bones.

Vietnamese women are more than beautiful, they are lovely. They have long black hair, which sets off delicate features. Their flowing two-toned sheer gowns and graceful dignified movements endow them with an ephemeral air.

Much to be happy about but I must fly out to Quang Ngai, my permanent outpost as a volunteer physician.

At the hospital in Quang Ngai, 600 patients a day, no sewage disposal, a trickle of water, naked light bulbs. I was shocked by this temple of misery, a whirlpool of blood and pus. The lines of sick and wounded trailing in and streams of refugees flowing out.

By the end of my first week in Vietnam, I was convinced Vietnamese medicine was a different profession from the one I practiced in the US. When I arrived at the hospital, the nurses informed me a lot of cataract surgery and amputations were done, "but don't worry, the nurses do them here." I was assured I had other duties that would require more skill.

My own place in the scheme of things in Quang Ngai was brought home to me in an unpleasant way one day as I walked to the hospital. Two Viet Cong men on bicycles rode past me, one on either side, and seeing I was obviously dressed like a Yank, they turned around, came back, and both, simultaneously, slapped me hard on my cheeks. It was really not much of a beating, and of course, it could have been worse. In retrospect, I'd say it was more like a warning, a tacit gesture which I clearly understood at once. It meant they knew who I was (their spies were everywhere), they could get tough whenever they felt like it, and I had better watch what I did or said in this hostile land.

I understood the background for all this as well. The young Vietnamese people had all left their villages to join one army or the other, leaving at home the small and defenseless. The Vietnamese doctors had already left to lead their troops. There were no caretakers left to care for the residents but us foreigners. This we did gladly, without manpower and supplies. We were volunteers and there was no need to reinforce our role with violence or threats, although the gallows humor had it all the time that in Vietnam they did not sue you for malpractice – they shot you.

I noticed, not only were the illnesses different in Vietnam, but the patients were also different, especially in their reactions to pain and death. When things were going badly and the severely wounded were dying on the wards, it became very quiet. You could tell when death had boldly threatened. The patients became increasingly withdrawn, still and silent. It was if their behavior were a rehearsal for the rapidly approaching drama of isolation and aloneness. I witnessed the opposite of this earlier in Manila, the Philippines, during World War II, where when things went badly, the wards became filled with shrill cries and loud moaning, with constant agitation among patients and staff.

In traveling about from Saigon to the river delta, I saw the hospitals were all overcrowded. I also noted there was one building with empty wards. With some indignation I asked why they had an empty ward. One of the nurses took me aside and said the monsoon rains would soon be upon us. I demanded, "Okay, so it's going to rain. So much for the weather report." She replied, "*Mon cher doctor,* with the rain come the rats who scramble into the houses." I said, "So now we have rain and rat, what of it?" She said, "Well, with the rain and the rats we get the fleas who ride on the rats and carry the plague. First the field workers get it, then they give it to everyone else. Overnight, every bed in the wards will be full. You have only to look at the patients' groins and you will see the big swollen inguinal nodes, the buboes. In a way they are lucky, they last longer." I queried, "Longer than whom?" Her reply, "Longer than the ones without the buboes. They are the ones with the pneumonia, and they die right away. Of course, there are some who first get the buboes and then the bacteria and then the pneumonia without treatment. When the epidemic is well launched, well, they could last a week." Seventy-two hours after this conversation, the rains came. Two weeks later I saw plague complications, common in many parts of Vietnam, and neither I nor my textbooks knew anything about it. Plague patients were losing their legs. Again, I was patiently instructed on what went on in Vietnam. It seemed the plague organism would spread to the femoral arteries of the legs, fill up and block the blood flow to the arteries, and to save the patient, the lifeless limbs had to be amputated, thus adding new conscripts to the army of crutch-bearers already recruited from the survivors of the land mines. The treatment of choice was streptomycin, but this had to be given paternally, and where did Third-World countries find a ready supply of such medication?

I don't know who said it, but it's a truism that the only decent place to be in a war is on the battlefield. Everything that flows from this source is inhuman: the thirst, the pain, the hunger, the critical sensibilities which distinguish man as a human being.

North Vietnam artillery unit relaxing during
Vietnam War. Photo Mum Kiem

Lawrence A. Smookler, MD
Field Director, VPVN Program
Saigon, Vietnam

When I took the position in September 1967, I understood I would be responsible for the administration of the program in the field and represent the American Medical Association (AMA) throughout South Vietnam. My duties would include assigning volunteers, sight inspection, evaluations, indoctrinations, providing transportation and housing, security, maintaining good working relationships with the multiple government agencies, military, and all volunteer agencies involved in medical care in Vietnam. I would also be responsible for security, publicity, helping with recruitment, and administrative functions involved in the handling of the personnel immediately under me in Saigon.

I visited many of the VPVN doctors and encountered many problems, and did my best to work solutions to increase the morale of the volunteers and the civilian and military personnel with whom they were working.

The assignment of VPVN is made very difficult due to continuous changes in security and the requirements at the different sites. Assigning volunteers to specific areas has been complicated by the uncertainty of the future status of the US Public Health Service teams and the various 'Free World' teams such as the Swiss, Spanish, Iranians, and Filipinos. The primary function of our volunteer program is to complement the aforementioned teams so that when one team falters it continually influences all the requirements of the remaining physicians. The general policy regarding security was, as far as I'm concerned, to be the responsibility of the local US military commanding officer. I note a considerable percentage of volunteers were found to have no evaluation reports nor any end-of-tour reports to the Saigon file. (Ed. Note: Hopefully, the VPVN doctors who responded herein with their wonderful reflections for *A Failure to Atone* help to finally complete the long-lost record.)

A close relationship between the United States Agency for International Development (USAID) was maintained. Briefing by the State Department covering past, present, political, economic, and military problems in Vietnam was important.

From William J. Rogers, III, MD
Da Nang, Vietnam

A Vietnamese female, wounded the night before, was brought to the hospital in Da Nang with an abdominal wound sufficiently large to allow the bowel to be extruded. It was covered by a soup dish maintained by bandaging about the torso. On the operating table the soup dish was removed and a large amount of compromised bowel was seen lying on the abdomen. Surgery consisted of debridement and resection of the bowel, which she tolerated well. The point of amazement occurred on opening the bowel specimen after resection. Within the bowel was a large, active roundworm, a common condition in the Vietnamese.

In late afternoon, a nine-year-old girl was brought to the hospital with a high-velocity missile wound to the leg about three inches above the ankle. She was fortunate she could be brought into the hospital within hours after being wounded. Most woundings occur in the early evening, and because of the VC activity at night, they are not usually brought to the hospital until the next day. Travel at night is not safe, and to be moving about in the dark is to invite trouble. A brief survey revealed the foot and- ankle to be attached to the leg only by a soft tissue pedicel about one inch side at the posteromedial aspect. This soft tissue pedicel, however, contained the posterior neurovascular bundle and the foot was still alive, although compromised. If the blood supply could be kept intact, the foot could be saved. Immediate surgery consisted of wound debridement with removal of loose bony fragments and devitalized soft tissue, and stabilization of the tibia and fibula. Heavy intra-medullary Steinman pins were placed. About three inches of bone was missing. By stabilizing the fracture and shortening the leg, fairly adequate skin for later closure was made available. The inevitable plaster cast completed the salvage. Amputation could have been done in minutes, but was avoided in this instance. That warm feeling crept over me because I felt I had been able to prevent this one amputation from happening.

As nearly as I can tell, there are many reasons for serving as a volunteer physician in Vietnam. In talking with American volunteers, I found the reasons for their being there could not be easily verbalized, but all said it was something they wanted to do, and maybe had to do, without being able to say why. These people are different. Their motivation is not quelled by riding the latest model luxury car, or by getting a hard-bargained-for salary raise, or gaining the position of no longer having to take a night call, or a thousand and one things that sometimes seem to be the ultimate goal for physicians.

Ferryboat loaded with Vietnamese slowly crosses Perfume River. When a bridge was destroyed in the war, some of these heavily overcrowded ferryboats sank, resulting in additional loss of life.

John McBratney, MD
Quy Nhon and Phang Rang, Vietnam

I was in Quy Nhon at the Catholic hospital in 1966. My room was right next to the delivery room and I didn't realize it for the first three weeks. And I'm not deaf either! Fifty milligrams of Demerol for nulliparous ladies and nothing for the rest. What a cultural difference.

At Phan Rang Bay the situation was very provincial. Lots of typhoid – perforations, lots of plague, lots of TB, and no medications to speak of. I would do my own spinals, and then I would scrub and do my own surgeries. A real eye-opener for a city boy. Lovely people and I always marveled at their ability to be clean, dressed, attractive, and wonderfully slender. Young people emerging each day from what appeared to be the most primitive conditions, dirt floors and all, with bright smiles and beautiful attire.

Victor S. Falk, MD
Vinh Binh, Vietnam

During our briefing in Saigon, we were told there were three reasons for our being there. The first was psychological impact, both on the Vietnamese, and the home front. The second was to teach and train the Vietnamese in the provincial hospitals to which we were assigned. Perhaps some of our methods and practices could rub off on the observers. The third was immediate medical care. The last proved to be the most important and consumed our time.

A small houseboat moves upriver in Vietnam

I was assigned to Vinh Binh in the Mekong Delta. In the hospital, which was built 70 years earlier by the French, aside from a small surgical suite, few changes had occurred. As a World War II surgeon I thought I had seen it all, but in one month in Vietnam I encountered more casualties than I had in all my service in World War II. Those ranged in age from breast-feeding infants of one year with a hand blown off to a 96-year-old woman who had sustained a bullet wound of the scalp. The wounds resulted from gunshots, grenades, mines, boobytraps, and air strikes. Mangling injuries of the hands and feet resulting in amputations were all too common. Compound fractures of the femur were frequently encountered and treated with skeletal traction. Surgery was usually kept to a minimum because of the extreme prevalence of infection. One of the most pathetic situations was a ten-year-old girl with four-quarter amputation because her shoulder had been shot away.

Several perineal injuries resulted from mine explosions with the loss of extensive tissue. These were initially treated by colostomy, and it is a matter of conjecture as to what the ultimate treatment would have been or where it would have been carried out. Countless gunshot wounds of the abdomen were explored, and perforations were encountered in the liver, spleen, stomach, small and large intestines, uterus, tubes, and ovaries. In exploring the bellies of those wounded, quite often intestinal parasites would be found wandering around the abdomen. Chest wounds were common, most treated with simple disposable tube and Heimlich valve. The response to this type of treatment and drainage was often dramatic. Pinch grafts proved satisfactory for skin grafting. Operation times were generally rapid because of the absence of adipose (good old American fat) tissue. Cesarean sections were carried out quite frequently because so many women were tiny and also because so many developed complications in grand multiparity.

Quite frequently, patients had been subjected to Chinese or Cambodian medicine before seeing the American doctors, most consisting of large suction cups over the affected areas with a lot of needles under the skin. A caustic paste used by the Cambodians was sometimes applied to the forehead if a person had a headache. One could quite often spot the illness by looking at the wounds the doctors had created.

I found the people warm, friendly, and appreciative. I became very attached to them. My experience was rewarding and gratifying and it's simply one I would not have missed.

Leonard M. Pickering, MD
Rach Gia and Hue, Vietnam

One of the striking stories I remember from Vietnam was that on a Monday morning when another American orthopedic specialist and I were reprimanding one of our Vietnamese technicians because he did not come in the Sunday before to do an enucleation of an eye. He was the individual who did all the enucleations for eye injuries on the Vietnamese people we were caring for. At the end of my reprimand I said to him, "After all, you were on call and you should have responded." He simply looked at me and said very quietly, "Doctor, I have been on call for fifteen years." He took the wind out of my sails and I walked away sheepishly.

My original assignment was Rach Gia in 1968 and a second tour to Hue in 1972. I certainly agree as you stated in your letter, it was a "very unusual experience." This is a poem I wrote regarding one of the fellow volunteers. We were sitting together on a hotel veranda in Saigon during my first tour.

He was a skinny ... bespectacled ... physician
who fell in love ... with a Saigon street walker ...
In his early forties ... enthusiastic ... tickled ...
His excitement was pervasive ...
The air around him ... was impregnated ... with the fragrance ...
Of love ...

He confides to me ...
Though married many years ...
It is the first time ... he has felt warmth from a woman ...

I salute his elation ...
For I know unhappiness awaits him ...
One his age cannot stand the onslaught of initial love ...
Only youth can bear its burden ...
Only the young ... can heal that broad wound ... inflicted gently ...
Yet unwillingly ... upon one's soul

William P. Levonian, MD
Nha Trang, Vietnam

Arrived alone and a little scared in Nha Trang. No one at the airport to meet me. Not sure I even got off the plane in the right town. No one around who spoke English, having no idea which way to town. Hitched ride with suitcase in hand to Provincial Hospital, having no idea who was VC or otherwise. The hospital thought I was to arrive the next day.

First day doing a cut-down on a child with dehydration of cholera. Only one source of light being the fading outdoor light of dusk since the power was off, with flies from the open windows landing on my incision and no water for cleansing.

A lot of plague patients came to me, extremely ill. The thrill of rapid recovery with treatment. The pride of riding a motorbike to town and having little kids, who used to be my patients, call out *Bac Si My* (American doctor) as I would pass by.

I will never be quite sure why I volunteered. The State Department Agency for International Development planned to help civilians in Vietnam. I just thought it was the right thing to do. I was unsure if I had the right to risk sacrificing the happiness and future well-being of my entire family as I waved goodbye through the airplane window. My wife and kids standing there waving goodbye gave me good reason to question my judgment. Why go? I served my time in World War II.

Well, about a week and a half of my tour into Nha Trang, a cholera epidemic broke out and all bedlam broke loose. Families laid their sick ones all over the floors of the wards, into the hallways and corridors or whatever. The hospital generator was out, as was often the case. No lights, no running water. The water pump was dependent on the power. There was vomit and diarrhea all over the cots and the floor. The hospital windows were devoid of screens and outside dust and flies everywhere. I was writing medication, intravenous fluid, and electrolyte orders as rapidly as I could in French. In the midst of all this crisis, I again pondered how it was that I got into this chaotic foreign world. I had been sitting in my peaceful little medical office in beautiful Santa Cruz, California, without a care in the world. I was horrified to find, the next day, the IV fluids were depleted and would soon be exhausted. Without IV many, many would die. By courier pouch of the US government, I sent word to Saigon of my crisis in Nha Trang, wondering if anyone would ever get the message or if they would even care. I could not believe the miracle. By the next morning, the U.S. military flew an entire cargo plane of IV fluids up to us to save the day for me and my patients.

Only one child died in this cholera-related tragedy. By the end of the epidemic, it was heating up on the nearby battlefields. In that emergency, I was asked to be evacuated, but I told them I had work to do and I would catch up with them later on my motorbike. The isolation I felt after lingering on was overwhelming. I got the last patients cleared away. Before I fully appreciated the aloneness of being the only remaining American on the compound, I then realized I had no idea where the evacuation center was located, what roads were blockaded and how to get out. There was no one to ask. Up to this time, I had no real anxieties about my safety. I had been treating civilians from both sides of the conflict including VC prisoners with no questions asked.

It chokes me up when I think of what our military did that day when they sent out the desperately needed IV fluids for the civilians of Nha Trang. It was truly an answer to prayer. The shameful My Lai behavior had to be the exception.

*Certificate of Appreciation given Dr. Hassan and other VPVN
doctors for service at Quang Tri Hospital by Ministry of Health
in the Republic of South Vietnam.*

Richard F. Harper, MD
Moc Hoa, Vietnam

I served in Moc Hoa, a small town 50 km west of Saigon in the Plain of
Reeds on the Cambodian border in late 1966. I did surgery in the
small hospital and was quite busy with wounds, infections, and other
surgical emergencies.

I have trouble remembering any events of extraordinary
courage, but have no shortage of examples of man's inhumanity to man.
After one firefight near our town, the VC cut off the arms of a small girl
(about two) and I had the job of closing the amputations. She was alive
when I left there, but I wonder how she could live with no arms.

I was brought a young woman who had been shot in the
perineum after being raped - she died shortly after she arrived.

I doubt if you would want any of my stories since they are so
depressing. I remember the crowded orphanages and the intense
suffering of the people - but I also saw the spirit of the people who were
determined to survive and try to keep their dignity.

Frank Van Orden, MD
Moc Hoa, Vietnam

I was present during the Tet offensive of 1968 at Moc Hoa, only 3.5 miles from the Cambodian border, near Parrot's Beak (named because of its shape).

The security in the town was as far as the eye could see on the Plain of Reeds; that is, considerable distance during the day but nil at night. Viet Cong forays drew great hails of fire, flares, and spooky, the US plane that poured bullets into an area six inches apart. The people of this beautiful area were considered to be thirty percent VC. The women were beautiful and graceful, the children exquisite. The suffering of the ill and wounded was borne, generally with quiet dignity. One eighty-five-year-old man with a gunshot wound to his mid-tibia walked fifteen miles to us for treatment. Ward rounds were difficult due to the language barrier and the relative lack of equipment and laboratory facilities. No x-rays, no contrast studies. The wounded came in waves, corresponding to attacks from either side. We did "meatball surgery," with a circulating nurse turning the pages of a surgery textbook. We opened abdomens, but sent head and chest wounds to Can Tho.

Getting the Vietnamese to give blood was tough. I gave blood once during my stay, as did many Americans. In desperation, we aspirated blood from a chest cavity and reinfused it into the patient with good results.

Physicians, including myself, had a high degree of confidence in the enlisted men in the US Army's MILPHAP. These men had been trained as corpsmen, etc. They attended minor, and some major, problems.

The attitude of the non-medical US military personnel toward the Vietnamese was generally appalling. The "slopes" were regarded as subhuman beings put in the way of competent Americans trying to do their jobs. When a VC attack loomed, U.S. military were pulled out of nearby villages where their presence had made the villages a target. The VC came in, killed the Vietnamese who had collaborated with the Americans, and left upon the Americans return. Once in my presence, U.S. medics expressed sympathy for the Vietnamese civilians who had been shot up. An American officer nearby replied wryly and with apparent sincerity, "Civilians are expendable."

Thomas Felix Oram, MD
My Tho and Da Nang, Vietnam

I was born in the heart of London, and my father was a medical officer in the Royal Army Medical Corps. The Second Battalion Coldstream Guards are my godparents.

After Cambridge Medical School, I went to Malaysia as a medical officer serving for five years. I returned to England to be told that there are 5,000 too many doctors, and that gave me a chance to escape to the USA. In 1967 I got an invitation to go to Vietnam, first at the old French Hospital at My Tho and later at Da Nang.

The medicine was similar to that which I had practiced in Malaysia. Malaria, pneumonia, typhoid, gastroenteritis. Most of the surgeons were the least experienced, especially in dealing with bullet wounds. We had a great many abdominal wounds.

Excerpt from my diary: "*Another day at Da Nang. Yesterday was classed as a heavy-casualty load. I understand we got one load of war casualties from an outlying area, wounded the day before, and also a group who had been injured when a bus went off the road. One died of brain damage on the table and several had severe scalp lacerations. A hundred more artillery rounds heard with large numbers of planes bombing and strafing nearby. It is quite dark now and maybe they are just trying to keep the VC honest. The MACV advisor stated we needed a million or more troops in the country to accomplish very much. I know the Marines around Da Nang and I-Corps are here in large numbers and have been taking severe casualties of late. This past week, they were reportedly double the number killed or wounded as the week before, over 1,700. It gives pause. Paul Meyer, MD, evidently a local advisor, stated, 'We are now taking a new stance. If the local population are not with you, they are to be treated as though they are against you.'*"

I went to Vietnam somewhat skeptical as to what we (the US) were doing in Vietnam. I came away convinced we had made the wrong move. I felt the following:

1. The US in its determination to put down Communism would back ANY anti-Communist regime anywhere.

2. The US decided to back a series of governments in Vietnam which were corrupt and had NO following among the vast majority of Vietnamese in general.

3. In backing the South Vietnamese Army, it was an army with little backbone and little well-articulated plan for fighting the Viet Cong.

4. Advisors had been replaced by an ever-increasing number of American troops with an ever-increasing number of weapons and air power – with an ever-decreasing clear directive of what was to be done.

5. Fighting a war with a hand behind the back. The air power could have almost wiped out North Vietnam from the map, but North Vietnam was off limits.

6. Most importantly – it should have been clear that the Vietnamese people neither respected nor feared the Viet Cong far more than they respected or feared their own forces.

7. The South Vietnamese people showed no hate of Communism.

8. The amount of sheer corruption that Americans were involved in probably will never be known. There were Americans who wished that the war would continue; otherwise, some of their sources of money would dry up.

9. 50,000 American lives were lost in a war that was ignominiously lost for no clear cause.

10. Many South Vietnamese almost looked on America as another colonial power only interested in their own ideas.

William Shaw, MD
Nha Trang, Vietnam

Dr. Shaw's son, Alvin Shaw, contributed the following information from his father. He said his father went to Vietnam in 1965 with the first team of volunteer physicians under Project Vietnam. Dr. William Shaw died June 22, 1973, at the age of eighty, after receiving many honors as a family physician and military surgeon. Alvin Shaw said his father had this to say about his service in Vietnam:

"President Johnson requested help from the medical profession of the US in caring for civilians in Vietnam where doctors are in radically short supply. Physicians from Australia, New Zealand, Philippines, Korea, Italy, and Iran were already present. Most of these teams functioned as surgical teams. In a country with seventeen million people, there were only seven hundred licensed Vietnamese physicians, five hundred of whom were serving in the armed forces. We worked with Vietnamese medical personnel and the various visiting surgical teams at those hospitals. The supply of civilian physicians rapidly diminished as the war accelerated. The first five family physicians were assigned to provincial hospitals in Nha Trang, Qui Nhon, Bien Hoa, and Da Nang. There was no available method for doctors to maintain contact with each other or compare problems. We were given a list of ten leading causes of illness and death including malaria, meningitis, typhoid fever, beri-beri, dysentery, diphtheria, influenza, trachoma, tuberculosis, whooping cough, amebiasis, pneumonia, measles, plus high early infancy risk.

Vietnam has one physician per 25,000 persons concentrated in the cities. In the rural areas, it is closer to one per 100,000. Compared to the US ratio of one to 700, Japan's ratio of one to 920. It is felt the ratio in Vietnam is one and one-half per thousand people. The US has a ratio of one to nine persons. Japan has a one-to-five person ratio.

In one month in my hospital, diseases included hepatitis, tonsilitis, diphtheria, Ascaris, leprosy, encephalitis, bubonic plague, myopathy, dysentery, malnutrition, cholera, and worms. On the survey of my surgical ward of thirty, thirteen of the group were listed as battle casualties. Generally fifty percent of our patients were battle casualties, but many times the number of casualties we saw died before being admitted to the hospital. In one instance, four out of six injured civilians died before surgery could be done. We were trying to improve our activities related to malaria control and eradication. The scope of this program and the challenge it faced can only be understood if one looks at the problems in the villages and among the vast rural population which includes the Montagnard hill tribes, who speak another language, the 800,000 refugees from North Vietnam, and the ever-present guerillas. Routine immunization has largely been neglected because of the more pressing needs of medical care.

The reaction of the patients, their families, and friends to American assistance is extremely gratifying. Doctors of Project Vietnam have a healthy regard for the citizens of that country and a real sympathy for the magnitude of their health problems."

Marvin H. Lottman, MD
Go Cong, Vietnam

September 18, 1966: Stayed in one of the finest hotels I've ever seen, the Peninsula Hotel, Hong Kong. This will be the calm before the storm as in the morning depart for Saigon and then to Go Cong on the Mekong delta where there is a medical team from Spain in need of a surgeon. I have been assigned because I speak some Spanish.

Now begins probably the most depressing point in my entire medical career. The only instruments available are old, rusty, and poorly sterilized. What there is available is for abdominal surgery along with some GU and rectal instruments. There are no orthopedic tools at all. There is no traction available. Little or no suture is present and what's there is #3 Linen. The only antibiotics available were those I brought with me. The x-ray department consists of a 15 milli-amp machine. The x-ray film is American but the cassettes are French, so because of the difference in measurement, no x-rays. There is no ventilation in the wards, no IV solution, no blood bank, no hygiene – the more I look, the more problems become apparent. It will probably get worse as I learn more about it.

Most medicine in Vietnam is practiced using the five senses only. It is amazing how dependent you become upon pulse, "a horse and buggy technique." It would pay to be a veterinarian.

More depression mounts in our decrepit, unsanitary hospital surroundings. The babies are constantly dying on the wards from pneumonia primarily because of the lack of any oxygen and/or respirator or IV fluids without antibiotics. I spend time reading reprints on tropical and infectious diseases and helping translate parts to the Spanish teams.

The sad thing is that the Vietnamese people here do their best. It's just that they are so used to working with garbage and doing things the wrong way for so long that they've just learned to put up with it.

I love the people here. They are all very warm, grateful, and friendly. The hierarchies in the system are the things to be condemned.

Stanley M. Garstka, MD
Nha Trang and Ban Ma Thout, Vietnam

Perspective from June 24, 1968, and included in the *US Congressional Record:*

"Although the Vietnamese appreciate our medical help, they are not rating our medical teams as number one. They say we are sending very good and very bad doctors to Vietnam; and they resent being replaced by American medical teams instead of being helped. The Vietnamese are observing us as much as we are observing them, and they are making conclusions about us as much as we are about them. They resent being exposed to young American doctors just after internship, insecure but aggressive and arrogant. They also resent when a capable American surgeon is doing a radical surgery, like a radical neck or total pelvic exoneration, in a provincial hospital where there is no setup for an appropriate post-operative care. These patients then die because of poor post-op care. They resent the impulsive and uncoordinated surgical activities in civilian hospitals by various American and military doctors, done ad hoc without planned action and with no lasting benefit to the patients. This applies, particularly, to orthopedic, neurosurgical, and urological cases where continuous supervision is mandatory in the post-operative care.

"There is an urgent need to recognize we have failed, dismally, in Vietnam, not because we lacked capability or motivation, but because the department of state and its agencies have been instrumental to create confusion, corruption, and frustration among the Vietnamese and Americans alike. This is the basic cause of our bankruptcy in Vietnam.

"We have failed to eradicate, through a compulsory nationwide vaccination program, diphtheria, polio, smallpox, pertussis, and tetanus. We have failed to diminish the incidence of venereal disease, cholera, typhoid, paratyphoid, malaria, plague, meliodosis, and intestinal infestations.

"Since war casualties account for sixty to seventy percent of major surgical procedure, thoraco-abdominal injuries predominating, without exception all patients with intra-abdominal injuries were offered the benefit of operative surgical treatment. None were denied based solely on the seriousness of the injury. The magnitude and seriousness of injury secondary to missile would depend, primarily, upon the site of injury and upon velocity of the missile. In comparing the severity of liver injury, alone, with other organs seen during this time, and with those cared for in civilian life in both large charity and private hospitals, it is apparent that for the most part the severity of injuries seen during this time exceeded those encountered in civilian practice. The high mortality rate post-missile wound and surgical intervention are not related to surgery, but to inadequate follow-up care."

Three Montagnard children, Vietnam, 1999.

J. Clyde Ralph, MD
Nha Trang, Vietnam

Before I left for Vietnam in 1968, I felt our involvement there was a blunder, not only morally, but politically, militarily, and economically as well. I thought this country's best course would be immediate withdrawal. When I left Vietnam I felt the same way, but with one exception. I felt we should win the war as quickly as possible.

I was quite unprepared for the beauty of Nha Trang. It had been painted as a town of 40,000 inhabitants of whom fifty percent were deemed sympathetic to the occupying armies (US, Korean, ARVN) and the other fifty percent loyal to the VC. My estimate was that ten percent were loyal to each side and the remaining eighty percent were indifferent. Both sides were supposed to use the area as a rest and recreation center, so that relative quiet encompassed the town even though daily bombing and shelling went on in the hills surrounding the town some fifteen miles distant – a not unusual situation in the war that envelops Vietnam. The semi-tropical town is neatly circumscribed by lush rice paddies and tree-covered mountains on one side and the warm blue South China Sea on the other side. Far different from the jungle-centered thatched hut in which I expected to be practicing. The borders of the hospital have red splotches up and down them, not from blood as was a first impression, but from the expectorations of the people (the chewers!). Almost all the older people seemed to chew betel nuts. These are narcotic-type nuts that help people get through the misery of the day. Dinginess, drabness, grayness, and dirtiness intensify as you enter the hospital. The halls were poorly lighted and also the wards. All rooms have high windows, screened and forever open to admit whatever breeze and light are available, both needed and welcomed. Some of the wealthier patients bring in rubber mattresses to replace the bamboo mats. Others string small hammocks between the head-rails to put their small infants in. Buddhists frequently set up altars on the small bed-stands which separate each one from its neighbor, burning incense and creating much smoke. Precooked food is brought to the midway landing and served from a warm hibachi-type stove where all patients flock at serving time, bowls in hand, to get their rice and a few small fish on top. There was always plenty of fruit around, bananas, apples, oranges, and more. These are not a badly nourished people. Even the scraggliest have good hemoglobin and tissue turgor, the exception being those with underlying disease (tuberculosis, worms, malaria, etc.). This is a hospital of many odors. A constant fight goes on to prevent the foul ones from taking complete mastery. Feces and urine are deposited freely, anywhere. They seem to live among it, and with it, free of any negative attitudes. It is as it is, and why fuss about waste, ashes, and orange peels they leave behind, under and alongside the beds, in the halls and certainly in every dark corner. Generally their skin rebels with the most awful rashes, yet they look at soap as something that will remove the old familiar and protective cover. There are those who do manage to keep their infants, the bed, bed area and themselves spotlessly clean. How they do this, under the circumstances, is beyond me since I could not be as clean as they are under those circumstances.

Still, in spite of their sanitary problems, I love these people. They seem genuinely suited to life, happy-go-lucky in a life situation, which, on the surface, would seem to offer little to be happy about. I contrast them with the stiff and overly rigid Guatemalan Indians we worked with. Those youngsters did not even seem free to swing entirely loose. Not so these kids. They run around with their bottom halves naked, squat when they need to no matter where, and keep impish and genuinely happy smiles almost always. Their dark eyes sparkle with a kind of keen awareness of the good of just being alive. Adulthood seems to change this quickly. They become more reserved and less spontaneous, more suspicious and less sure of the goodness of life, but isn't that true of all people? We all start out innocent, and life does its best to take this away from us. We all end up with a certain amount of corruption and, sadly, that loss of innocence.

The diseases and tropical medicine book clearly states that strict isolation of the plague patient, in a separate insect-proof room, is essential. I have four cases of plague in a big open ward, side-by-side with typhoid cholera, tuberculosis, meningitis, septicemia, and various assortments of pneumonia, enteritis, and tetanus.

Not infrequently, a mother arrives with her dead infant in her arms (still warm, but dead). Once I put my stethoscope on the chest when the heart stopped beating. We went through all these heroic measures of external cardiac compression, intra-cardiac adrenalin, Coramine, and immediate IV with plasma extender (even our carefully hoarded oxygen). For a while it looked like we might pull it off. Three hours later he died for keeps. Grief comes hard when you've put your all into it. You have to keep reminding yourself, it isn't the US. Don't expect stateside performance. Still you know it could be better than it is.

I leave the hospital at the end of the day and see a rice farmer plowing his paddy with oxen-drawn wooden plow – two small boys pumping water with a primitive device, a bucket suspended between two ropes. As the boys fall back away from each other, the full bucket is pulled up and emptied. As they relax their pull, it falls back for refilling. Crude, primitive, but pretty damned efficient. Hard to feel any emotion except wonder at it all. Wonder at the bright happy smiles of the Vietnamese children, wonder at the beautiful poise and dignity of their women. Wonder at the senselessness of this war that surrounds them and adds to the painfulness of their lives. Wonder at the inhumanity of man to man and the lopsided unfairness of the distribution of life's wealth and abundance. But does it really matter? These people have a reality in their lives that keeps them happy. I wonder if we can improve on that.

Paul Spray, MD
Da Nang and Can Tho, Vietnam
Volunteer doctor Da Nang, 1967, and Can Tho, 1972.

Orthopedic surgery in civilian provincial hospitals is almost entirely traumatic surgery. At least in Can Tho. Its provincial hospital is the largest in the region, with about 500 patients. Most fractures, simple or compound, were treated with casts and traction in the civilian hospital. The military hospital, better equipped, did more open reductions. Amputations were still so common that they were being done mostly by medical student interns.

There were many traumatic aneurism and peripheral nerve injuries and, of course, a lot of traumatic osteomyelitis. There were some flies, gnats, and mosquitoes in the operating room, but they were less present than in other hospitals. Leprosy, in Vietnam, was treated in separate hospitals.

Some of the doctors who helped us came through the Medico-Care Program which was developed by Tom Dooley, MD, in Quang Ngai in the 1950s. After the fall of Dien Bien Phu in 1954, Dooley was assigned to help transfer Vietnamese families (mostly Catholics) from the North to the South, rather than live under the Communist regime that had defeated the French.

Another organization, Project Hope, was started in the 1950s by William Walsh, MD, of Washington, DC. This humanitarian group recruited medical volunteers to serve aboard the former World War II hospital ship USS *Hope*. This particular ship, along with the USS *Sanctuary*, stood off the coast of South Vietnam during most of the Vietnam War to take care of complex surgeries and acutely ill Americans with difficult-to-diagnose, difficult-to-treat diseases.

This is an excerpt from a presentation I made to the annual meeting of the Tennessee Orthopedic Association meeting in Memphis, April 1973, that concludes with comments about Vietnamese traditional medicine:

"There has been a lot of discussion in the journals and newspapers in the last year or two about the use of acupuncture. Another traditional system used in Vietnam, especially for backache, is "cupping." I am assured, by both Vietnamese and American patients, that this is effective. In view of the lack of success in treating certain backache patients with the methods currently in use in our country, perhaps we should add this to our armamentarium. The cups, made of either glass or bamboo, are heated and then applied to the skin. As they cool, a vacuum forms inside the cup, which draws up the skin and subcutaneous tissue. The rationale may be as obscure as that of acupuncture, but anyway, it seems to help."

David F. Goldstone, MD
Quang Tri and Quy Nhon, Vietnam

The Vietnam period between February and August 1972 indoctrinated me from a physician green behind the ears into a physician more aware of world suffering and misfortune.

Rather than highlight a roasted shrimp evening, bathing in the South China Sea, an offshore barbeque, and off-hour interludes traversing Vietnam, I would most emphasize the patients that I remember. Perhaps the most notable is that child of eight who died of respiratory arrest and the mother looking at me with solace. Perhaps the girl with bubonic plague that became well. Perhaps the leper colony congregating in isolation removed from normality. Perhaps the nuns serving graciously their time in the sun with those less fortunate souls. Perhaps it was the time in Saigon that I tested Vietnam physically with food, mentally with the people, and emotionally with their plight. Perhaps is the only word to define an unnecessary sojourn assisting the necessities of my raw and untested training. Compassion and fortitude were then ill-defined in my psyche. Understanding political game-playing was not a conscious reality.

My conclusion is that the round eye and the slanted eye are no different than the window upon which the soul shines forth. Had the round eye not implanted himself upon this tarnished soil, the slanted eye might have learned far more about defending his own soil than the round eye learned in defending someone else's soil. Only in absentia thirty years after the fact may we reflect upon their lifestyle before the fact. That can be said about any human intervention upon any soil other than our own. A reflection upon the past is seen only in the mirror of our own existence. The mirror of this other existence is a 180-degree rotation of consciousness. Perhaps the reflection should be reversed.

When the rain began to cease and the heat began
to swelter
And the smell of one's remains began to tell
When we shouldered our own decision and
blocked it from the past
And saw our lives unfolding
in a form of hell
When we felt a lack of standing
may have crowded the next one out
From biding time from life's entombment

in doing less than what we shout
Then, it was time from that beginning to start again

Carnes Weeks, MD
Phan Rang, Vietnam

June through August 1967, I was involved in a very busy rural practice. I was 43 and thinking of having a midlife crisis. I had it by going to Vietnam as a volunteer for two months. My patients did not seem to object, as I would be doing needed work for a medically under-served population. I ended up in Phan Rang, South Vietnam, with a population of about 50,000.

There were no doctors around. They were serving with the armed forces. The need was great. A lot of us went, including some freshly minted US physicians to help mentor and exercise reason in dispensing state-of-the-art U.S. medicine in 1967. We had some of the basics, including even an EKG machine, but since the Vietnamese rarely have heart disease it was never used.

The first day was my hardest. I suffered acute gastroenteritis, made worse by the smell of the hospital population, a line of patients stretching for three blocks (many traveling all night by foot and ox cart). On this day I was very happy and thankful for the local custom of siesta during the hot afternoon. I had a chance to lie down for a couple of hours and get rehydrated.

In the next month, we became quite adept at triaging, improvising and empathizing. The Vietnamese language was impossible to learn in a short time. We treated bubonic plague, cholera, tetanus, polio, and TB, to name a few. Diarrhea was a major killer, although in theory we were good at treating it. Fortunately, the patient families stayed and cooked their foods. The nurses could then give them their medicine.

In the evenings, I would study up on tropical diseases I had seen during the day. We could not go back to the hospital at night since the VC owned the town after dark. Before daybreak, it was considered too dangerous for any American to be on the streets (this was never mentioned in the doctor recruitment literature).

Rounds in the morning showed many patients missing. If they died, they were taken home to their village. Likewise, if they had gotten slightly better, they discharged themselves on their own, and their families took them home. We had to ask the night nurse, if she hadn't left already, what happened to whom, when, and why. Oddly enough, there were many overdoses, as the pharmacies did not require a prescription blank for sedatives or narcotics. On weekends, we made chopper visits to outlying villages, mostly a goodwill gesture. The village water was often contaminated with organisms such as endamoeba histolytism. One could certainly see the need for a public health program with the ever-present polio and tetanus – rampant is the word!

It was a tremendous learning experience for me. I probably got more than I gave.

An open air market in Vietnam.

R.B. Richards, MD
Ban Mi Thout, Vietnam

The population is made up of tribal people and Vietnamese citizens. Hospitals and facilities were very crude, resulting in poor sanitation. I went in 1968 because I felt the United States was getting an inaccurate report from the news media, and being there maybe I would be exposed to the truth.

I spent my spare time reviewing and condensing a book on tropical illnesses. I had published a book of tropical diseases for the VPVN.

I had an exceptionally good nurse. I was planning to drain the swollen inguinal lymph node of a bubonic plague patient. The following morning, as I was getting ready to incise the node, I found the nurse had completed the procedure. I congratulated her on a job well done.

Customarily several family members would remain with their patients during their hospitalization. They would cook their meals on a small fire on the ground. Frequently, on making my rounds, I found one or two very ill patients were not in the ward. I asked the nurse what happened. She said that the family had taken the patients away to die at home rather than in the hospital. The hospital had mats on which the patients would lie. One time, I visited and inspected an outlying area that had a renovated medical unit. They had a shipment of hospital beds with inner spring mattresses. I noted patients were not using the mattresses, but lie on mats as that was what they were accustomed to.

The Vietnamese people I came in contact with were very nice, and wanted essentially the same things Americans wanted. I had two young Vietnamese men acting as interpreters. One day they seemed to be out of sorts, and wanted to know if it was true that the US President was going to withdraw its soldiers from Vietnam. They were extremely frightened over such a thing, as they would come under Communist rule.

The children of Ban Mi Thout were all smoking and begging for cigarettes from US Army personnel, who freely gave them out. The thought struck me that, some years hence, they were all going to have big problems with lung disease.

John McCann, MD
Phu Vinh, Vietnam

When I first hit the ground at my Mekong Delta hospital, I saw a lady lying on a stretcher just outside with her right arm severed below the shoulder joint. No dressing had been applied. According to the interpreter, the Viet Cong had questioned this lady at great length. They felt she had some knowledge they needed, but she stubbornly refused to answer their questions, so the VC cut off her arm. They left her to bleed to death. Her family carried her many miles to the hospital. She was eighty-three years old and she did survive. Whether she had any information of value to the Viet Cong, I will never know, but her unwillingness to cooperate with them certainly impressed me.

On my tour of duty, I met a young first lieutenant. His nickname was "Snoopy." Snoopy's picture was painted on the nose of his aircraft.

The lieutenant used a light plane, a Cub or a Cessna type for reconnaissance flights. He flew to watch for troop movement and to sight the Viet Cong. I saw his plane close up and counted numerous bullet holes in the wings and fuselage. To my knowledge, he had no armor on the plane. One day on a routine flight he sighted a long line of native women walking a jungle trail. All were carrying baskets on their heads. He radioed this information to battalion (I suppose he was suspicious of small arms or ammunition being moved) and received the following message back. Within a few minutes, he had the answer: "Fish."

B.L. Tom, MD
Dalat, Vietnam

Dr. Tom writing home from Dalat during the Vietnam War:

We are in a pretty mountain resort area 100 km north of Saigon. My Vietnamese patients are extremely courteous and friendly. I have a very intelligent interpreter, Azma, who is half Vietnamese and half East Indian. He is fluent in French as well.

There is no television, radio or phonograph, but we amuse ourselves with down-home entertainment. The dining room has a huge fireplace that makes the room look like a ski lodge. We all gather around in the evening to sing and listen to a couple of our Montagnard friends play guitar. Many of the tribes have been converted to Christianity and the missionaries who have been in the area a long time join in singing hymns. The Vietnamese are mostly Buddhists but enjoy listening to music. When we are not pulling Jeeps out of the mud, we see fifty or more patients every morning lined up at the clinic. The monsoon season leaves everyone drenched almost every day. We see terrible abscesses, tuberculosis, and a fair amount of trauma. One morning, a little old man came in and squatted down in front of me, beamed a toothless grin at me, and used the remains of the stubs of his fingers to point to his swollen ankles and toes which had fallen off. He had leprosy and wanted to know if I could help him.

I have been doing a lot of reading recently (books of all kind since no one bothers to write to me anymore!). I've been inspired by Dr. Tom Dooley's writings, as well as his life in Vietnam. In one essay he wrote, "Dedicate some of your life to others. Your dedication will not be sacrifice. It will be an exhilarating experience because it is intense effort applied toward meaningful end ... and you will know the happiness that comes of serving others who have nothing."

From James R. Wiant, MD
Quang Tri, Vietnam

"I was interested to read you [Dr. Hassan] had been in Quang Tri. I was there in the winter of 1969. It was a terrible shock to see the pictures of Quang Tri destroyed in the offensive of 1972. If you were in Quang Tri anytime close to my stay, I would like to hear about it. Good luck with your book.

(Ed. Note: Shortly after receiving this letter, Dr. Hassan called Dr. Wiant. He told him of the broad outlines of *Failure to Atone*, including the execution of the babies and the veiled threat of the CIA. When Dr. Hassan asked, "Would you think any of the other volunteer doctors would be offended in any way?" Dr. Wiant replied, "I would be offended if you did *not* include it in your book."

22

Volunteers for America

$\mathcal{T}$he following men and women served in the American Medical Association's Volunteer Physicians for Vietnam program which began in July 1966 and continued through June 1973. Many physicians served two tours of duty, and some doctors returned to Vietnam for as many as eight tours. Altogether, 774 US-licensed doctors served 1,029 tours as volunteer doctors in Vietnam.

Adams, John M., Winchester, Virginia
Adams, Willard E., Garland, Texas
Adelman, Jack, Camarillo, California
Adler, Robert E., Fremont, California
Albert, Richard O., Alice, Texas
Albracht, William R., College Station, Texas
Aldis, William, Fort Scott, Kansas
Alexander, Clifton, Tucson, Arizona
Almond, Carl H., Columbia, Missouri
Amlin, Kenneth M., Arnold, California
Ammentorp, Peter A., Middletown, Ohio
Andersen, Edward P., North Providence, Rhode Island
Anderson, Donald P., Los Angeles, California
Anderson, Roy W., Cordell, Oklahoma
Auchincloss, Hugh, Ridgewood, New Jersey
Ayer, John L., Syracuse, New York
Ayers, Marion E., Indianapolis, Indiana

Bacevich, Andrew, Hammond, Indiana
Bailey, Thomas E., Indianapolis, Indiana
Bains, Jerry W., Charlottesville, Virginia
Baker, John H., Bethesda, Maryland
Baker, Julia McVicar, Campos Eliseos 81, Mexico
Baldwin, Jack P., Cincinnati, Ohio
Balkissoon, Basdeo M., Washington, D.C.
Ballou, John B., Salem, Massachusetts
Bannon, Ann E., St. Louis, Missouri
Barber, C. Richard, Glen Falls, New York
Bard, James W., Lexington, Kentucky
Barratt, William, Painesville, Ohio
Barrett, Howard T., Minonk, Illinois
Batdorf, John W., Las Vegas, Nevada
Baugh, Robert F., Detroit, Michigan
Baum, Mark, Idaho Falls, Idaho
Bear, Edward S., Jersey City, New Jersey
Becker, Folke, Birmingham, Alabama
Beckjord, Philip R., New Orleans, Lousiana
Beggs, John H., Lake City, Florida
Bell, Exter F., Jr., Houston, Texas
Bender, John M., Goshen, Indiana
Benjamin, Charles I., St. Paul, Minnesota
Bennett, J.B., Warren, Indiana
Bennett, John F., Rome, New York
Bennett, Truett V., Kailua, Hawaii
Beno, Thomas J., Green Bay, Wisconsin
Benson, Raymond, Billings, Montana
Benson, Roger L., Woodstock, Illinois
Berezney, Paul L., Big Spring, Texas
Berg, Frank P., Mt. Kisco, New York
Berglund, Paul N., San Francisco, California
Berkley, Kelly M., Mt. Vernon, Illinois
Berkman, Eugene, Beaver, Pennsylvania
Bernadett, Faustino, Chico, California
Berry, Charles, Atlanta, Georgia
Berry, Herbert Lee, McLean, Virginia
Bernstein, Joseph I., San Francisco, California
Betancourt, Sergio E., Balboa, Canal Zone
Beychok, Irving A., Sarasota, Florida
Blankenship, Billy Jim, Harlingen, Texas
Bloom, George R., Elkhart, Indiana
Bloom, Irving B., Placerville, California
Boe, John R., Grants Pass, Oregon
Boekelheide, Priscilla D., Marawi City, Philippines
Boese, Robert K., New York, New York
Bogardus, George M., Bellevue, Washington
Bolivar, Juan C., Indianpolis, Indiana
Bonser, Quentin, Placerville, California
Bontley, Jack R., Columbus, Ohio
Bort, Robert F., Ann Arbor, Michigan
Bowers, C. Richard, Anderson, Indiana
Bowers, James H., Clemson, South Carolina
Brackney, Edwin L., Augusta, Georgia

Bradham, Gilbert, Charleston, South Carolina
Bradley, James V. L., Pinedale, California
Bradley, Martin R., Phoenix, Arizona
Bradley, Matthew H., Miami Beach, Florida
Bragg, Leroy P., Hampton, Virginia
Braile, Louis E., Seattle, Washington
Brandfass, Carl F., Jr., Amherst, Massachusetts
Braun, Harold A., Missoula, Montana
Brenner, Susan J., McDowell, Kentucky
Brewer, Ray L., Houston, Texas
Brindle, William D., Rio Pedras, Puerto Rico
Brinker, David B., Oklahoma City, Oklahoma
Brinker, William R., Ravenna, Ohio
Brittain, Robert S., Englewood, Colorado
Brockman, George, III, Greenville, Kentucky
Brooks, Daniel H., Pittsburgh, Pennsylvania
Brown, Arthur, Perry, Oklahoma
Brown, Merril W., Albuquerque, New Mexico
Brown, Robert O., Atchison, Kansas
Brownlee, William H., Tulare, California
Bryant, Joe F., Lebanon, Tennessee
Burgess, Joan C., Philadelphia, Pennsylvania
Burgoon, Edwin B., Big Piney, Wyoming
Burke, Joseph A., Cincinnati, Ohio
Burnett, Waldo E., Middletown, New York
Burns, Cornelius, Sumter, South Carolina
Burns, Craig A., Westwood, California
Burns, E., Murray, Portland, Oregon
Butler, Thomas C., Baltimore, Maryland
Burwell, Edward L., Falmouth, Massachusetts
Butterfield, Donald E., Wauwatosa, Wisconsin
Buxton, Julian T., Jr., Charleston, South Carolina
Byerly, W. Grimes, Jr., Hickory, North Carolina
Cabrera, Eusebio E., Torrance, California
Cahill, Robert C., Attica, Ohio
Caine, Curtis W., Jackson, Mississippi
Caldwell, Bruce F., Clinton, North Carolina
Call, Cyril C., Phoenix, Arizona
Callahan, Dan, Warner Robbins, Georgia
Carpenter, Lawrence O., Point Arena, California
Calta, Edward C., Renton, Washington
Camm, Elizabeth G., Ormond Beach, Florida
Cammack, Kirk V., Las Vegas, Nevada
Canfield, Merritt C., San Diego, California
Caplan, Benjamin B., Columbus, Ohio
Carey, Thomas A., Englewood, Colorado
Carlberg, Dale L., Jeffersonville, Indiana
Carlin, Jean E., Irvine, California
Carlson, Paul A., Fresno, California
Carlson, Paul E., Bozeman, Montana
Casselman, Bernard W., Marina Del Rey, California
Cassem, Edwin H., Cambridge, Maine
Cates, Charles H., Washington, DC
Caumartin, Hugh T., Saginaw, Michigan

Cavanagh, James G., Carmichael, California
Ceriani, Ernest G., Kremmling, Colorado
Chapman, Daniel D., Ann Arbor, Michigan
Chasler, Charles N., Pittsburgh, Pennsylvania
Chastain, William B., Empire, California
Cheever, Donald H., Bozeman, Montana
Childress, Max E., San Francisco, California
Chisholm, Thomas P., Ft. Benning, Georgia
Christian, George P., Cambridge, Massachusetts
Chua, Benjamin E., Pittsburgh, Pennsylvania
Church, Reynold E., Bronxville, New York
Clark, Thomas W., Morton, Illinois
Charke, Michael J., Springfield, Missouri
Clinton, Philip H., Vallejo, California
Cloud, Lawrence P., Boston, Massachusetts
Cobb, William T., Newberry, Florida
Coes, Harold V., Sussex, New Jersey
Coffin, G.S., Eldridge, California
Colizzo, Francis P., Scranton, Pennsylvania
Comer, Thomas P., Bakersfield, California
Conley, Richard A., Watonga, Oklahoma
Connolly, John V., Corpus Christi, Texas
Cooke, Robert E., Addyston, Ohio
Cope, John R., Greensburg, Pennsylvania
Cotter, Lloyd H., Santa Ana, California
Craig, Carol, South Hadley, Massachusetts
Craig, Harry L., Huntingburg, Indiana
Craig, Rufus H., Alexandria, Louisiana
Crain, James W., Branson, Missouri
Crawford, Hugh, Santa Ana, California
Creamer, David M., Bellaire, Ohio
Creer, Stephen M., Spanish Fork, Utah
Cross, Charles J., Columbus, Ohio
Curran, William S., Albuquerque, New Mexico
Currie, Richard A., Baltimore, Maryland
Curtis, Charles P., Fairfield, Connecticut
Davis, Harry R., Boiling Springs, Pennsylvania
Day, Marvin B., Darien, Connecticut
Dayer, Roger S., Buffalo, New York
Detwiler, Howard F., Van Nuys, California
Devito, James, St. Augustine, Florida
Dill, James E., San Francisco, California
Dolehide, Eugene F., Chicago, Illinois
Dominguez, Fernando, Huntington, West Virginia
Donahue, Walter W., Salem Massachusetts
Doremus, William P., New York, New York
Dorgan, James Q., Jr., Columbus, Ohio
Doria, Alberto, Concord, California
Douglas, Herschel L., San Antonio, Texas
Dowling, Jerry J., Waipanu, Hawaii
Drogowski, Matthew J., West Palm Beach, Florida
Dudley, Charles C., Jr., Elkin, North Carolina
Duncan, John, Stanwood, Washington
Dunn, James R., Jr., Tarboro, North Carolina

Eby, Charles E., Tucson, Arizona
Eby, Robert E., College Park, Maryland
Eckert, Wade R., Mammoth Lakes, California
Eggerstedt, Charles, Eureka, California
Elliot, J. Colin, Chula Vista, California
Ellis, Franklin H., Jr., Boston, Massachusetts
Elstrom, John A., Tunis, Tunisia
Emory, Emerson, Dallas, Texas
Emory, Mayo L., New Orleans, Louisiana
Engstrom, Perry H., Wahpeton, North Dakota
Ennis, Arthur L, Decatur, Illinois
Erben, John J., Scottsdale, Arizona
Erdman, Helga M., New York, New York
Espen, Lloyd, Redwood City, California
Espey, Dan, Jr., Hickory, North Carolina
Ezekiel, Gerald A., Jr., San Diego, California
Faber, Dorian R., Merced, California
Fazekas, Joseph F., Washington, DC
Falk, Leo J., Charlottesville, Virginia
Falk, Victor S., Edgerton, Wisconsin
Farish, Henry G., Whittier, California
Farrell, Elliston, Laguna Hills, California
Farrell, Joseph P., Yuba City, California
Fenenga, Adriana, Las Cruces, New Mexico
Ferguson, James H., Miami, Florida
Fesus, Andre V., Baltimore, Maryland
Fiedler, Dolores E., Middle Village, New York
Fink, Joseph G., New York, New York
Finkelmeier, Louis J., Celina, Ohio
Fischer, Don A., Champaign, Illinois
Fisher, Neal R., Covina, California
Fisher, Robert E., Woodland, California
Fitts, Charles T., Charleston, South Carolina
Fitzhugh, Alexander S., Little Rock, Arkansas
Fitzsimons, Richard M., Anaheim, California
Fixott, Richard S., Colorado Springs, Colorado
Fly, Sterling, Uvalde, Texas
Flynn, George W., Petaluma, California
Flynn, Michael B., Houston, Texas
Forlenza, Ronald S., Buffalo, New York
Forlenza, Susan W., Jacksonville, Texas
Foster, Robert M., Youngstown, Ohio
Foster, Wayne K., Cecilton, Maryland
France, Richard, Nashville, Tennessee
Franken, Robert, San Angelo, Texas
Frewing, Harry L., Bend, Oregon
Frick, Henry Clay II, New York, New York
Fuller, Robert E., Placerville, California
Funderburk, William W., Washington, D.C.
Funk, Martin A., Prospect Heights, Illinois
Furman, George J., Reno, Nevada
Galgano, Anthony R., Port Angeles, Washington
Gallagher, William B., La Crosse, Wisconsin
Gamwell, John W., Atlanta, Georgia

Gantenbein, Calvin E., Portland, Oregon
Garcia-Rivera, Carlos, San Francisco, California
Garnello, John M., Honolulu, Hawaii
Garstka, Stanley M., Riverside, California
Gaskin, John S., Jr., Albemarle, North Carolina
Gassaway, Franklin D., Pittsburgh, Pennsylvania
Gates, Dennis J., Chicago, Illinois
Gaudreault, Joseph H., Hinckley, Ohio
Gauthier, Joseph W., Foxboro, Massachusetts
Gaytan, Ralph G., El Monte, California
Gee, Vernon R., Redding, California
Geier, Fred J., Washington, DC
Gerrits, James F., St. Clair, Michigan
Ghicadus, Christie J., Laramie, Wyoming
Gilbert, Robert F., San Francisco, California
Gilbertson, F.E., Red Bank, New Jersey
Gildea, Robert T., Tupper Lake, New York
Gillette, Harriet E., Buffalo, New York
Gillette, Warren, Boulder, Colorado
Girod, Arthur H., Decatur, Indiana
Gius, John A., Pomona, California
Glasser, David, New York, New York
Gleichman, Theodore K., Denver, Colorado
Gloeckner, Fred H., Buckley, Washington
Godfrey, John, Olean, New York
Godfrey, Merle F., St. Helena, California
Godsey, John W., San Francisco, California
Goldstone, David F., Baltimore, Maryland
Goodhope, C. Richard, Edmond, Washington
Goodman, Harold F., New York, New York
Gordon, Glenn M., Eugene, Oregon
Grab, John A., Madison, Wisconsin
Grady, Joseph A., Detroit, Michigan
Graham, James E., Springfield, Illinois
Grant, Albert J., Hannibal, Missouri
Grant, John P., Jr., Englewood, New Jersey
Grasse, John M., Jr., Topeka, Kansas
Grassi, Robert M., Alexandria, Virginia
Green, Charles E., Lawton, Oklahoma
Green, Edward W., Indio, California
Green, Leonard J., Valparaiso, Indiana
Greenbaum, James K., Kittanning, Pennsylvania
Greene, Mark H., Salt Lake City, Utah
Gregorie, H. B., Jr., Charleston, South Carolina
Griffin, George D., Palo Alto, California
Griffith, Joseph B., Sewickley, Pennsylvania
Grollman, Aaron E., Cincinnati, Ohio
Grubman, David, Berkeley, California
Grufferman, Sue Kim, San Francisco, California
Guinan, Patrick D., Oak Lawn, Illinois
Gutsche, Brett, Philadelphia, Pennsylvania
Haan, Robert E., El Paso, Texas
Hadfield, Dale, Bremerton, Washington
Hagedorn, Albert B., Rochester, Minnesota

Hagen, Kristofer N., Edina, Minnesota
Haines, William F., Malvern, Pennsylvania
Hall, Donald T., Seattle, Washington
Hall, William A., Princeton, New Jersey
Hallaba, Moheb A.S., Joplin, Missouri
Hallett, George W., Jr., Portland, Maine
Hallman, Jerry M., Wills Point, Texas
Halpin, Jack D., Ventura, California
Hannum, Thomas L., Brigham City, Utah
Harbaugh, Oril S., San Diego, California
Harper, Richard F., Pawhuska, Oklahoma
Harper, Samuel B., Madison, Wisconsin
Harris, William A., Honolulu, Hawaii
Hartin, Richard B., Garland, Texas
Hartman, J.B. Leith, Marblehead, Massachusetts
Hartman, John J., Angola, Indiana
Harvey, David N., Warner Robins, Georgia
Hase, Charles W., Sherman, Texas
Hassan, Allen, Carmichael, California
Hasselblad, Oliver W., New York, New York
Healey, Edward W., Canal Zone
Heath, Joe D., Kermit, Texas
Heilbrunn, Ilse, Rolla, Missouri
Heins, Otto, Raymondville, Texas
Helfant, Murray H., Framingham Massachusetts
Heller, Henry K., Bethlehem, Pennsylvania
Helvey, William M., Los Altos, California
Hemphill, Wayne A., Victorville, California
Henderson, James A., Denver, Colorado
Hendricks, James Y., Clear Lake, Iowa
Hendrickson, Merlin A., Rialto, California
Hennemann, Jack G., Seattle, Washington
Henner, Charles M., Santa Anna, Texas
Hensley, Cline D., Wichita, Kansas
Herbelin, J. Ted, Pine Ridge, South Dakota
Hershey, John E., Spokane, Washington
Herz, Elisabeth, Vienna, Austria
Hesla, Inman A., Austin, Minesotta
Hiller, Carl J., New Bern, North Carolina
Hineburg, Paul A., Hollywood, Florida
Hogkinson, Bernard J., Boston, Massachusetts
Hoekenga, Mark T., Cincinnati, Ohio
Hoffman, William F., III, New York, New York
Hollingsworth, Gerald M., Fort Walton Beach, Florida
Holmes, Dorothy B., Washington, DC
Holswade, George R., New York, New York
Homay, Alan, Anchorage, Alaska
Hoover, Norman W., APO San Francisco, California
Hopkins, Charles E., Madison, Eisconsin
Horn, John E., Tulsa, Oklahoma
Horsch, Robert F., Westfield, New York
Howe, Luke A., Townshend, Vermont
Hoy, Ronald J., Pittsburgh, Pennsylvania
Huibregtse, Willard G., Sheboygan, Wisconsin

Hume, David H., Rochester Minnesota
Humphrey, Thomas, Los Angeles, California
Hutchins, Earl C., Greeley, Colorado
Hyde, Howard P., Phoenix, Arizona
Hyder, Nat E., Jr., Erwin, Tennessee
Iverson, Roland K., Marysville, California
James, Russell B., Imola, California
Jenson, Mark B., Provo, Utah
Jeric, William H., Cleveland, Ohio
Jewell, Ross L., Coffeyville, Kansas
Johnson, Douglas, Little Falls, Minnesota
Johnson, Hugh A., Rockford, Illinois
Johnson, William A., Longview, Washington
Jones, Clarence W., Longview, Washington
Jones, James, San Jose, California
Jones, Reverdy H., Jr., Fairmont, West Virginia
Jordan, Curtis R., Palestine, Texas
Kaiser, Walter H., Los Angeles, California
Kalb, Sam W., East Orange, New Jersey
Karam, Adib, New York, New York
Keagy, Charles L., Delano, California
Keary, Frank V., Rochester, New York
Keffler, Richard, Lubbock, Texas
Keiger, Richard F., San Diego, California
Knefick, Thomas P., San Francisco, California
Kenessey, George, Ewa Beach, Hawaii
Kenyon, Barbara A., Nashville, Tennessee
Kerner, Donald J., Naval Hospital FPO New York
Ketchum, William F., Needham, Massachusetts
Kiely, Joseph M., Rochester, Minnesota
Kilgore, William R., Taos, New Mexico
Kimball, Gale R., Oklahoma City, Oklahoma
Kimbell, Jo Erle, Los Angeles, California
Kimbrough, Edward E., III, Columbia, South Carolina
Kimmich, Haydee J., Springfield, Illinois
Kindar, Adam, Amsterdam, New York
King, John N., Norfolk, Virginia
King, Robert T., Mobile, Alabama
Kitchen, Benjamin F., Jr., Houston, Texas
Kitowski, Vincent J., Houston, Texas
Klickstein, Gilbert D., Brooklyn, New York
Knight, McGregor, Kitchener, Ontario, Canada
Koehl, Michael F., San Antonio, Texas
Kradjian, Robert M., Long Beach, Calfironia
Krevsky, Seymour, Detroit, Michigan
Krombach, Julius D., Henderson, New York
Kuehnle, John C., Philadelphia, Pennsylvania
Lackore, Leonard K., Willmar, Minnesota
LaDage, Leo H., Long Beach, California
Lane, Robert E., Tacoma, Washington
La Sorsa, Armand M., Manistique, Michigan
Leake, James R., Littleton, Colorado
Lee, Gilbert, Palm Springs, California
Lee, James H., Baltimore, Maryland

Lee, Martin L., Danville, Pennsylvania
Leeper, Ben M., Cheyenne, Wyoming
Lefevre, Ira D., Coeymans, New York
Lehman, Kenneth M., Topeka, Indiana
Leibold, Edwin F., Forks, Washington
Leiby, George M., Albemarle, North Carolina
Leighty, Ralph G., Swissvale, Pennsylvania
Lekisch, Kurt, Midland, Texas
Lesser, Albert, Garden City, New York
Levitan, Morton E., Ft. Harrison, Montana
Levonian, William P., Santa Cruz, California
Lewis, Harold, Hilo, Hawaii
Libertson, William, Rochester, New York
Liepins, Kurts W., Crestwood, Illinois
Link, Richard B., American Lake, Washington
Lipinski, John J., Kalispell, Montana
Lipsey, Donald, Okemos, Michigan
Lipsey, James H., Asheville, North Carolina
Littler, J. William, New York, New York
Livingston, Charles E., Salina, Kansas
Lockwood, Wayne B., Oklahoma City, Oklahoma
Lokvam, Leif H., Kenosha, Wisconsin
Long, John C., Plainview, Texas
Lottman, Marvin, Anaheim, California
Lowe, George H., Jr., Ogden, Utah
Lowell, Russell H., Santee, California
Lowry, Frederick, Austin, Texas
Luschinsky, Walter, Ringtown, Pennsylvania
Mackenzie, James, Hamilton, Ontario, Canada
Maher, Robert C., Spokane, Wahington
Maloney, Christopher T., Tucson, Arizona
Manwell, Claire C., Northampton, Massachusetts
Manwell, Edward J., Northampton, Massachusetts
Marians, Mark, El Paso, Texas
Marshall, Foster, II, Washington, DC
Marshall, William H., Palo Alto, California
Martin, William J., Ventura, California
Martinetti, Dominic J., Hurley, Wisconsin
Mauger, Theodore F., Chatsworth, Illinois
May, Robert D., Greenville, North Carolina
McAninch, David L., Glendale, California
McBratney, John, G., New Bedford, Massachusetts
McCann, John P., Parkston, South Dakota
McCord, Colin, W., New York, New York
McCormack, George A., Medford, Massachusetts
McDermott, John J., Claremont, California
McFadden, John W., West Point, Mississippi
McLaughlin, Robert W., Eaton, Pennsylvania
McGown, Curtis, Clarksville, Tennessee
McGuirk, Justin, Randolph, Massachusetts
McKinley, Robert A., Delmar, New York
McLaren, Daniel E., Indianapolis, Indiana
McRoberts, Robert L., Rochester, Minnesota
Meaders, Robert H., San Francisco, California

Mebane, William C., Wilmington, North Carolina
Meehan, Donald J., Springville, New York
Mehta, Bal R., Honolulu, Hawaii
Mercer, Marshall M., Los Angeles, California
Merrill, Marion T., Plainfield, Vermont
Meyer, Paul R., Jr., Chicago, Illinois
Meyer, Paul R., Sr., Port Arthur, Texas
Milde, Paul A., Cleveland, Ohio
Miller, Alexander, Cleveland Heights, Ohio
Miller, Arthur, Hollywood, California
Miller, Diebert J., Morenci, Arizona
Miller, Galen R., Elkhart, Indiana
Miller, James B., Colorado Springs, Colorado
Miller, Samuel L., San Francisco, California
Milligan, John O., Salinas, California
Mills, Samuel W., Jr., Middletown, New York
Mitchell, Thomas H., Vicksburg, Mississippi
Mitchell, William F., Columbus, Ohio
Moglen, Leslie J., San Francisco, California
Moller, Christopher J., Rapillion, Nebraska
Moller, Jurgen J., St. Paul, Minnesota
Monahan, Robert, St. Paul, Minnesota
Moore, Ronald E., Cristobal, Canal Zone
Moorman, Claude T., II, Savannah, Georgia
Morgan, Edward S., Pendleton, Oregon
Morgan, Loran, Torrington, Wyoming
Morris, Thomas E., Jr., Portland, Oregon
Northland, William E., Bearsville, New York
Morvant, Richard A., Thibodaux, Lousiana
Mosley, Patricia K., Indianapolis, Indiana
Mulder, Lambertus, Muskegon, Michigan
Mulligan, Wallace J., Cleveland, Ohio
Mulloy, William P., Philadelphia, Pennsylvania
Munsey, Franklin A., Rockford, Illinois
Murphy, Joseph P., Casper, Wyoming
Murray, Douglas M., Ft. Collins, Colorado
Mutty, Lawrence, Glen Falls, New York
Nagy, Stephen M., Jr., Woodland, California
Nahigian, Stanley H., Cleveland, Ohio
Nassif, Anthony C., Cleveland, Ohio
Nathan, Peter A., Portland, Oregon
Neal, William B., Los Angeles, California
Neerken, Adrian J., Kalamazoo, Michigan
Neher, Lauren M., Jerome, Idaho
Neilson, Robert W., Bluefield, West Virginia
Nelson, Charles H., Tucson, Arizona
Nelson, John D., Dallas, Texas
Nelson, Kenneth E., Broomfield, Colorado
Nelson, Robert H., Benson, Minnesota
Nesemann, Reynold M., Kewaunee, Wisconsin
Nettles, Joe, Savannah, Georgia
Newell, Frank, Summit, New Jersey
Newton, Walter M., Jr., Pinehurst, North Carolina
Ney, Julian J., Harrisonberg, Virginia

Nixon, Richard, Long Beach, California
Norman, Edward C., New Orleans, Louisiana
Norton, Jay F., Corpus Christi, Texas
Novak, Lumir F., San Antonio, Texas
Oba, Calvin, Scottsbluff, Nebraska
Oder, Lawrence G., Vandalia, Illinois
O'Keefe, John B., Biloxi, Mississippi
Oldham, William D., San Francisco, California
Olson, John H., Colrain, Massachusetts
Olsson, Carl A., Boston, Massachusetts
O'Neill, Ann, San Leandro, California
Oram, Thomas F., Schenectady, New York
Overmyer, Jay Wilbur, San Jose, California
Owen, Charles A., Riverside, California
Owen, William E., St. Ansgar, Iowa
Owens, Jennings K., Jr., Bennettsville, South Carolina
Padovano, Louis, New York, New York
Pakusch, Rainer S., Frankfurt, APO New York
Palmer, Mahlon, Springvale, Maine
Pannell, Harlan C., San Francisco, California
Para, Andrew W., Big Spring, Texas
Parker, Wayne G., Garden City, Kansas
Parkinson, Richard P., Indio, California
Parshall, William A., Eugene, Oregon
Passafaro, Ronald A., Dunkirk, New York
Patrick, James K., Fayetteville, Arkansas
Patterson, James B., Lorain, Ohio
Pawley, Ralph E., Palm Desert, California
Pearson, Bror F., Shakopee, Minnesota
Pedone, Pietro, Long Island, New York
Pendall, Magda, G., St. Croix, Virgin Islands
Peppard, Raymond W., Laconia, New Hampshire
Perry, Richard E., St. Petersburg, Florida
Pezzi, Pio J., Abington, Pennsylvania
Phelps, James H., Upland, California
Pfeiffer, Paul, Togus, Maine
Piburn, Marvin F., Wichita, Kansas
Pickering, Leonard, Southgate, Michigan
Pierce, Alson F., Colorado Springs, Colorado
Pillsbury, R. Cree, Mountain View, California
Pleune, Frederick G., Rochester, New York
Pope, William N., Seattle, Washington
Porter, Robert, Des Moines, Iowa
Potter, Robert T., Brooklyn, New York
Powell, Thomas H., Baltimore, Maryland
Prescott, Thomas, Tucumcari, New Mexico
Prespare, Charles J., Tupperlake, New York
Presto, Andrew J., Flushing, New York
Price, Robert B., Batavia, New York
Price, Steve F., Lake Charles, Louisiana
Pritel, Philip A., Vancouver, Washington
Puls, Gerald E., Fort Collins, Colorado
Pyle, William W., Franklin, Tennessee
Quiring, Dennis L., Los Angeles, California

Ragde, Haakon, Seattle, Washington
Raitt, Grant, Billings, Montana
Ralph, J. Clyde, Sacramento, California
Rambo, William, Charleston, South Carolina
Rasor, Robert W., Colorado Springs, Colorado
Rawling, John C., St. Petersburg, Florida
Rayson, Glendon E., Baltimore, Maryland
Reardon, Patrick A., Hilo, Hawaii
Redman, Jack C., Albuquerque, New Mexico
Reed, John M., Carmichael, California
Reid, James W., Rockville, Maryland
Reinecke, Robert D., Albany, New York
Rettig, Arthur C., Laguna Beach, California
Reznichek, Richard C., Torrance, California
Rhomberg, Bernard B., Milwaukee, Wisconsin
Ricci, Henry N., Martinez, California
Rice, Joseph F., Savannah, Georgia
Richards, Robert B., Ft. Morgan, Colorado
Ricketts, E. Tyson, Talladega, Alabama
Rielly, Thomas V., San Diego, California
Riker, Robert P., Fairview, Massachusetts
Riley, Francis D., Los Angeles, California
Risley, Donald R., Mt. Carmel, Illinois
Ritter, John A., Harlan, Kentucky
Roberts, C. Reid, Worcester, Massachusetts
Roberts, James A., Big Spring, Texas
Rodgers, James B., New York, New York
Rodman, Charles, Salt Lake City, Utah
Rogers, William J., III, Tonowanda, New York
Rosen, Albert M., Taos, New Mexico
Rosenberg, Jerry C., Detroit, Michigan
Rosenberg, Murray D., St. Paul, Minnesota
Ross, Warren B., Nampa, Idaho
Roth, Robert L., San Jose, California
Rowe, Robert B., Madera, California
Rozendaal, Hendrik, M., Schenectady, New York
Ruppert, Karl D., Olympia, Washington
Ryals, Jarvis, D., Charleston, South Carolina
Ryan, James E., Louisville, Kentucky
Ryan, Robert A., Lake Forest, Illinois
Sacry, Gayle F., Cordova, Alaska
Saint, Charles L., Pineville, Louisiana
Salladay, Isaiah R., Pierre, South Dakota
Sanborn, Alvin L., Fontana, California
Sanchez, Jose S., West St. Paul, Minnesota
Sanford, Jay P., Dallas, Texas
Sauer, Donald C., St. Louis, Missouri
Saviers, George, Sun Valley, Idaho
Schadler, John A., Las Cruces, New Mexico
Schafer, Ted A., Houston, Texas
Scharnweber, Henry C., Sanford, Michigan
Schiess, Herman L., Seattle, Washington
Schissel, Gregory, Minneapolis, Minnesota
Schlosman, Robert C., Rochester, New Y9rk

Schmidt, John R., Asuncion, Paraguay
Schmitz, Paul L., North Miami, Florida
Schnee, Charles F., Setauket, New York
Scholten, Roger A., Kalamazoo, Michagan
Schultz, Isadore H., Mazomanie, Wisconsin
Schulze, Roscoe A., Flatonia, Texas
Scott, William N., Long Beach, California
Segal, Myran I., Hollywood, Florida
Serino, Arthur B., Cambridge, Massachusetts
Servid, Lester P., Lynden Washington
Seybold, Marjorie E., Baltimore, Maryland
Shaw, William J., Fayette , Missouri
Shaw, Wilson W., Jamestown, New York
Shay, Robert D., Canal Zone
Sheris, Edward, Wilton, New Hampshire
Sherwin, Richard N., Prineville, Oregon
Shields, Charles D., Buffalo, New York
Shonkwiler, Jack D., Oklahoma City, Oklahoma
Short, Joan K., Beckley, West Virginia
Shouse, Samuel S., Lexington, Kentucky
Singleton, Edward B., Houston, Texas
Skivolocki, William P., Columbus, Ohio
Sloane, G. Harvey I., Louisville, Kentucky
Slosser, Paul J., Yuma, Arizona
Sluis, Joost, Santa Cruz, California
Smilkstein, Gabriel, Claremont, California
Smith, Elmer M., Des Moines, Iowa
Smith, Merle E., San Antonio, Texas
Smith, Robert G., Circleville, Ohio
Smith-T, Joanne, Tuskegee, Alabama
Smookler, Lawrence A., San Francisco, California
Sooy, Robert E., Kettering, Ohio
Sorsky, Eliot D., Fresno, California
Soskis, Elbert J., Tampa, Florida
Sparger, Charles, Pampa, Texas
Spray, Paul, Oak Ridge, Tennessee
Springer, Joseph P., Durand, Wisconsin
Stanmar, Stanley C., Forest Hill, Illinois
Stark, Merritt W., Denver, Colorado
Stark, Richard B., New York, New York
Steinmetz, Hermann J., Salem, Virginia
Stephens, John E., Columbus, Ohio
Stewart, David M., Bellows Falls, Vermont
Stewart, James, Cascade, Idaho
Stewart, Robert J., Denver, Colorado
Stickler, Joseph H., Bosbee, Arizona
Stone, William C., Roanake, Virginia
Strait, Herbert S., Minneapolis, Minnesota
Strandjork, Nels M., Kansas City, Kansas
Strizich, John W. Helena, Montana
Sulfridge, Hugh L., Saginaw, Michigan
Suter, Max, Jacksonville, Florida
Sutton, John, Columbia, South Carolina
Swanson, Alfred B., Grand Rapids, Michigan

Swenson, Harold B., Long Beach, California
Taghavi, Bijan, New York, New York
Taintor, Zebulon, Buffalo, New York
Tatem, William H., Walpole, New Hampshire
Taylor, Howard C., Burlington, Vermont
Taylor, John W., Seattle, Washington
Taylor, William W., Dallas, Texas
Teasley, Jack L., Milwaukee, Wisconsin
Teschner, Bernard M., White Plaines, New York
Thill, Roger A., Harbor City, California
Thompson, A. Frank., Jr., Concord, North Carolina
Thompson, John, Caldwell, New Jersey
Thrower, Ann E., Madison, New Jersey
Tierney, Jon P., Minneapolis, Minnesota
Tinker, Richard V., Seattle, Washington
Toch, Rudolf, Milton, Massachusetts
Tolentino, Ernestino A., Glen Burnie, Maryland
Tom, Betty Lou, Los Angeles, California
Tom, Lloyd, Palo Alto, California
Toomin, Leonard A., Beaumont, Texas
Trembly, Diane L., Chicago, Illinois
Trott, Clinton W., Kettering, Ohio
Truax, Wayne, Beverly Hills, California
Tschanz, Vance, W., Anaheim, California
Tucker, Harry E., Chino, California
Tumolo, Mauro A., Brooklyn, New York
Tuchy, James L., Ft. Lee, Virginia
Tupper, Jack W., Oakland, California
Turner, Charles W., Northridge, California
Updegrove, John H., Easton, Pennsylvania
Upson, James F., Buffalo, New York
Vanderhoof, Edward S., La Grange, Georgia
Van der Vlugt, Gerald, Arlington, Virginia
Van Orden, Frank, San Francisco, California
Vence, Carlos A., College Park, Maryland
Vicencio, Antonio B., Cebu City, Philippines
Victor, Irving, Savannah, Georgia
Vidziunas, Joseph, Lexington, Illinois
Vigorita, John L., New York, New York
Villarreal, Virgilio, Flint, Michigan
Vincent, Edward H., Colorado Springs, Colorado
Vincent, Ronald G., Buffalo, New York
Visscher, Lois H., Kasganj, U.P., India
Voyles, Carl M., St. Petersburg, Florida
Wabrek, Alan J., Hartford, Connecticut
Wade, Franklin V., Flint, Michigan
Wagner, John M., Clarks Summit, Pennsylvania
Waitt, Paul M., Noblesville, Indiana
Walker, John A., Bradford, New Hampshire
Walker, Samuel, H., Asheville, North Carolina
Wall, Emmett D., St. Louis, Missouri
Wallace, Donald K., Columbia, Maryland
Wallerstein, Ladislao K., Toledo, Ohio
Walsh, Redmond B., Bronx, New York

Walsh, Robert, Jr., Summit, New Jersey
Walstad, Paul M., Harlan, Kentucky
Walters, Felix A., Nederland, Texas
Wampler, Frederick W., Williamson, West Virginia
Wanebo, Harold, New York, New York
Washburn, Willard W., Boiling Springs, North Carolina
Walters, Ronald F., South Laguna, California
Watson, David F., Muskogee, Oklahoma
Weaver, Donald S., Carmichael, California
Weaver, John L. Pueblo, Colorado
Wedum, Bernice G., Washington, DC
Weeks, Carnes, Jr., Amenia, New York
Weed, Chester A., W. Hartford, Connecticut
Weir, Matthew J., Virginia, Minnesota
Weiss, Joseph J., Kabul, Afghanistan
Weitzner, George M., Monticello, New York
Welch, Richard B., San Francisco, California
Wells, Arthur H., Duluth, Minnesota
Wells, E. Robert, Walla Walla, Washington
Welsh, Jack D., Oklahoma City, Oklahoma
Wenke, Leo L., Sun City, Arizona
White, Daniel B., Rochester, Michigan
White, Gilbert H., Jr.., Hammond, Indiana
Whitmire, James E., Sumner, Iowa
Whittaker, Loria D., Jr., Peoria Illinois
Wiant, James R., University City, Missouri
Wick, Robert L., Worthington, Ohio
Wike, Charles C., Amarillo, Texas
Wilcox, William A., Minneapolis, Minnesota
Wilk, Herbert J., Birmingham, Alabama
Wilson, Hal T., Winston-Salem, North Carolina
Wilson, Robert, Jr., Charleston, South Carolina
Wipperman, Rudolph P., Hilo, Hawaii
Wolaver, John H., Knoxville, Tennessee
Wood, Harold A., Brownsville, Texas
Woodruff, William E., Vallejo, California
Woodruff, William H., Aurora, Illinois
Woodward, Celeste L., Baltimore, Maryland
Woodward, William W., Kansas City, Missouri
Wray, Charles H., Augusta, Georgia
Wright, William A., Wilmington, Delaware
Wu, Lan Sing, Concord, California
Wyman, Edwin T., Jr., Weston, Massachusetts
Young, David G., Las Vegas, Nevada
Young, Ralf I., Long Beach, California
Young, Richard W., Baton Rouge, Louisiana
Younger, Lewis I., Winona, Minnesota
Yuskaitis, Anthony J., New London, New Hampshire
Zalter, Rudolf, New York, New York
Zeier, Frances G., Evansville, Indiana
Zerzavy, Frederick M., San Francisco, California
Zimmerman, Lois R., Clairsville, Ohio
Zimmerman, Wayne, Tacoma, Washington
Zubero, Jose L., Jacksonville, Florida

About the Author

*D*r. Allen Clarence Hassan is a physician, a surgeon, a lawyer, and an educator. A native of Red Oak, Iowa, he served in the US Marine Corps from 1954-1957, being promoted to sergeant, and he became a full Commander in the US Coast Guard in 1986. He received a DVM from Iowa State University in 1962, and an MD from the University of Iowa in 1966. As a physician and surgeon, Dr. Hassan served two tours of duty in Vietnam, the first as a representative of the American Medical Association's Volunteer Physicians for Vietnam program, and the second as a representative of the Committee of Responsibility. He received his JD from Lincoln University in 1978. One of only a small number people to hold both a medical and legal degree, Dr. Hassan served as president of the Academy of Family Physicians in 1977, and president of the Academy of Law in Medicine in 1983. He served as a clinical instructor in family practice at the University of California—Davis medical school in Davis, California, from 1976-1986. He is a diplomate with the American Board of Family Practice, the American College of Legal Medicine, the American Board of Forensic Examiners, and the American Academy of Experts in Traumatic Stress. Dr. Hassan is also board-certified in sports medicine. His publications include the book *Evaluation, Treatment and Prevention of Head and/or Spinal Injury Problems*, edited by Gervase Flick, MD, JD, published in 1996. His publications include the book *Evaluation, Treatment and Prevention of Head and/or Spinal Injury Problems*, edited by Gervase Flick, MD, JD, published in 1996, and he is at work on another book, tentatively titled *Invisible Wounds*, detailing war injuries and benefits to surviving veterans. Dr. Hassan currently practices medicine and law in Sacramento, California.

"The End"

THE FAILURE TO ATONE PLEDGE

With the publication of Failure to Atone,
we pledge to donate 10 percent of all profits from
the book to charitable organizations which help children
who have been injured, maimed or displaced by war.

To order additional copies, visit our Website:

www.vietnamfailuretoatone.com